Writing and Literacy in the World of Ancient Israel

Society of Biblical Literature

Archaeology and Biblical Studies

Tammi Schneider, Editor

Number 11
Writing and Literacy in the World of Ancient Israel
Epigraphic Evidence from the Iron Age

Writing and Literacy in the World of Ancient Israel
Epigraphic Evidence from the Iron Age

by

Christopher A. Rollston

Society of Biblical Literature
Atlanta

Writing and Literacy in the World of Ancient Israel
Epigraphic Evidence from the Iron Age

Library of Congress Cataloging-in-Publication Data

Rollston, Chris A.
    Writing and literacy in the world of ancient Israel : epigraphic evidence from the Iron Age / by Christopher A. Rollston.
        p. cm. — (Archaeology and biblical studies ; no. 11)
    Includes bibliographical references and index.
    ISBN 978-1-58983-107-0 (paper binding : alk. paper)
    1. Inscriptions, Semitic. 2. Semitic languages, Northwest. 3. Bible. O.T.—Criticism, interpretation, etc. 4. Middle Eastern literature—Relation to the Old Testament. 5. Palestine—Languages. I. Title.
    PJ3085.R65 2010
    492—dc22

2010033450

Printed on acid-free, recycled paper conforming to ANSI/NISO Z39.48-1992 (R1997) and ISO 9706:1994 standards for paper permanence.

Das Mittelmeer

Logia about scripts from days of yore
arcana mundi vom distant shore
the meer, the yam, the middle sea
beloved gift of humanity

CONTENTS

List of Illustrations

ACKNOWLEDGMENTS

The Department of Near Eastern Studies at Johns Hopkins University provided research and travel funding for me on numerous occasions. The Society of Biblical Literature also awarded me a generous grant. With these sources of funding, I was able to collate a large number of epigraphs in Jerusalem, Tel Aviv, Damascus, Aleppo, London, Boston, and Philadelphia. The National Endowment for the Humanities gave me a substantial fellowship and this funded much of my research in Amman, Salt, Madaba, Beirut, and Byblos. During my time in the Middle East, I have benefited from the libraries and accommodations at the American Center of Oriental Research (Amman) and the Albright Institute of Archaeological Research (Jerusalem).

    I am especially indebted to Hava Katz of the Israel Antiquities Authority, Michal Dayagi-Mendels of the Israel Museum, Fawwaz al-Khraysheh of the Department of Antiquities of Jordan, Frederic Husseini of the Department of Antiquities of Lebanon for their support of my research. In addition, I am grateful to the Rockefeller Museum (Jerusalem), the British Museum, the University of Pennsylvania Museum, Harvard Semitic Museum, and Tel Aviv University for permission to collate inscriptions within their collections. The library staff of Emmanuel School of Religion has assisted my research in various ways, Chris Quillen has my special gratitude for her constant alacrity. In addition, Emmanuel has provided me with some superb research assistants through the years, especially Heather Dana Davis Parker, Alan Dyson, Katya Ivanova, W. G. Hulbert, Stephen Paul, Liesl Huhn, Nathaniel Greene, Adam Bean, C. J. Frisina, and Ra Lovingsworth.

    During the course of time, Jo Ann Hackett, Ivan Kaufman, Lawrence Stager, Helene Sader, Benjamin Sass, Yitzhaq Beit-Arieh, Anson Rainey, Zeev Herzog, David Ussishkin, Israel Finekstein, Amihai Mazar, William Dever, and Avraham Biran have been gracious in working to ensure the fact that I was granted access to various epigraphic texts and corpora, or photographic images thereof. Moreover, I have often worked closely on symbiotic photographic and digital projects with Bruce Zuckerman and Marilyn Lundberg of West Semitic Research, and this work has always been enjoyable and productive. Annalisa Azzoni, Joel Burnett, and Doug Emery have been frequent sources of fertile discussion. Frank Moore Cross and Joseph Naveh have been mentors and dialogue partners through the years and I have benefited much from their writings and from their personal support. My Doktorvater, P. Kyle McCarter, Jr., has been a paradigmatic teacher, sage, conversation partner, and cherished friend. From him I have learned most and best.

PREFACE

This book is designed to be a non-technical volume focusing on the Iron Age Northwest Semitic epigraphic (written) record. Yet, the purpose of this volume is not simply to analyze or summarize this epigraphic evidence; rather the work intends to discuss the epigraphic evidence so as to provide a window into the world of ancient Israelite scribalism, writing, and literacy. For a number of the subjects treated in this volume, I have authored technical articles; therefore, specialists are encouraged to consult the nuanced data in these articles, as well as the bibliography cited therein.

The ordering of the chapters in this volume conveys, in a sequential manner, certain critical aspects of the depth, diversity, and development of writing practices and literacy in the broader Levantine world (i.e., Syria-Palestine). That is, because ancient Israel did not exist in a cultural vacuum, one must analyze writing and literacy in ancient Israel within the broader cultural milieu. The volume thus begins with a brief discussion of Early Alphabetic writing during the early 2nd millennium BCE and then turns to a discussion of the rise of the Phoenician script during the late 2nd millennium, as well as its usage during the early 1st millennium.

After discussing the invention of the alphabet, the use of the early Phoenician script, and the rise of the national scripts, I provide a synopsis of some of the major and minor Northwest Semitic inscriptions from the Iron Age. This section of the volume reveals some of the depth and diversity of the corpus. At times I have also included in this section some reference to linguistic isoglosses, that is, features that distinguish an Aramaic text from a Phoenician or Hebrew text. At this point, the reader should have a strong sense for the form and function of the epigraphic record, as well as some of the features that distinguish the Iron Age dialects of Syria-Palestine. The discussion is not exhaustive, but is representative.

The volume then focuses on the writers responsible for the production of the lion's share of the Old Hebrew epigraphic corpus: the Israelite scribe. Rejecting the view that the Old Hebrew writing system was so facile that it required minimal training, I conclude that the Old Hebrew epigraphic evidence reflects the type of sophistication that requires the positing of some sort of formal, standardized education. Along these lines, I find that it is naïve to assume that a child learning her or his first alphabetic system could have done so in a matter of days or weeks. Indeed, I use modern analyses from the field(s) of educational psychology to demonstrate the difficulties inherent in assumptions about the pace at which a first writing system can be learned. The Israelite scribe, I contend, was a thoroughly educated member of the elite classes.

At this point in the book I present a discussion of the extent of literacy in ancient Israel. Some scholars have previously concluded that because ancient Israel used a "facile" alphabetic system that literacy rates of the populace were necessarily high. Such experts have thus assumed that people from various strata of society could read and write. Obviously, I do not agree. I contend that literacy rates in Israel were not high. To be sure, I do not believe that the evidence suggests that just the scribes were literate. Rather, I believe that the Old Hebrew epigraphic evidence (and the evidence from the Hebrew Bible) demonstrates that various elite officials (including military officers) were often capable of reading and writing as well. Nevertheless, the epigraphic evidence simply does not support the contention that the average pastoralist or agriculturalist in Israelite society was literate. This is a marvelous romantic notion, but I simply do not find credible evidence for widespread literacy of the non-elite masses.

Finally, I conclude the volume with some reference to the fact that the Northwest Semitic epigraphic corpus has been flooded with inscriptions from the market. I urge caution with regard to the use of inscriptions from the market. After all, some of these inscriptions are modern forgeries. Sometimes forgeries are readily detectable (e.g., when the forger makes significant mistakes with the script, orthography, etc.), but I have seen some that are virtually perfect. Therefore, I caution against using data from the market as the basis for constructs about the past, including assumptions about writing and literacy.

ABBREVIATIONS

GENERAL

Ø	signifies an inscription that comes from the antiquities market, not an excavation
Ad	Arad
ca.	circa
C^{14}	carbon-14
Gn	Gibeon
GSI	Geological Survey of Israel
Lh	Lachish
Mh	Mesad Hashavyahu (= Yavneh Yam)
obv	obverse (front side of an inscription)
r.	ruled
rev	reverse (back side of an inscription)
SA	Samaria
SA.JE.BL	the Barley Letter from the Joint Expedition to Samaria
SEM-EDS	Scanning Electron Microscope with Energy Dispersive X-ray Spectroscopy
TL	thermoluminescence dating

BIBLIOGRAPHIC

AASOR	The Annual of the American Schools of Oriental Research
AAT	Ägypten und Altes Testament
AOS	American Oriental Series
ASOR	American Schools of Oriental Research
BA	*Biblical Archaeologist*
BASOR	*Bulletin of the American Schools of Oriental Research*

BES	Brown Egyptological Studies
BibOr	*Biblica et orientalia*
BZAW	*Beiheft zur Zeitschrift für die alttestamentliche Wissenschaft*
CBQMS	Catholic Biblical Quarterly Monograph Series
CM	Cuneiform Monographs
DJD	Discoveries in the Judean Desert
HSM	Harvard Semitic Monographs
HSS	Harvard Semitic Series
HTR	*Harvard Theological Review*
HTS	Harvard Theological Studies
HUCA	*Hebrew Union College Annual*
IEJ	*Israel Exploration Journal*
JAOS	*Journal of the American Oriental Society*
JBL	*Journal of Biblical Literature*
JCS	*Journal of Cuneiform Studies*
JEA	*The Journal of Egyptian Archaeology*
JSOTSup	Journal for the Study of the Old Testament Supplement Series
KAI	Kanaanäische und aramäische Inschriften
NEA	*Near Eastern Archaeology*
OBO	Orbis Biblicus et Orientalis
OLA	Orientalia Lovaniensia Analecta
PEFQS	*Palestine Exploration Fund Quarterly Statement*
PIHANS	Publications de l'Institut historique-archéologique néerlandais de Stamboul
RB	*Revue Biblique*
SBLABS	Society of Biblical Literature Archaeology and Biblical Studies Series
SBLWAW	Society of Biblical Literature Writings from the Ancient World Series
SBLRBS	Society of Biblical Literature Resources for Biblical Study Series
SHANE	Studies in the History of the Ancient Near East
STDJ	Studies on the Texts of the Desert of Judah
UISK	Untersuchungen zur indogermanischen Sprach- und Kulturwissenschaft
VT	*Vetus Testamentum*
WMANT	Wissenschaftliche Monographien zum Alten und Neuen Testament

ZA   *Zeitschrift für Assyriologie*
ZDPV   *Zeitschrift des deutschen Palästina-Vereins*

Introduction:
The Importance of Archaeological Context
for Analyses of Inscriptions

The focus of this volume is the Northwest Semitic epigraphic corpus of the Iron Age. The Iron Age inscriptions discussed herein do not hail from a contextual vacuum. Rather, they were written in a particular place and time, for a particular purpose, in a particular language. Furthermore, the inscriptions discussed in this volume were, for the most part, excavated, and so there is an archaeological context for them as well. Often the archaeological context will provide data that can assist the modern interpreter (archaeologist, epigrapher, or historian). To be sure, the importance of an archaeological context for epigraphic materials has sometimes been marginalized in various, sometimes radical, ways. For example, Deutsch and Heltzer have stated that "in the case of epigraphical material, the provenance and the exact context and locus are of significantly minor importance, as the items are 'loaded' with information" (1994, 7). Nevertheless, most specialists within the fields of archaeology and epigraphy would strongly affirm the value of understanding the archaeological context of an inscription. Therefore, as a point of departure, I will summarize some of the ways that knowledge of the archaeological context can assist the modern interpreter of the epigraphic data (see also Rollston 2004).

First, excavated Northwest Semitic epigraphic materials are of enormous importance for the reconstruction of various aspects of ancient Levantine society and history. Note, for example, that the Reisner Samaria Ostraca reveal some information about state administration in the capital city of the Northern Kingdom of Israel during the early-eighth century (Reisner, Fisher, and Lyon 1924). The Lachish II ostraca contain information about the troop movements (e.g., of the Judean army commander Conyahu to Egypt), rations, and prophetic warnings that were reported to officials (e.g., Ya'ush) at the fortified royal bastion of Lachish during the period immediately preceding this strategic Judean city's destruction in the early-sixth century B.C.E. (Tur-Sinai, Harding, Lewis, and Starkey 1938). The Old Hebrew epigraphs from Arad (Aharoni 1981) provide the name of the Judean military leader (Malkiyahu) of the Arad stratum VIII fortress and those of two of his subordinates (Gemaryahu and Nehemyahu). In addition, these epigraphs state the name of the military leader of the stratum VII–VI fortress as well ('Eliashib ben 'Ishyahu). The Aramaic ostraca from Tel Arad (Aharoni 1981) contain critical information about Arad, including its function as a "way station" supplying barley to horsemen during the Persian period, and suggest ethnic diversity at the site as well.

Epigraphs from scores of additional sites could be mentioned, but the point is that the knowledge of the provenance and archaeological context of inscriptions enables and facilitates various types of site-specific historical analyses, including ancient bureaucracy, the presence of literacy, some of the nature of scribal activities, and the names of military leaders at specific sites in certain periods, as well as military movements in precise regions, ethnic diversity within specific populations or regions, and regional interactions of various sorts. These sorts of foundational data are of peerless importance for detailed historical reconstruction and analysis of the epigraphic data. Without provenance and archaeological context, however, the information derived from these corpora would be diminished significantly, and those attempting to interpret the significance of these corpora would often be forced to resort to generalities and tenuous speculations because the essential *Sitz im Leben* would not be known.

Second, the archaeological context is also of fundamental importance for the reconstruction of regional differences within "dialects" or "languages." For example, we can state with some confidence that the word for "year" was *št* in northern Israelite, but *šnh* in Judahite. Similarly, in northern Israelite the diphthong *ay* contracted to *ê* and the diphthong *aw* contracted to *ô*; however, in the Judahite dialect these diphthongs remained uncontracted in all positions (Cross and Freedman 1952; Garr 1985; Rollston 2006). Knowledge of provenance facilitates these sorts of analyses of "dialects" and "languages." That is, the field of Northwest Semitic dialect geography is heavily dependent on provenanced epigraphic data.

Third, the science of palaeography should be based on the best data, and it is readily apparent that provenance and archaeological context is often of fundamental importance for this (Cross 2003; Peckham 1968; Naveh 1987a; Rollston 1999; 2003a; 2006). For example, it is a fact that there are differences between the seventh-century script employed in Ammon and the seventh-century script employed in Judah. Moreover, there are distinct differences between the Aramaic script of the seventh century and the Phoenician script of the seventh century. The reason these sorts of things can be affirmed with certitude is because of the provenanced exemplars from Syria-Palestine during the Iron Age. For the purposes of this volume, therefore, I affirm as an *Ausgangspunkt* that the archaeological context is of fundamental importance for someone attempting to distill data about ancient scribal education, writing, and literacy.

Scripts and Languages: Two Very Different Things

Within this volume, there will be references to various languages and various scripts. Non-specialists sometimes assume that "script" and "language" are the same thing. This is, however, not the case at all. Thus, the alphabet used to write most European languages is the Latin alphabet. For example, the sentence "*Rien ne l'intéresse*" ("Nothing interests him") is written in the French language, but the script is Latin. Similarly, the sentence "*Daar wil ik niets mee te doen hebben*" ("I will have nothing to do with that") is written in the Dutch language, but the script is Latin. That is, the script used to write these languages is the same script used to write the Latin sentence "*Bis das si cito das*" ("You give twice if you give quickly"). Similarly, this sentence from Philo "Ἡ μὲν προτέρα σύνταξίς ἐστι περὶ γενέσεως τῆς Μωυσέως" ("But the former treatise is about the generation of Moses") is written in the Greek language and the Greek script, but "Νετ-μοουτ" ("those who are dead") is written in the Greek script, but the Coptic language. The same phenomenon is attested in Northwest Semitic. For example, there are texts written in the Aramaic language but the Phoenician script. Throughout these pages, therefore, readers must be very attentive to the terms "script" and "language." They are, after all, not synonymous.

Script Types

Various linear alphabetic inscriptions from the Iron Age will be considered in this volume. For these inscriptions, two broad primary categories of scripts are evidenced, namely, lapidary and cursive. The dominant features of a lapidary script are its graphic arrangement, letter clarity, uniformity of letter form and size, and general conservativeness (i.e., retarded development). Lapidary inscriptions are normally found on surfaces that were carefully prepared (e.g., stone) and, in general, they were intended to be permanent. The primary features of a cursive script (often written on surfaces such as papyrus and pottery) are the rapidity with which it can be written and its adaptability. For a cursive script, variations in letter form and size are common, stroke curvature tends to be more prominent, letter spacing is more compact, semi-ligatures are more common, and development occurs more rapidly. Writing instruments and media are of fundamental importance in this regard, but not always determinative (e.g., because cursive scripts can be employed on stone). For the scripts that constitute the focus of this volume, both lapidary and cursive traditions are attested.

Drawings of various inscriptions, on various media (metal, pottery, stone), with various writing instruments (chisel, incising tool, brush and ink) are included to demonstrate some of the diversity of the epigraphic material in Iron Age Northwest Semitic scripts. Some photographs are also provided to augment the reader's understanding of the media and script.

Epigraphic Method: Some Basic Principles

Northwest Semitic epigraphy is a data-driven field and trained epigraphers should operate on the basis of certain basic epigraphic methodological principles, as follows:

1) First and foremost, modern translations of an ancient Northwest Semitic language are subject to the same caveats and provisos of any translated text. That is, *translations are approximations*. I definitely do not believe that any translation can capture all of the nuances of meaning that are present in the original text (ancient or modern). There are often multiple defensible ways of understanding and rendering words. Obviously, part of this results from the fact that the same word in different contexts will have different semantic ranges and the modern epigrapher must attempt to determine, so much as is possible, the precise nuance of a root in a particular context. That is, I find myself in substantial agreement with the ancient sentiments penned in the prologue to Ben Sira: translations are interpretive approximations.

2) *Determining the operative lexeme is not always a simple task.* That is, a ponderous aspect of language interpretation for various languages (including Northwest Semitic languages) is making determinations regarding the intended lexeme. For example, there are different lexemes consisting of the same two letters: *qṣ*. Thus, the letters *qṣ* could signify a nominal lexeme meaning "summer fruit," but the letters *qṣ* could also signify a nominal lexeme meaning "end" (arguably there is a word play on these words in Amos 8:1–2). Similarly, the letters ʾ*lp* could plausibly be understood in multiple different ways, including ʾ*lp* "to write," "to be instructed"; ʾ*lp* "ox"; ʾ*lp* "thousand," "to produce by the thousand." Deterimination of the actual lexeme is, therefore, a critical component of the epigrapher's responsibility, since there are scores of times when this can be an issue in an epigraphic (or non-epigraphic) text. Epigraphers, therefore, must consider the linguistic context and make a reasonable decision about the lexeme that the scribe intended.

3) Sometimes there will be no real debate about the root, but there will be debate about the way to understand the root (e.g., as a verb, as this noun or that noun, or as an adjective). For example, Lachish 3 (Tur-Sinai, Harding, Lewis, and Starkey 1938) contains multiple occurrences of the root *spr*. At times, there has been some debate about whether this or that occurrence should be understood

as the noun "scribe," the noun "book," or the verb "write." *Often context will be useful in assisting the modern translator, but the context is not always decisive.*

4) *Faded and abraded letters are common, but restoring such letters often cannot be done with absolute certainty.* Sometimes a single letter will be faded or abraded and a plausible reading can be posited on the basis of the traces (of the faded or abraded letter) and the surrounding letters. That is, the lexicon (or one's lexical knowledge) can be used to assist in determining the probable reading for the faded or abraded letter. Nevertheless, even in such cases, certitude is often elusive, as there are frequently multiple viable lexical options.

5) *Restorations of multiple letters, entire words, or even phrases are normally precarious ventures.* To be sure, there are a number of tools in the epigrapher's "toolbox" that can be of some use in this situation. For example, a line of a text that contains repetitious language can sometimes be restored with some certitude. Moreover, a formulaic text (e.g., a legal text, such as a contract) can sometimes be restored based on its use of traditional formulaic words and phrases. A critical component of this sort of venture is attempting to measure the lacuna(e) and determine the number of missing letters. Nevertheless, restorations are often speculative and I am normally disinclined to restore much more than a letter or two.

6) Scholars who wish to argue that a person known from the biblical text is also known in an epigraphic text should be very careful. Prosopography is a very scientific venture, but there is a history of people arguing for positive identifications on the basis of tenuous of evidence (see Rollston 2009).

Palaeographic Method: Some Essential Features

The premise of the field of palaeography (and all the typological sciences) is that artifacts develop through time and that this development can be discerned in an empirical fashion, described, and used as the basis for typologies (Cross 1982; Rollston 2003a, 150–57; cf. Kaufman 1986; Zuckerman 2003). New finds serve to augment, refine, and revise typologies (e.g., for a script series or pottery sequence). Using the most pristine extant ancient evidence, palaeography focuses on the establishment of: (1) the morphology of the letters of a script series, relative size of the letters, letter environment (e.g., horizontal proximity and relative vertical positioning of the letters), stance of a letter (e.g., the way a letter is "leaning"), ductus of a letter (i.e., number, order, and direction of strokes), as well as the relationship of the various letters to the ceiling line (Northwest Semitic inscriptions were normally "hung" from a ceiling line, rather than written on a base line); (2) the similarities and differences between the various components of a script series, such as the lapidary and cursives of a script series; issues of media and writing instrument must be factored in as well (e.g., ink on pottery, chiseled in stone); (3) and the diachronic development and synchronic variation within a script series, including things such as script innovations, preservations, and individual scribal idiosyncrasies. For this reason, palaeographic analyses made on the basis of a larger number of letters will be more secure than those made on the basis of a small number of letters. Thus, the longer an inscription is, the more precise and secure the palaeographic analysis can be). (4) In this connection, it should be noted that within a script series, different letters can (and do) develop at different paces. That is, within a script series of a certain chronological horizon some letters will develop rapidly, but some letters will develop very slowly. The pace of development can be cataloged and factored into palaeographic typologies.

The amount of the provenanced epigraphic data is of critical importance for the science of palaeography (and, of course, for epigraphy in general). That is, statements made on the basis of a large(r) number of inscriptions for a script series are more definitive than statements made on the basis of modest amounts of data (i.e., because the extant epigraphic remains of a script series are a fraction of the epigraphic material produced, larger sample sizes permit more definitive conclusions).

Also of great importance is the general quality of the data. Inscriptions (or exemplars of letters within an inscription) that are clear (i.e., not very faded or abraded) are the most valuable. Moreover, inscriptions that contain a date formula, or were found in a primary stratigraphic context (or are dateable via some other means), or contain historical data revealing the date or era of composition are most helpful in establishing chronological "benchmarks" for a script typology. Multiple inscriptions found in secure primary contexts in sequential strata of the same tell are often of particular import, because the chronological sequencing is arguably more secure.

In addition, the geographic and chronological distribution of the data must be factored in to the assessment as well. That is, analyses of the "targeted" script series that are based on palaeograpic data from various sites and multiple horizons provide the best window on the diagnostic features, developments, and variation within a script series. Based on these cumulative data, a reliable script typology can be developed for a script series. It should be noted that the more sophisticated the analysis and the more rigorous the method, the more reliable the conclusions; that is, not all palaeographers are equal and not all palaeographic analyses are equal. Of course on some occasions an ancient inscription will nuance epigraphic knowledge (e.g., script typologies, orthography, etc.) in rather dramatic ways. This was the case with the Tell Fakhariyeh bilingual (fig. 2.9; Cross 1995; Naveh 1987b; Rollston 2008b; cf. Kaufman 1982), with its archaizing script (fig. 2.9). New palaeographic data such as those of Tell Fakhariyeh are not problematic, but rather serve to complement previous conceptions.

Often within an *editio princeps*, hand drawings of faded or abraded letters are included. This is appropriate. However, hand drawings of faded or abraded letters are not to be the basis of a script typology because of the poor quality of the data. That is, a script typology must be based on the clearest exemplars of a script series. Finally, and with rare exceptions, it is methodologically imprudent to use inscriptions from the antiquities market as the basis for palaeographic typologies (Rollston 2004).

It is interesting that some archaeologists consider palaeographic typology to be very imprecise, or even "smoke and mirrors," but, nevertheless, affirm the substantial accuracy of pottery typologies. The fact of the matter is that palaeographic typologies can be as reliable as pottery typologies. Obviously, the amount of extant pottery of a specific horizon within a pottery series is exponentially larger than that of the epigraphic remains of a specific horizon within a script series, but the palaeographic epigraphic evidence for the horizons of many script series is not negligible, and (most importantly) the innumerable intricacies of the morphology of the letters of a horizon of a script series contain enormous amounts of data that can be analyzed and documented in an empirical manner by a trained palaeographer. It is also intriguing that some non-palaeographers will refer to variation in the writing of a modern script (e.g., the Latin cursive used in American English), note the presence of radical variation often present in the modern period, and *assume* that this is a relevant means of evaluating the accuracy of palaeography. This is hardly, however, a compelling argument. Analyses of an ancient script series must be based on the extant ancient evidence of a series and the synchronic variation and diachronic development attested for that ancient series. Modern analogies of variation for a modern script series are of negligible value, as much more script variation is tolerated within the modern period.

PART 1
THE EPIGRAPHIC RECORD: THE BROAD TABLEAU

Chapter 1

The Origins of Alphabetic Writing:
A Summary of the Salient Features

The alphabet was invented once, and this occurred during the early-second millennium B.C.E. All alphabets derive, in some fashion, from this original alphabet. Writing itself had already been invented during the late-fourth millennium B.C.E., in the cultural centers of Mesopotamia and Egypt. Sumerian is Mesopotamia's (and the world's) first recorded language, a fact enshrined in the title of Kramer's famed monograph *History Begins at Sumer* (1981). The earliest Sumerian inscriptions demonstrate that the Sumerian writing system was initially pictographic in nature. During the third millennium B.C.E., texts in the Akkadian language become common, but without displacing Sumerian. Because a predominant feature of the writing systems used for Sumerian and Akkadian is the "wedge-shaped sign," the writing system is normally referred to as cuneiform (from Latin *cuneus* "wedge"). Of course, the system that was predominant in Egypt is referred to as hieroglyphics (from Greek *hiero* "sacred" and Greek *gluph* "carving"). Nevertheless, these writing systems of Mesopotamia and Egypt are not alphabetic. Instead, they use logograms, that is, a sign that represents an entire word rather than just a single sound. They also use signs that represent combinations of consonants and vowels (syllables) rather than a single consonant. In addition, Mesopotamian cuneiform and Egyptian hieroglyphics use determinatives, that is, signs that identify the semantic category of the associated word; examples include "deity," "person," "metal," "wood," and so on. An alphabetic writing system, on the other hand, is a system in which a single grapheme (i.e., letter) is used to signify a single phoneme (i.e., meaningful unit of sound).

Origins of the Alphabet: Basic Synopsis

Research on the early alphabet began in earnest during the first two decades of the twentieth century. Sir Flinders Petrie had discovered, in a temple in Serabiṭ el-Ḥadem (in the Sinai), various hieroglyphic inscriptions. However, he also discovered some inscriptions that he considered enigmatic. He referred to these inscriptions as a "local barbarism" (Gardiner 1906, 129–32). However, Gardiner soon began to analyze this corpus of inscriptions and became convinced that the script was alphabetic, not some "local barbarism." He rapidly made major strides forward in the decipherment of these inscriptions (often referred to as "Proto-Sinaitic"), based on his assumption that "the acrophonic principle" was operative. Moreover, he also argued that the intellectual soil that facilitated the invention was certain aspects of the ancient Egyptian writing system (Gardiner 1916, 1–16), including various Egyptian signs that represented single consonants. In addition, he became convinced that although these early alphabetic signs "are not in Egyptian Hieroglyphic … many of the signs are obviously borrowed from that source" (14). Ultimately, based on the date of some of the hieroglyphic inscriptions in the region of Serabiṭ el-Ḥadem as well as the morphological similarities between these early alphabetic signs and certain hieroglyphic signs, Gardiner stated that he believed that it was reasonable to assign the alphabetic inscriptions to the latter portion of the Egyptian Twelfth Dynasty (i.e., early-eighteenth century B.C.E.). Nevertheless, because of a dearth of data, he did not rule out a date some three centuries later than this (13). Regarding the writers of these texts, Gardiner proposed that because these early alphabetic texts were written in a Semitic language, the authors were Semites. Moreover, Gardiner argued, because of the similarities between certain hieroglyphic signs and early alphabetic letters, that these Semites were familiar with Egyptian hieroglyphics. Furthermore, he believed that these Semites were connected in some fashion with the Egyptian turquoise mines in this region.

Ultimately, Gardiner was able to decipher accurately a number of letters and this allowed him to read certain portions of some of these early alphabetic texts from the Sinai. Among the most convincing of Gardiner's readings were the words *tnt lbʿlt* "gift for the lady," with *bʿlt* being a reference to a goddess, that is, the feminine form of the divine name "Baʿal" (fig. 1.1). Some five decades after Gardiner's initial progress, Albright built on his seminal work and published his own analysis of these inscriptions, positing that he could read twenty-three of the posited twenty-seven letters of the script (fig. 1.2; Albright 1966), and dating the inscriptions to ca. 1550–1450 B.C.E.

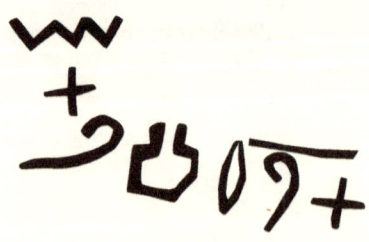

Fig. 1.1. Serabiṭ 346T. Drawing by the author.

Phon. Value	Schematic Forms	Early North-west Semitic	Early South Semitic	Early Letter Names	Meaning of Names
ʾ		✗ (16th) ⸲ (13th)	(Jamme)	ʾalp-	ox-head
b		□ (17th) (13th)	П	bêt-	house
g		⌒ (15th) ⟩ (12th)	⅂Γ	gaml-	throw-stick
d		◁ (10th)	(Jamme)	digg-	fish
ḏ		?	H N (Jamme)	?	?
h		∃ (10th)		hô(?)	man calling
w		Y (10th)	⊕ (? used for y)	wô(waw)	mace
z		F (16th) I (10th)		zê(n-)	?
ḥ		III (12th) ᛐ (10th)		ḥê(t-)	fence (?)
ḫ		?	(Jamme)	ḫa( )	hank of yarn
ṭ		(10th) ⊕ (10th)	⊞	ṭê(t-)	spindle?
y		(13th) (10th)	(orig w)	yad-	arm
k		(17th) (13th)		kapp-	palm
l		(14th) (13th)	(Jamme)	lamd-	ox-goad
m		ᴍ (15th) (13th)	(9th) (8th)	mêm-	water
n		(14th) (12th)		naḥš-	snake
ś		(10th)		(samk-?)	?
ʿ		☉ (12th) O (10th)	o	ʿên-	eye
ḡ		(15th)	(Jamme)	ḡa( )	?
p		) (10th)		puʾt-(?)	corner?
ṣ/ẓ		(10th)		ṣa(d-)	plant
ḍ		?		?	?
q		(14th) φ (10th)	(Jamme)	qu(p-)	?
r		(16th–14th)	) (	naʾš-	head of man
ś/ṯ		(13th) w (10th)		ṯann·	composite bow
š		?	(Jamme)	?	?
t		+ X (13th)	X + (Jamme)	tô(taw)	owner's mark

Fig. 1.2. Albright's chart of the proto-Sinaitic letters.

Two alphabetic inscriptions discovered at Wadi el-Hol in Egypt (fig. 1.3) were recently published (Darnell, Dobbs-Allsopp, Lundberg, McCarter, and Zuckerman 2005) and it has been argued that these can be dated to the same basic chronological horizon as the early alphabetic texts from Serabiṭ el-Ḥadem. Significantly, however, the data from the inscriptions at Wadi el-Hol converge to suggest that Albright's dates were low, and that Gardiner's original sense regarding the dates was correct. After all, various hieroglyphic inscriptions were discovered in the vicinity of the Wadi el-Hol alphabetic inscriptions and these

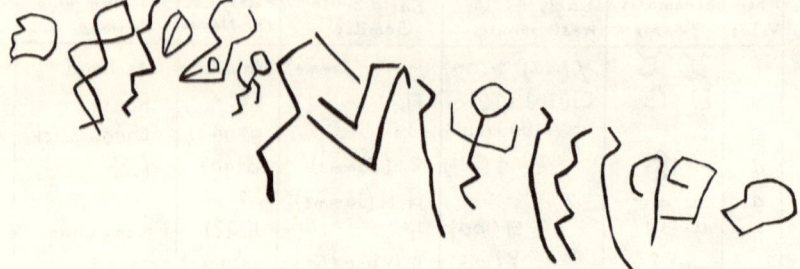

Fig. 1.3. The Wadi el-Hol inscription. Drawing by the author.

hieroglyphic inscriptions hail, for the most part, from the Middle Kingdom and Second Intermediate period. Moreover, there is evidence for a rise in contact between the Egyptians and Asiatics during the early part of the Middle Kingdom.

Finally, the palaeographic profile for the alphabetic script and its precursors in the Egyptian hieroglyphic and hieratic scripts are reflective of a date in the Middle Kingdom (Darnell, Dobbs-Allsopp, Lundberg, McCarter, and Zuckerman 2005, 86–87; Hamilton 2006). Some time ago, Sass (1988) argued for this chronological horizon (i.e., ca. eighteenth century B.C.E.) and his position has been strengthened with the discovery and publication of the alphabetic inscriptions from Wadi el-Hol.

THE ACROPHONIC PRINCIPLE AND THE ALPHABET: PRELIMINARY CONSIDERATIONS

The inscriptions from Wadi el-Hol and Serabiṭ el-Ḥadem are pictographic in nature and employ what is often referred to as the acrophonic principle. So, for example, one of the letters attested has the appearance of a human head. The word for a human head in Semitic is *rʾš*. This pictographic letter stood for the phoneme "r." That is, because the first sound of the word for head (*rʾš*) is "r," a pictographic depiction of a head was intended to signify the "r" sound. Similarly, the word for water in Semitic is *mym*. Therefore, this pictographic letter, which has, in some respects, the appearance of flowing water, stood for the phoneme "m." That is, because the first sound of the word for water (*mym*) is "m," a graphic depiction of water was intended to signify the "m" sound. Similarly, the word for a snake in Semitic is *nḥš*. The pictographic depiction of a snake (*nḥš*) stood for the phoneme "n." Or again, the word for the palm of the hand (including the fingers) in Semitic is *kp*. Therefore, the pictographic depiction of a hand (*kp*) stood for the phoneme "k," that is, the first sound in the word for hand (*kp*).

Fig. 1.4. Gezer sherd. Drawing by the author.

The acrophonic principle is the fundamental component of early alphabetic writing.

It should be emphasized strongly here that early alphabetic inscriptions are attested not only in Egypt, but also in Palestine. For example, an inscribed potsherd from Gezer dating to the Middle Bronze Age II (ca. 1800–1630 B.C.E.; fig. 1.4) contains three early alphabetic letters. The first letter depicts a hand and so can be read with confidence as a *kap*. The third letter depicts a house (Semitic *bayt*) and so can be read with substantial certitude as a *bet*. There has been some discussion about the letter in the middle. It is sometimes understood to be the pictoral sign for the "ox-goad" that represented the letter "l" (that is, *lamed*). This would yield a fine reading, namely, the word *klb* "dog," a self-designation that secondary and tertiary members of a hierarchy used in communications with superiors (e.g., in the letters from el-Amarna). However, this second sign is most readily understood as the sign for a "mace," that is, the letter *waw*, and the word "dog" is not preserved on this sherd. In short, there is no consensus regarding the putative meaning of these letters, or if the letters are even part of a single word, or the direction of writing.

Similarly, a stunning inscribed bronze dagger was discovered at Lachish (fig. 1.5). Four alphabetic signs are inscribed on the metal. Based on similar epigraphs from vari-

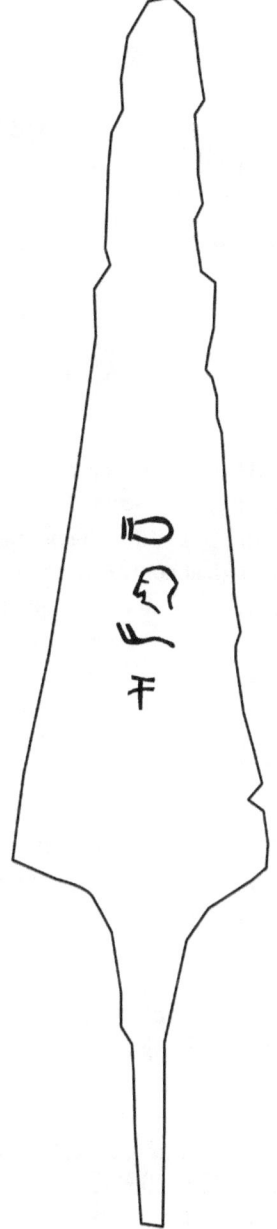

Fig. 1.5. Bronze dagger from Lachish. Drawing by the author.

Fig. 1.6. Qubur Walaydah bowl. Drawing by the author.

ous periods, it is to reasonable to suggest that the letters constitute a personal name. Also, an inscribed bowl was discovered during the final quarter of the twentieth century at a site near Gaza known as Qubur 'el-Walaydah (fig. 1.6). The archaeological context of the bowl (e.g., associated pottery) and the bowl itself have been dated to the terminal portion of the Late Bronze II Age or the beginning of Iron I. Although the entire inscription has not been preserved, a number of letters have been. Cross has argued that it was written from left to right, that is, dextrograde. He dates the inscription to ca. 1200 B.C.E. (1980, 1–20; 2003, 213–30, esp. 213–16) and reads it as follows: *šmpʿl. ʾyʾl.š*. At this juncture, it can be emphasized that the earliest of the early alphabetic linear inscriptions hail from the early-second millennium B.C.E. and the latest of the early alphabetic comes from the late-second millennium B.C.E.

The Alphabet at Ugarit

During the third quarter of the second millennium there was a distinct and important development: the invention and use of alphabetic cuneiform (not to be confused with Mesopotamian syllabic cuneiform). The Mesopotamian cuneiform script was certainly the prestige script in Syro-Mesopotamia during the second millennium B.C.E. The ancient city of Ugarit (Raš Šamra) was a powerful urban center during the second millennium and Mesopotamian cuneiform is very well-attested at Ugarit (as is also Hittite and even some Hurrian). However, the alphabet itself was also known at Ugarit (fig. 1.7). Rather than employing the linear alphabet such as was used at Wadi el-Hol, Serabiṭ el-Ḥadem, Gezer, Lachish, and so on, the scribes at Ugarit used a variant thereof. Namely, they employed a special system of "alphabetic cuneiform" letters. That is, they used the alphabet, but they employed wedge-shaped letters to write the alphabet rather than using the pictographic or linear forms, presumably because there was a certain cache associated with the cuneiform script, but not with the alphabetic script. Moreover, alphabetic cuneiform tablets have been found not just at Syrian Ugarit (and Ras Ibn Hani and Tell Negi Mend), but also in Lebanon (Sarepta) and Israel (Taanach, Beth-Shemesh, and Nahal Tavor); therefore, the use of alphabetic cuneiform during the mid- to late-second millennium was certainly not confined to the region of Ugarit.

Several remaining facets of the early history of the alphabet merit mention here. (1) A number of the signs of the cuneiform alphabet are modeled after the morphology of the early alphabetic signs. So, for example, the Ugaritic *šin* bears a striking resemblance to the linear alphabetic *šin*. Similarly, the Ugaritic ʿ*ayin* is reminiscent of the linear alphabetic ʿ*ayin*. Moreover, the Ugaritic *samek* is a cuneiform version of the linear *samek*. Ultimately, it is convincing to affirm that alphabetic cuneiform was developed later than, and on the basis of, linear early alphabetic.

(2) The evidence of ancient abecedaries (lists of the alphabet) in alphabetic cuneiform, indicates that there were two major variant sequences of the letters of the alphabet during the second millennium. That is, someone writing out the alphabet during the second millennium ostensibly had two basic options. One option was: ʾa, b g, ḫ, d, h, w, z, ḥ, ṭ, y, k, š, l, m, ḏ, n, ṯ, s, ʿ, p, ṣ, q, r, ṱ, ġ, t, ʾi, ʾu, ś. The other option was: h, l, ḥ, m. q, w, s₂ (š or ṯ), r, b, t, s₁ (š or ṯ), k, n, ḫ, ṣ, s₃ (s), p, ʾ, ʿ, d, ġ, ṭ, z, ḏ, y, ṱ, ṯ. The first of these is often called the "Abgad" order and the second of these is often called the "Halḥam" order. During the succeeding centuries, the former order became predominant in Northwest Semitic (e.g., the acrostics in the Hebrew Bible and at Kuntillet ʿAjrud), but the latter (halḥam)

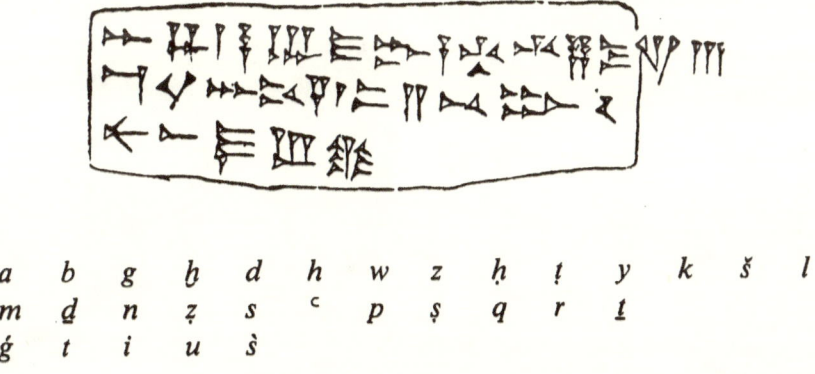

a	*b*	*g*	*ḫ*	*d*	*h*	*w*	*z*	*ḥ*	*ṭ*	*y*	*k*	*š*	*l*
m	*ḏ*	*n*	*ẓ*	*s*	ʿ	*p*	*ṣ*	*q*	*r*	*ṱ*			
ġ	*t*	*i*	*u*	*ṡ*									

Fig. 1.7. Chart with Ugaritic alphabet.

order became predominant in South Semitic (e.g., Ethiopic). However, during the second millennium B.C.E., both orders are attested.

(3) During the terminal horizons of the Late Bronze Age, there were a number of consonantal mergers in Northwest Semitic. That is, some of the consonants attested in early alphabetic and Ugaritic merged with some of the other consonants attested in early alphabetic and Ugaritic. For example, ḫ merges with ḥ and, therefore, a distinct grapheme ("letter") for ḫ is not attested in Northwest Semitic during the Iron Age. Moreover, ġ merges with ʿ and, therefore, a distinct grapheme for ġ is not attested in Northwest Semitic during the Iron Age. Because of the various consonantal mergers, Iron Age Northwest Semitic, beginning with Phoenician, consists of just twenty-two letters.

CHAPTER 2

THE USE OF THE PHOENICIAN SCRIPT DURING THE IRON AGE AND THE RISE OF THE LEVANTINE NATIONAL SCRIPTS

Throughout much of the second millennium B.C.E. there was a Northwest Semitic script tradition ("early alphabetic") but the variations present within the script were often quite significant: there was certainly no standardized Northwest Semitic script tradition. Rather, there was much variation in stance, including the direction of the "face" of the letters. The direction of writing could vary, with sinistrograde (right-to-left), dextrograde (left-to-right), boustrophedon (i.e., consecutive lines written from left-to-right, then right-to-left), and columnar writing all attested. Moreover, there was a larger stock of consonants available, arguably as many as twenty-seven or twenty-eight during the earliest periods of the alphabet (i.e., not just the twenty-two letters of the later Phoenician alphabet). This period of the script has been the subject of several substantive studies (Albright 1966; Cross 2003, 195–343; Sass 1988; Darnell, Dobbs-Allsopp, Lundberg, McCarter, and Zuckerman 2005; Hamilton 2006).

During the terminal horizons of the second millennium, however, several developments occurred: (1) The stance of the letters became more stabilized and standardized; (2) the direction of writing was consistently sinistrograde; and, (3) because of a number of consonant mergers, the number of consonants was reduced to twenty-two. From this point on, because of these three developments, the convention within the field of Northwest Semitic epigraphy is to refer to this stage of the script as Phoenician rather than early alphabetic. Naveh reflects the consensus of the field with his statement that the transition from early alphabetic to Phoenician "took place in the mid-eleventh century B.C." (1987a, 42). Note that these changes did not occur simultaneously, however. That is, the changes occurred over the course of time, but all were complete by about the mid-eleventh century.

The Iron Age Phoenician Script:
The *Mutterschrift* in the Homeland

There are a number of Phoenician inscriptions from the Phoenician homeland (modern Lebanon) that provide substantial data about the Phoenician script of the late-eleventh, tenth, and early-ninth centuries (Rollston 2008a; 2008b). Moreover, there are a number of important Phoenician inscriptions that were produced outside of the borders of Phoenicia during this early period as well. Among the most important of the early Phoenician inscriptions from the homeland is the Azarbaʿal Inscription, often referred to as the Bronze Spatula Inscription (fig. 2.1; Dunand 1945, 155–57). This prestige object was discovered during controlled excavations at Byblos (ancient Gebal, in Phoenicia). Six lines of Phoenician text (often considered enigmatic) are etched into the metal. The script reflects archaic features, such as the trident *kap*, the *mem* with a strong vertical stance, *samek* with a short vertical shaft (i.e., not extending much below the bottom horizontal), and the box-shaped *ḥet*. The five strokes of *mem* are of the same approximate length, as are the three strokes of *nun*; these are early features. Some have argued that this inscription reflects the terminal horizon of the eleventh century, but a date in the (early-)tenth century is also possible.

There are several early royal Phoenician inscriptions from Byblos. Among the most impressive of these is that of the Ahiram Sarcophagus (fig. 2.2), an inscription commissioned by Ahiram's son Ittobaʿal (Dussaud 1924; Lehmann 2005; Lundberg 2004). The majority of this inscription is written on the lid of the sarcophagus (the long edge), but the initial component of the inscription is written on the end of the sarcophagus itself (i.e., not on the lid). Most of the letters were chiseled with care and substantial precision, although there is a diminution of letter size that is visible (and quantifiable) in the terminal portions of the inscription. Space constraints probably necessitated the diminution. That is,

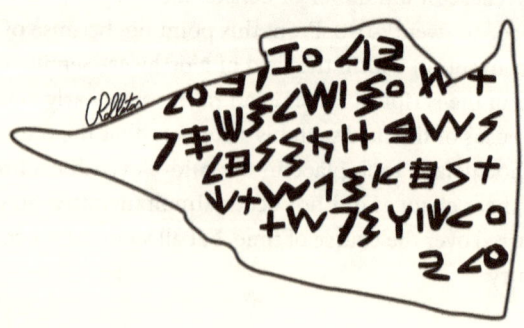

Fig. 2.1. The bronze
Azarbaʿal inscription.
Drawing by the author.

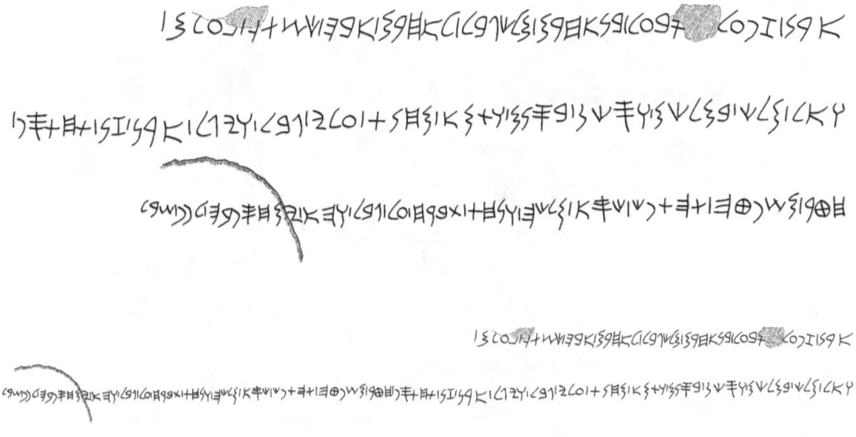

Fig. 2.2. The Ahiram sarcophagus inscription. Drawing by Marilyn Lundberg. Above: Line 1 = side 1; lines 2–3 = side 2. Below: Transcription with side 2 in one line.

as the scribe realized that there was not sufficient space to complete the entire inscription using such large letters he began to reduce the sizes of the letters.

The Phoenician script of the Ahiram Sarcophagus can be distinguished from the script of the Azarbaʻal Inscription by the presence of some discernible and diagnostic typological differences, or developments, that indicate that the script of this inscription is later than that of the Azarbaʻal Inscription. The differences that are among the most important are the distinct lengthening of the vertical shaft of *samek*, the occasional lengthening of the fifth stroke of *mem*, the occasional lengthening of the third stroke of *nun*, and the lengthening of the verticals of *ḥet* (i.e., no longer box-shaped). Note, however, that *kap* remains trident-shaped (the trident form of *kap* is an early feature). Based on the script, I consider this inscription to be dateable with substantial certitude to the tenth century B.C.E. (Rollston 2008a; 2008b).

Hailing also from Byblos during this same basic horizon are the Yehimilk Inscription (fig. 2.3), the Abibaʻal Inscription, and the Elibaʻal Inscription. Yehimilk is a monumental Byblian inscription, chiseled into a stone tablet (Dunand 1930, 321–31). The Abibaʻal Inscription is inscribed on a statue of Pharaoh Sheshonk I (reigned ca. 945–924 B.C.E.) and so it is among the most interesting and important of the early Byblian (Phoenician) lapidary inscriptions (Clermont-Ganneau 1903, 378–83). Similarly, the Byblian inscription of Elibaʻal (Dussaud 1925, 101–17) was inscribed on a bust of Pharaoh Osorkon I (reigned ca. 924–

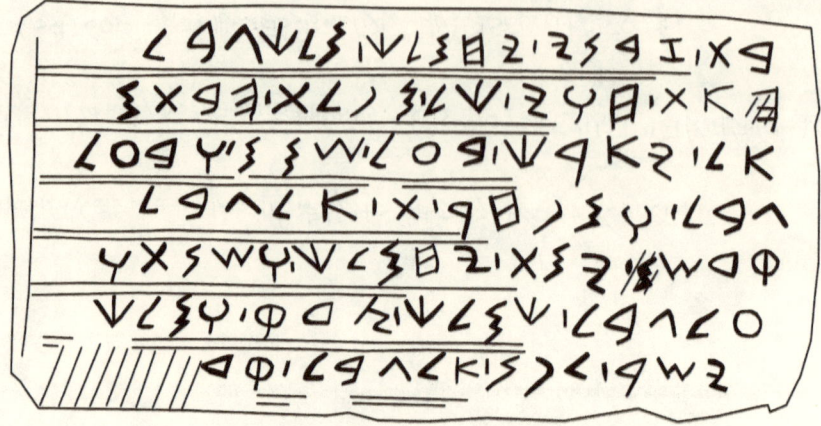

Fig. 2.3. Yehimilk inscription. Drawing by the author.

889).[1] Of consequence is the fact that within this inscription, Eliba'al provides his father's name: Yehi[milk]. The inscriptions of Yehimilk, Abiba'al, and Eliba'al reflect the same basic script typology as that of the Ahiram Sarcophagus Inscription. For example, the vertical stroke of 'alep is at the leftmost extreme of the vertex of the two horizontal crossbars; this is an early feature. Moreover, *kap* continues to be trident-shaped; this too is an early feature.

Some modest typological differences are present in the inscriptions of Ahiram, Yehimilk, Abiba'al, and Eliba'al. Among the most interesting is the length of the final stroke of *mem* and *nun*. Here is the way that I would summarize the palaeographic data. Within early Phoenician, the *mem* consists of five oblique downstrokes and the *nun* consists of three oblique downstrokes. The *mem* of the Ahiram Sarcophagus Inscription, Yehimilk, Abiba'al, and Eliba'al has a strong vertical stance. Often (but not always) the five strokes of the *mem* are all about the same length and often (but not always) the three strokes of the *nun* are all about the same length. Thus, the five strokes of the *mem* and the three strokes of the *nun* in the Eliba'al Inscription are each about the same length, with some modest variation. However, the fifth stroke of *mem* and the third stroke of *nun* in the Ahiram Sarcophagus and the Yehimilk Inscription do sometimes exhibit

---

1. Note that the names in the cartouches of these statues of Sheshonq and Osorkon are those of Sheshonq I and Osorkon I. That is, it would be problematic for someone to suggest that these statues were those of Sheshonq II (r. ca. 890 B.C.E.) and Osorkon II (r. ca. 874–850 B.C.E.), as the readings of the latter two are quite different (Beckerath 1999, 185). I am grateful to James Hoffmeier for discussing this issue with me and providing this reference.

Fig. 2.4. Shipitba'al inscription. Drawing by the author.

some lengthening (i.e, the final stroke of each letter is often slightly longer than the preceding strokes). The slight lengthening of the final stroke would be classified as being slightly more advanced typologically. Nonetheless, the variations are not such that I would be inclined to date these inscriptions to different periods. Rather, I consider the Ahiram Sarcophagus, the Yehimilk Inscription, the Abiba'al Inscription and the Eliba'al Inscription all to hail from the same chronological horizon, namely, Byblos of the tenth century.

The script of the Shipitba'al Inscription from Byblos (fig. 2.4; Dunand 1945, 146–51) contains features that reflect further typological development (i.e., when compared with the script of the Ahiram, Yehimilk, Abiba'al, and Eliba'al inscriptions). For example, the fifth stroke of *mem* has lengthened considerably and it is readily apparent that some rotation of the head has begun (sometimes incipient, sometimes significant). Furthermore, the third stroke of *nun* has lengthened substantially and there is some rotation of its head as well. The Shipitba'al Inscription can be classed as the latest of the great early Byblian royal inscriptions. From this

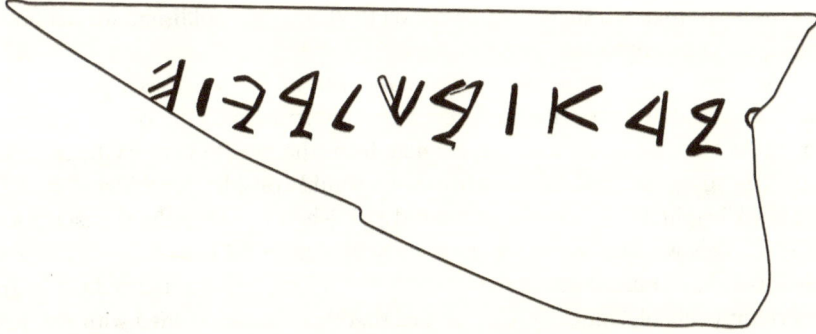

Fig. 2.5. 'Abda sherd. Drawing by the author.

chronological horizon also comes the ʿAbda Sherd (fig. 2.5). Note that the morphology of *bet* in these two inscriptions is the same; this feature was ephemeral. In sum, during the tenth and very-early-ninth centuries, the Phoenician script is well attested in the Phoenician homeland and Shipitbaʿal is the latest of the early Byblian royal inscriptions.

DEBATES ABOUT DATES OF EARLY PHOENICIAN INSCRIPTIONS

There has been some criticism of the standard dates of the early Byblian royal inscriptions, with some scholars arguing that they date to the ninth and eighth centuries B.C.E. (e.g., Sass 2005). For this reason, some reference to the sequence of finds, the progress of scholarship during the first half of the twentieth century, and the rationale for the standard dating, should be instructive.

The Abibaʿal Inscription (on a statue of Sheshonq) was published in 1903 (Clermont-Ganneau 1903, 378–83), but the entire text was not deciphered (because scholars had misunderstood the archaic *kap* as a *šin*). Nevertheless, even though the text was not deciphered in its entirety, the fact that it was inscribed on a statue of Sheshonq I (r. ca. 945–924 B.C.E.) resulted in its being dated to the late-tenth century B.C.E. The Ahiram Sarcophagus was discovered in 1923 (Dussaud 1924). Because two fragments of alabaster vases in the tomb of Ahiram bore the name of Ramesses II, the Ahiram Sarcophagus Inscription was initially believed to have hailed from that chronological horizon (i.e., the thirteenth century B.C.E.). However, because the script of the Abibaʿal Inscription and that of the Ahiram Sarcophagus Inscription were so similar, it soon began to be argued that the Ahiram Sarcophagus Inscription must be dated to the tenth century, not the thirteenth century. Two years after the discovery of the Ahiram Sarcophagus, Dussaud (1925, 101–17) published fragments of the Elibaʿal Inscription, inscribed on a statue of Osorkon I (r. ca. 924–889 B.C.E.). The Phoenician script of this inscription was very similar to that of the Abibaʿal and Ahiram Sarcophagus Inscriptions. Soon thereafter, Dunand (1930, 321–31) published the Yehimilk Inscription from Byblos.

Albright had been active in the analysis of all of these inscriptions. Initially, he had dated the Ahiram Sarcophagus Inscription to the twelfth century, but he had subsequently lowered his date from the twelfth century to ca. 1000 B.C.E. He suggested that the lowest date he would consider tenable was ca. 975 B.C.E. (Albright 1947, 153–54). Dunand published the Shipitbaʿal Inscription in 1945. This was the last of the great early Byblian royal inscriptions (Dunand 1945, 146–51). Dunand stated that the Shipitbaʿal Inscription antedated the "autre inscriptions Phéniciennes" and he argued that this was established with absolute decisiveness on the basis of script. Indeed, he argued that it was plausible to date this inscription to the end of the eighteenth century B.C.E. or the beginning of the seventeenth century (Dunand 1945, 150–51). Dunand's early dating of Shipitba'al had few followers, however. Albright stated that in his judgment "there is no need to date any of [the early Byblian royal inscriptions] after the beginning of the ninth century, and the group as a whole belongs to the tenth century" (1947, 154). Regarding the fact that there was initially such diversity of opinion among epigraphers and archaeologists regarding the dating of these inscriptions, Albright noted that "when the first documents of this category were published there was much less external evidence bearing on grammar, lexicography and spelling than there is today. All scholars made numerous mistakes" (155). Behind Albright's statement is the fact that a strong scholarly consensus had emerged by, or during, the 1940s. Of course, Albright was among those who contributed in a substantive manner to the discussion and his views represented the consensus.

Albright's dates for the kings of the early Byblian royal inscriptions are as follows (160): (1) Ahiram, ca. 1000 B.C.E.; (2) Ittoba'al (son of Ahiram), ca. 975 B.C.E.; (3) Yehimilk, ca. 950 B.C.E.; (4) Abiba'al (son of Yehimilk?), ca. 930 B.C.E.; (5) Eliba'al (son of Yehimilk), ca. 920 B.C.E.; (6) Shipitba'al (son of Eliba'al), ca. 900 B.C.E. Since Albright's era, the dates for which he argued have normally been accepted. Within McCarter's detailed analysis of these inscriptions he posited the following dates: (1) Ahiram, fl. 1000 B.C.E.; (2) Ittoba'al, fl. 980 B.C.E.; (3) Yehimilk, fl. 960 B.C.E.; (4) Abiba'al, fl. 940 B.C.E.; (5) Eliba'al, fl. 920 B.C.E.; (6) Shipitba'al, fl. 900 B.C.E. (1975, 34). Some might not wish to be as precise in assigning dates as Albright and McCarter, but the fact remains that a tenth century date for the early Byblian royal inscriptions has stood the test of time (Rollston 2008b).

The reasons for the persistence of the standard chronology of the early Byblian royal inscriptions, however, should be reiterated. (1) Monumental inscriptions such as the Mesha Stele and the Tel Dan Stele can be dated securely on the basis of historical content to the ninth century. The scripts of these inscriptions are typologically later than the scripts of the early Byblian royal inscriptions. (2) The inscription of Abiba'al was inscribed on a statue of the Egyptian King Sheshonq I. (3) The inscription of Eliba'al was inscribed on a statue of the Egyptian King Osorkon I. (4) The Ahiram Sarcophagus refers to Ittoba'al as the son of Ahiram. Thus, in terms of royal chronology, it can be affirmed that Ahiram was succeeded by his son Ittoba'al. (5) The Shipitba'al inscription contains a three-generation genealogy: Shipitba'al, king of Byblos; son of Eliba'al, king of Byblos; son of Yehimilk, king of Byblos. Thus, in terms of royal chronology, the following sequence can be affirmed: Yehimilk, then Eliba'al, and then Shipitba'al. (6) In terms of script typology, the script of the Shipitba'al Inscription is definitely the most developed of all of the early Byblian royal inscriptions. That is, the script of this inscription can be affirmed to be the latest of the early Byblian royal inscriptions.

Thus, at this juncture, there are two sets of royal sequences that can be discerned on the basis of the early Byblian royal inscriptions:

Ahiram	Yehimilk
Ittoba'al	Eliba'al
	Shipitba'al

Because the script of the Shipitba'al Inscription is definitively the most developed (i.e., typologically latest), it has been considered reasonable to argue that the sequence that includes Shipitba'al should be understood as the later of the two royal sequences. This then yields the following combined chronology:

Ahiram – Ittoba'al – Yehimilk – Eliba'al – Shipitba'al

At this point in the reconstruction, the early Byblian royal inscriptions of Ahiram, Yehimilk, Eliba'al, and Shipitba'al have been factored into the discussion. However, for the Abiba'al Inscription, there is no preserved patronymic; therefore, the question of placement of Abiba'al within the royal sequence cannot be known with certitude. Certain things can be noted, however. First, the script of the Abiba'al Inscription is not as late as that of the Shipitba'al inscription, so the palaeographic evidence would militate strongly against placing the reign of Abiba'al after that of Shipitba'al. Second, the Eliba'al Inscription is on a statue of Osorkon I and the Abiba'al Inscription is on a statue of Sheshonq I. Sheshonq I reigned before Osorkon I; therefore, it can be reasonably postulated that Abiba'al reigned before Eliba'al. Although it might be tempting to suggest that Abiba'al reigned before Ahiram, in light of the fact that the inscription of Abiba'al was inscribed on a statue of Sheshonq I (who was the immediate predecessor of Osorkon I) it is arguably most convincing to posit that he was the immediate predecessor of Eliba'al. The sequence then is as follows:

Ahiram – Ittoba'al – Yehimilk – Abiba'al – Eliba'al – Shipitba'al

Of course, an issue that arises in this connection is the paternity of Abiba'al. Because there is no preserved patronymic, it is not possible to answer this question with confidence. However, Albright's tentative proposal (1947, 160; see also Donner and Röllig, 1973–79, vol. 2, 8) that Abiba'al and Eliba'al were brothers (and thus both sons of Yehimilk) is plausible (cf. Kings Jehoahaz and Jehoiakim, both sons of King Josiah, 2 Kgs 23:30, 34). Nevertheless, the precise placement of Abiba'al within the sequence is not a critical component of the tenth century dating of the early Byblian royal inscriptions. Rather, in various ways, it is an ancillary component. In any case, the main point is that the standard chronology of the early Byblian royal inscriptions is based on the convergence of a constellation of compelling data; therefore, the standard dating is the most cogent position (Rollston 2008b; contra Sass 2005).

THE USE OF THE PHOENICIAN SCRIPT OUTSIDE OF PHOENICIA

ISRAEL

The Kefar Veradim bowl is a stunning artifact, made of bronze, and fluted (fig. 2.6; Alexandre 2006). The inscription consists of just four words, all preserved quite well, with two word dividers present. The inscribed bowl was found in a burial cave at Kefar Veradim (Israel). Moreover, the script is definitively Phoenician, even though this inscription was found in Israel.

The excavator has stated that, according to the standard chronology, the associated archaeological materials (bowls, craters, including some black-on-red ware, etc.) can be dated to the tenth century (Alexandre 2006, 31), or early-ninth century (22–23). Alexandre contemplated the possibility that this bowl might have been an heirloom piece, but does not come down definitively on the subject (31). From my perspective, based on the quality of the bowl and the presence of an inscription, this is an obvious prestige item. Moreover, the script of this inscription reflects the work of a trained, consummate scribe. Its script reflects the same basic script morphology as that of the Azarba'al Inscription. For example, *kap* is trident-shaped, *samek* has the short vertical shaft, and the *ḥet* is box-shaped. Because of the medium (a bowl) it is difficult to place substantial emphasis upon the stance of *mem* and *nun*. However, the five strokes of *mem* and the three strokes of *nun* are of the same approximate length (although the scribe had some difficulty incising certain of the strokes of the *mem*). I consider this inscribed bowl to hail from the same basic chronological horizon as the Azarba'al Inscription. Based on the script, therefore, I am comfortable with an early-tenth century date for this inscription.

Note that Sass argues that the low chronology should be accepted and so he dates the artifacts from this tomb to the mid-ninth century. Furthermore, he argues against the possibility that the inscribed bowl is an heirloom piece (Sass 2005, 34–39, 50–74). At one point, with some deft (if problematic) rhetoric, he states that if the standard chronology for "West Semitic palaeography and Palestinian archaeology" is applied, "an absurd situation ensues: the Kefar Veradim inscription would be 200 years older than the bowl it is written on … the inscription would date to the eleventh century, the tomb assemblage to the tenth, and the

Fig. 2.6. Kefar Veradim bowl. Drawing by the author.

bowl to the ninth" (39). Sass's framing of the data, though, is a chimera. After all, Alexandre considers the tomb, the bowl, and the inscription all to be tenth century.

Nevertheless, I suppose that someone might suggest that none of the associated pottery can be dated to the early-tenth century, or conversely, that all of it must be dated to the late-tenth century (i.e., not the early-tenth century). For various reasons, however, this is not a serious dilemma. After all, there is always a plus or minus for pottery typologies, just as there is for palaeographic typologies. This must be factored in, I contend, to the composite picture. Furthermore, I cannot agree with Sass's strong disinclination to consider the possibility that a beautiful inscribed bowl could have been an heirloom piece (39). After all, the presence of "heirloom objects" in ancient Near Eastern archaeology is a well-attested phenomenon. For example, Marcus (1991; following Porada) has stated that some mosaic glass vessels from Hasanlu are heirlooms. Moreover, sometimes seals are retained as prestigious heirlooms and reused. Thus, it has been argued that dynastic seals (e.g., of the earlier Mitannian ruler Shaushtatar) were retained and reused during the Late Bronze Age at Tell Brak (Matthews 1997; Stein 1989). Furthermore, a tablet from the reign of the Neo-Assyrian king Esarhaddon was sealed with three dynastic seals from different periods, namely, a seal of an Old Assyrian king, a Middle Assyrian king, and a Neo-Assyrian king (Parker 1955; 1962; Albenda 1978). Because of the quality of the Kefar Veradim inscribed bronze bowl, it would be difficult to state that it could not have been an heirloom, but rather quite the contrary. Ultimately, therefore, I believe that the excavator's date in the tenth century for the tomb and bowl is cogent. Also, a palaeographic date in the tenth century is convincing. Moreover, it is entirely possible that this piece was an heirloom piece and thus was inscribed earlier in the tenth century and then deposited in the tomb later during the tenth century. In short, the archaeological data and palaeographic data dovetail just fine.

Fig. 2.7. The Gezer Calendar. From Naveh 1987a, fig. 54.

On an ancillary note, I should like to state that some might suggest that they are surprised that a Phoenician inscription would be found in Israel. Actually, however, this should not be surprising. After all, Phoenician inscriptions are found throughout much of the Levant and Mediterranean (see below). Moreover, the biblical text itself (e.g., 1–2 Kings) affirms that there was substantial cultural contact between Phoenicia and Israel. Furthermore, the archaeological remains often confirm this (Lipiński 1991). Thus, the fact that multiple Phoenician inscriptions have been discovered in Israel during the "early period" was predictable. In sum, the Kefar Veradim bronze bowl is a superb exemplar of the usage of the Phoenician script in early Israel, a reflection of the fact that Israelite scribes first wrote with the Phoenician script (not the Old Hebrew script).

A small limestone "tablet" was discovered in 1908 at Gezer during Macalister's excavations (fig. 2.7), in debris from his "Fourth Semitic," a period Albright associated with Iron I (Macalister 1908; Albright 1943). Because the contents of the inscription revolve around seasonal agricultural activities (e.g., sowing, harvesting, and processing of flax and barley), it is often considered to be some sort of an agricultural "calendar." Naveh has stated that "the script of the Gezer Calendar, thought to be the earliest Hebrew inscription known to date, resembles the writing of the tenth-century B.C. Phoenician inscriptions from Byblos." He then goes on to state that "at this stage no specifically Hebrew characters can be distinguished, and the Hebrew followed the scribal tradition current in Canaan" (Naveh 1987a, 65). Cross considers the Gezer Calendar to be written in the Hebrew language (Cross and Freedman 1952, 46–47). Pardee, however, has recently argued that the language is indeed Phoenician (Pardee in press). In any case, regarding the script of the Gezer Calendar, Cross has written that "so similar are Phoenician and Hebrew in the tenth century that it has been difficult for epigraphists to establish whether the Gezer Calendar was written in a Hebrew or in a Phoenician script." Cross continues and states that "I believe that the first rudimentary innovations that will mark the emergent Hebrew script can be perceived in the Gezer Calendar, but they are faint at best." Cross then affirms that "these rudimentary features include the elongation of the vertical strokes or legs of such letters as ʾalep, waw, kap, mem, and reš." To be sure, Cross has not come down hard on this subject, though. Rather, again, he has stated that he believes the features that distinguish the fledgling Old Hebrew script from the Phoenician *Mutterschrift* are "faint at best" (Cross 1980; 2003, 226).

Ultimately, though, and with all due respect, I must differ with Cross. That is, I consider the script of the Gezer Calendar to be Phoenician. My reasons are basically twofold: (1) Elongation is a feature that is already present in Phoenician of the late-tenth century and the early-ninth century. Therefore, I cannot consider elongation to be a distinctive feature of the Old Hebrew script.[2] (2) Moreover, features such as the pronounced curvature of *kap*, *mem*, and *nun* that are markers of the Old Hebrew script (Naveh 1987a, 66) are absent in the Gezer Calendar. For these reasons, I consider the script of the Gezer Calendar to be pure Phoenician (Rollston 2008a, 77–87).[3]

Regarding its placement within the Phoenician series, I would state that certain basic features of the Gezer Calendar's script are typologically later than the majority of the Old Byblian inscriptions. For example, the *kap* is no longer trident-shaped (in the Gezer Calendar), as the right stroke of this letter has elongated forming a leg.[4] Although this sort of elongation (of this stroke) is attested in Phoenician of the ninth and eighth centuries, it is not attested in Shipitbaʿal (from the late-tenth or early-ninth century). The *waw* of Gezer is no longer the bowl-headed form that is the norm in the earliest of the Royal Byblian inscriptions, but is rather the more angular form (cf. the similar fledgling form in Shipitbaʿal, the latest of the Royal Byblian). Substantial elongation is also present in the final strokes of *mem* and *nun*, and the best parallels for this are in Shipitbaʿal and,

---

2. Within my discussion of the Tel Zayit abecedary (below), I provide more data about the phenomenon of elongation.

3. It is imperative to note that certain aspects of the Gezer Calendar are often argued to be indicative of the hand of a fledgling student. This is possible, but the fact remains that the letter forms reflect important typological features. Similar statements can be made about the Tel Zayit abecedary.

4. Note that although there is elongation in the *kap* of Izbet Sarteh, it is not a lengthening of the stroke on the right side.

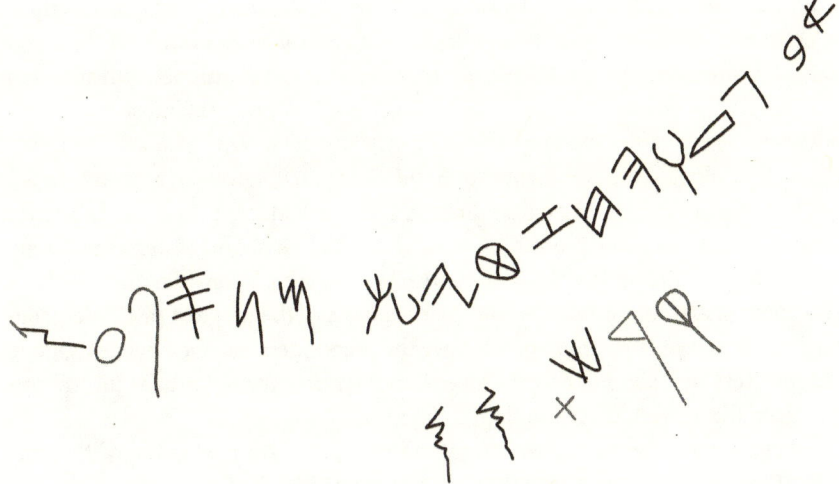

Fig. 2.8. Tel Zayit abcedery. Drawing of the two-line inscription by McCarter in Tappy and McCarter 2008, fig. 3.8.

of course, Phoenician texts from horizons after Shipitba'al. Note, however, that the stance of *mem* in the Gezer Calendar is still strongly vertical, more so than Shipitba'al. Note also that the main vertical shaft of *samek* exhibits elongation (but this sort of elongation is attested in Ahiram as well). Based on the constellation of script data, I date the Gezer Calendar to the same basic horizon as Shipitba'al, that is late-tenth or very-early-ninth century. Someone might wish to argue for an earlier date for this inscription, but I consider the combined evidence of the elongation of the *kap*, the morphology of the *waw*, and the substantial elongation of *mem* and *nun* to be solid evidence for a date in the late-tenth century or the very-early ninth century.

The Tel Zayit abecedary (fig. 2.8) hails from an archaeological context that Tappy considers to be tenth century (Tappy and McCarter 2008, 5–25). The inscription was carved into a stone. Although the second half of this abecedary is quite abraded, it is certain that it is a complete abecedary. The script of this inscription reflects typological developments not attested in the Kefar Veradim bowl inscription, the Azarba'al, Ahiram, Yehimilk, Abiba'al, or Eliba'al inscriptions. For example, *kap* is not trident shaped, but rather has developed a leg (note again that even Shipitba'al retains the trident-shaped *kap*). Moreover, the fifth stroke of *mem* and the third stroke of *nun* are elongated. In addition, the entire stance of *mem* exhibits development, as it has begun to rotate (note, therefore, that the *mem* of Zayit is typologically later than that of Gezer). These sorts of typological features reflect the fact that the Tel Zayit abecedary is typologically later than the inscriptions of Ahiram, Yehimilk, Abiba'al, and Eliba'al, and thus, of course, much later typologically than the Azarba'al Inscription and the Kefar Veradim bowl inscription. Of course, there are a modest number of features of the Tel Zayit abecedary that are typologically early. Among the most significant of these is *waw* (cf. the typologically later *waw* of the Gezer Calendar). Preservations of typologically older forms are to be anticipated, however, at times. Based on the constellation of palaeographic data, I date this inscription to the late-tenth century or the very-early-ninth century (i.e., I date it slightly later than Tappy desires to date the archaeological context). Moreover, I consider the Tel Zayit abecedary also to constitute another nice example of the usage of the Phoenician script in Iron Age Israel. Finally, I believe the preponderance of evidence suggests that the Tel Zayit abecedary, the Gezer Calendar, and the Shipitba'al Inscription hail from the same basic chronological horizon.

Regarding the script series, however, McCarter has argued in the *editio princeps* of the Tel Zayit abecedary that it is not written in the Phoenician script but rather a distinct south Canaanite script that derived from the Phoenician script.[5] Moreover, this south Canaanite script is affirmed to be a transitional script that "in the tenth century it already exhibits characteristics that anticipate the distinctive features of the mature Hebrew national script" (Tappy and McCarter 2008, 26, 28). This is considered to be "a major watershed in the evolution of alphabetic writing in southern Canaan at the outset of Iron Age IIA, and the principal result of this phenomenon emerged as the mature Hebrew national script of the first millennium" (42, *et passim*). Thus, within the *editio princeps*, it is affirmed that the script of the Tel Zayit abecedary is not that of the Phoenician script series, but rather is basically a nascent Old Hebrew script.

McCarter's position regarding the script of the Tel Zayit abecedary is important and nuanced. Nonetheless, I understand the data differently. That is, I consider the script of the Tel Zayit abecedary to fit nicely within the Phoenician script series. A major component of the McCarter's argument that this is not the Phoenician script is his contention that elongation is not a real feature of the Phoenician script during this horizon. To be precise, it is affirmed that "the elongation of *'alep, he, waw, kap, mem, nun,* and *reš*" argues against considering this Phoenician and is evidence for the fact that it is a transitional script that anticipates the distinctive "features of the mature Hebrew national script." Furthermore, it is argued that this resistance of elongation is "underscored by the persistence into the ninth century of a preference for compact, well-proportioned

---

5. Note that within the Tel Zayit abecedary there is just a single example of each letter, and some of these are not well preserved!

characters of the kind seen, for example, in maritime Phoenician inscriptions such as the so-called Honeyman inscriptions from Cyprus and the *taršiš* from Nora in Sardinia" (30).

However, I contend that it would be very difficult to suggest that the elongation of certain letters should be considered to be evidence for or against an inscription's status within a script series. That is, I do not consider elongation to be a distinctive marker of a particular national script series. The Phoenician, Aramaic, and Old Hebrew script series all reflect elongation (Peckham 1968 [Phoenician]; Naveh 1970 [Aramaic]; Rollston 1999; 2003a; 2006 [Old Hebrew]). For the sake of argument, I will focus here on elongation in Phoenician itself. For example, note the elongation present in *mem* and *nun* of Shipitba'al. That is, the elongation present in these letters in this early Byblian royal inscription is as great as that attested in the Tel Zayit abecedary. No one would suggest (because of the elongation in *mem* and *nun* in Shipitba'al) that Shipitba'al was written in the Old Hebrew script; therefore, it stands to reason that it would be a precarious basis for suggesting that the Tel Zayit abecedary is written in the Old Hebrew script. Note that the relative length of the vertical stroke of the *'alep* in the Tell Fakhariyeh Inscription (fig. 2.9) is as long as that of Zayit, and all would agree that the script of the Tell Fakhariyeh is Phoenician and typologically early (Cross 1995, 408; see also Naveh 1987b, 101–13).[6] Regarding the *he*, similar statements can be made. Note, for example, that the vertical stroke of *he* in the Tell Fakhariyeh Inscription reflects elongation, even though this is a typologically early Phoenician script. The *waw* of the Tell Fakhariyeh Inscription reflects elongation as well. Regarding *kap*, it is again critical to note that in the Tell Fakhariyeh Inscription, the *kap* reflects some elongation (i.e., it is no longer just the trident). Furthermore, and of fundamental importance, note that there is some significant elongation of *kap* in the sherd from Izbet Sarteh (Cross 1980, 8–14; 2002, 220–27) a sherd normally dated to the eleventh century B.C.E. This inscription is certainly not written in the Old Hebrew script. Notice also the pronounced elongation present in the Phoenician script of subsequent centuries, as revealed in the eighth century Kition Bowl (fig. 2.10). Again, then, it is very difficult to consider elongation to be a distinctive feature of the Old Hebrew, nascent Old Hebrew script, or a transitional South Canaanite script.

Furthermore, curvature of the vertical downstrokes of *kap, mem, nun* is an important marker of the Old Hebrew script (so also Naveh 1987a, 66), but this feature is absent in the script of the Tel Zayit abecedary. At the end of the day, I

---

6. Cross states that he does not think the Fakhariyeh Inscription shows much tendency "to lengthen final downstrokes" (1995, 407). Nonetheless, I would note that even his drawings reveal that there is some significant lengthening of some of the downstrokes in this inscription.

Fig. 2.9. Tell Fakhariyeh inscription.
Drawing by P. Bordreuil in Abou-Assaf,
Bordreuil, and Millard 1982, fig. 3.

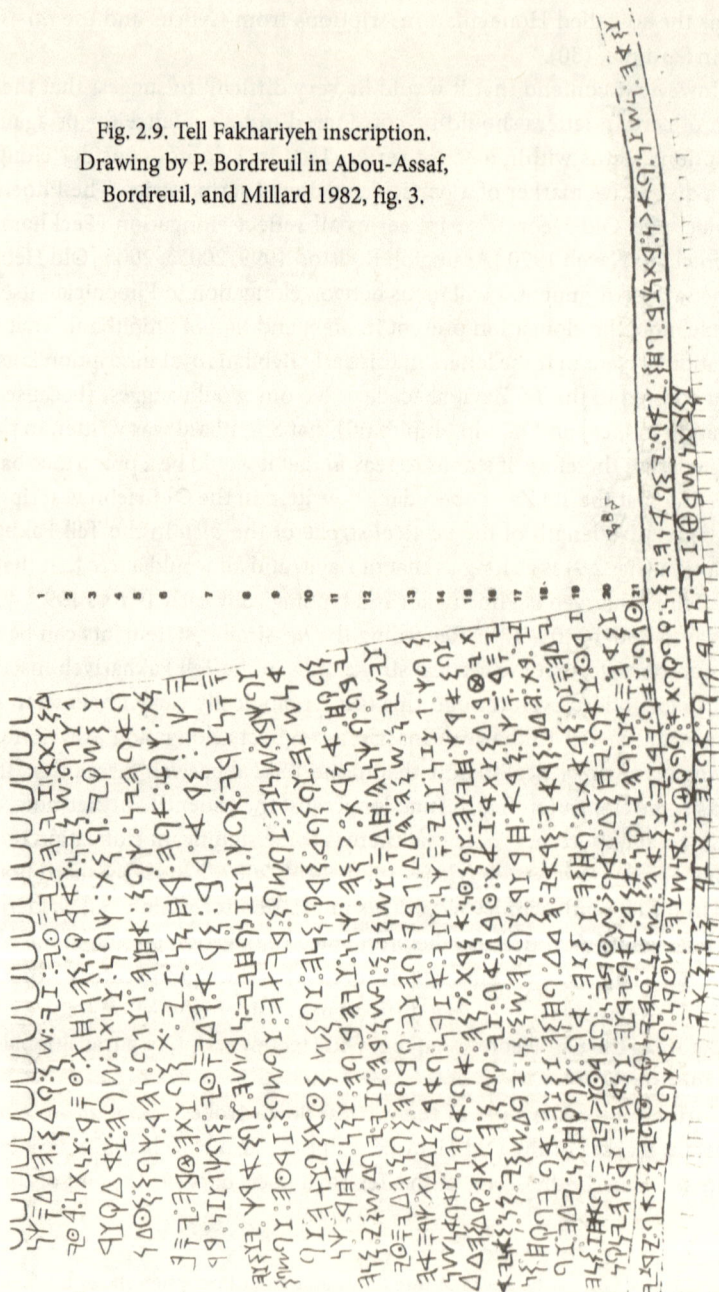

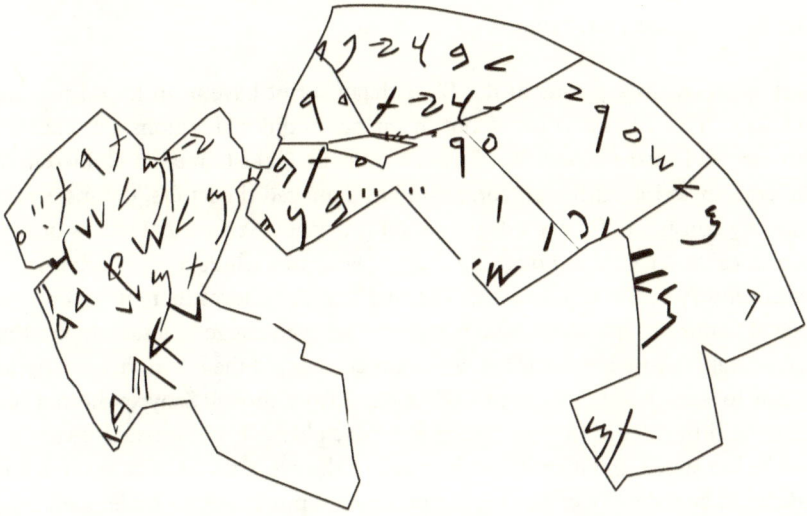

Fig. 2.10. Kition Bowl with Phoenician inscription. Drawing by the author.

am compelled to affirm that the script of the Tel Zayit abecedary is a fine Phoenician script of the late-tenth or very-early-ninth century B.C.E.[7]

Reference should be made to some additional "early" inscriptions that have been found in Israel and the script of these inscriptions, specifically those found at Hazor Stratum IX and Stratum VIII. Although fragmentary, I would suggest that it is readily apparent that none of these inscriptions reflects palaeographic features that are demonstrative of the Old Hebrew script, that is, there is nothing that is diagnostic of Old Hebrew (Rollston 2008a; 2008b). Similar statements can be made about the (fragmentary) inscriptions from Khirbet Roš Zayit, Beth Shemesh, and Tel Batash (Rollston 2008a; 2008b). Of course, some of the Arad ostraca are affirmed to have come from horizons antecedent to the ninth century (Aharoni 1981). Some of these ostraca are indeed early; however, the inscriptions from these early strata are normally faded, abraded, and fragmentary and so precarious bases for definitive statements about the script. Moreover, there has been substantial debate about the dates for the strata in which these inscriptions were discovered (Herzog 2002). Again, the fact that the Phoenician script persisted during the tenth and early-ninth centuries in Israelite territories is a demonstration that the Old Hebrew script had not yet been developed.

---

7. For a more detailed critique, see Rollston 2008a.

The Mediterranean, Syria, and Anatolia

Furthermore, inscriptions in the Phoenician script have been found not only in ancient Phoenicia and Israel, but in various additional regions. For example, Sznycer published a bronze bowl from a tomb in Tekke (Crete), inscribed in the Phoenician script. Although corrosion has damaged the letters, the inscription arguably consists of four words. Based on the script, Sznycer dated this inscription to ca. 900 B.C.E., although he did not wish to exclude a date earlier in the tenth century (1979, 91). Cross has argued that he believes there is "not a typological feature of the script which requires or even suggests a date lower than 1000 B.C.E." (Cross 1980; 2003, 229). Cross considered the *bet* in this inscription to date to some point prior to ca. 1000 B.C.E. Also, although Sznycer did not consider the fifth letter of the inscription to be decipherable, Cross read it as an *'ayin* and he has stated that it contains the pupil of the eye, a feature that is often considered to be reflective of an early script. Cross summarized his understanding of the script in the following manner: "the archaic forms of *'ayin* and *bet* require a date no later than the end of the eleventh century (ca. 1000 in round numbers), and the remaining clear letter forms conform to this dating" (1980, 17; also 2003, 229). The archaeological context of the tomb is Cretan Early Protogeometric (= Attic Late Protogeometric) and has been dated to ca. 950–900 B.C.E. (Catling 1977, 14).

Obviously, Cross knows that his dating of the inscription to ca. 1000 B.C.E. is rather close to the dating of the archaeological context, but nevertheless slightly earlier. He notes that there are two viable alternatives. The inscribed bowl may have been an heirloom piece, "a half century or so older than the main deposit in the Tomb." Cross draws attention to the fact that Lawrence Stager has suggested that there was a Late Minoan (LMIII) lentoid seal stone in the tomb and that it is "certainly an heirloom." Conversely, he suggests a second alternative is that "the dates of the Proto-geometric series may be raised a half-century. That is to say, the inscription may furnish new evidence that our chronology is in fact low" (Cross 1980, 18 n. 19; also 2003, 229 no. 49). I am sympathetic to Cross's desire to date the bowl to ca. 1000 B.C.E. Nevertheless, the morphology and stance of the Tekke *bet* could also be considered an acceptable tenth-century form, or even an acceptable ninth-century form (cf. the Nora Stone [fig. 2.14]). The general absence of elongation of the third stroke of *nun* is an archaic feature, however, and this argues for a date no later than the tenth or early-ninth century. Moreover, regarding the Tekke *'ayin*, I would note that the reading may not be correct, as the letter is corroded. In any case, it may be that the dotted *'ayin* persisted (especially outside the Phoenician homeland) into the tenth and ninth centuries. Based on the constellation of palaeographic data, I am comfortable dating this inscription to the tenth century, although I do not think that the evidence allows me to be more precise than this. In any case, the Tekke Bowl is a critically important Phoenician inscription and it hails not from the Phoenician homeland (Lebanon), but from Crete.

In addition, from the island of Cyprus hails the Honeyman Inscription, a monumental Phoenician inscription from the ninth century (Albright 1941). The script of this inscription is pure Phoenician. Similarly, the Nora Stone was found on the Mediterranean island of Sardinia, and can be dated with substantial certitude to the late-ninth century (Cross 1972; 2003, 250–53). Or again, the Kition Bowl (fig. 2.10) was found at Kition on Cyprus, and reflects a fine Phoenician cursive of the mid-eighth century (Dupont-Sommer 1970). Similarly, the Seville Statuette (Spain) dates to the second half of the eighth century and employs the Phoenician script. Also, the Malta Stele, from the late-eighth century, exhibits a fine Phoenician script (McCarter 1975). Obviously, the Phoenician script was used throughout much of the Mediterranean world. Thus, Israel's use of the Phoenician script was definitely part of a broader phenomenon.

The Phoenician script was also used in northern Syria. The script of the Tell Fakhariyeh statue is indicative of this (fig. 3.8). The languages of the Tell Fakhariyeh bilingual inscription are Assyrian (a dialect of Akkadian) and Aramaic. Within the field of Northwest Semitic palaeography, it is the linear script of the Aramaic text that has generated a substantial amount of discussion. Specifically, it has been argued that the linear script resembles the script of the eleventh and early-tenth century Phoenician inscriptions. However, various non-palaeographic data suggest a date in the ninth century. Regarding the script, Naveh has stated that it was "reminiscent of the Proto-Canaanite script of the eleventh century B.C.E." (1987b, 103). Naveh was very much cognizant of the fact that (in the *editio princeps*) Abou-Assaf, Bordreuil, and Millard (1982) had made a strong case, on the basis of historical, orthographic, and art historical data, for a date in the ninth century. Therefore, Naveh concluded that "the only possibility that can be taken into consideration is that we have here a very successful artificial archaizing script." He then continued and stated that "it is so extraordinary and out of context in the ninth century that it can only be explained by assuming that its set of letters was copied without a single failure from a stele of the eleventh century" (Naveh 1987b, 109).

Regarding the script of the Tell Fakhariyeh Inscription, Cross has stated that it "is typologically pure Phoenician, the Phoenician character of the end of the eleventh century B.C.E." However, with some reluctance, he was willing to concede that the text was composed in the ninth century B.C.E. Therefore, he argued that the script should be considered a "triumph of archaism" (1995, 409). Regarding the precise mechanism that resulted in the archaizing script of the Tell

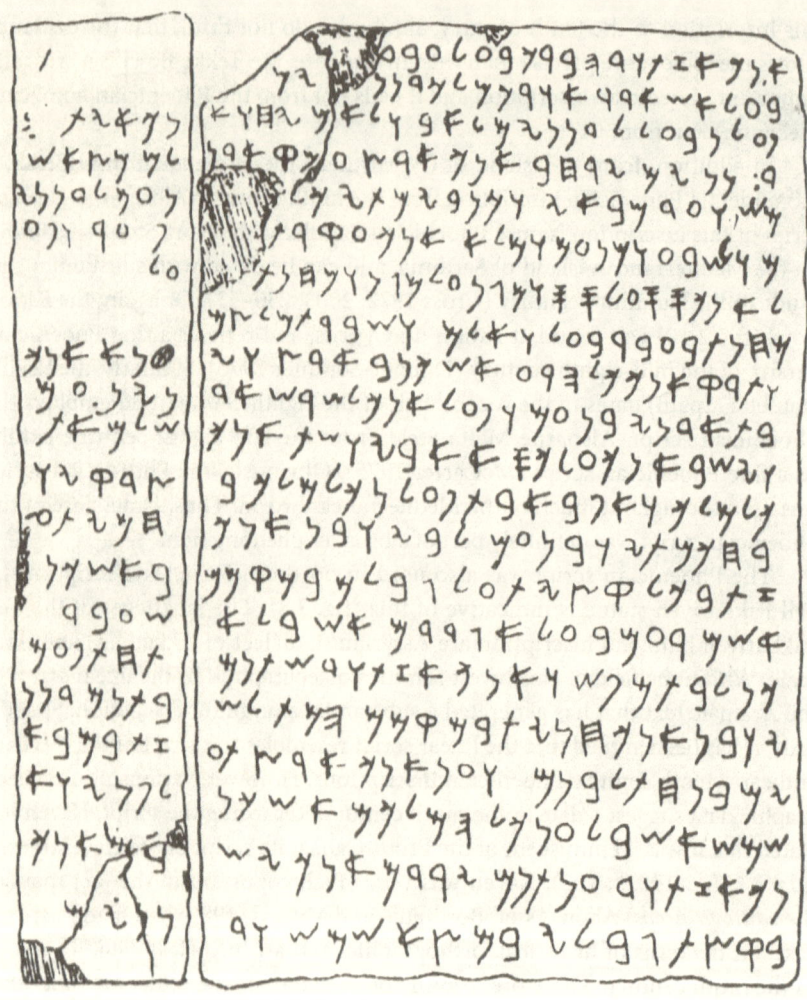

Fig. 2.11. A section of the Karatepe inscription (Phoenician). From Naveh 1987a, fig. 46.

Fakhariyeh Inscription, Cross has stated that a "ninth-century scribe copied earlier script models from Aramaic monuments of the late eleventh century…. He ignored the Aramaic script used by contemporary [ninth-century] scribes" (408).

Conversely, Kaufman has argued that the script of the Fakhariyeh Inscription should be understood as a Phoenician script that was used in that region (1982, 142–45). That is, Kaufman wished to posit that there were "Peripheral Phoenician scripts" and also a contemporaneous "Standard Phoenician script." Cross, however, has argued that he believes there is a problem with this proposal. Thus, after discussing various minor problems with the notion of a non-standard script in geographic peripheries, he states that "an even greater hindrance to the notion of a peripheral pocket of archaism is the existence of the Gozan Pedestal Inscription" (1995, 396). This inscription dates to the late-tenth or early-ninth century and uses the standard script of the late-tenth and early-ninth century. Gozan (Tell Halaf) and Tell Fakhariyeh are separated by about 4 kilometers. Cross believes, therefore, that if this region were actually employing a peripheral script that perpetuated archaic forms, then the Gozan Pedestal Inscription, which antedates the Fakhariyeh Inscription, should have employed the postulated peripheral script. However, because it did not employ the same archaic script as Tell Fakhariyeh, Cross affirms that the Fakhariyeh Inscription should be considered an archaizing script, not a peripheral archaic script. Sass has also stated that he considers the Fakhariyeh Inscription to be "archaizing" (2005, 34, 52, 58).

I concur with the affirmation that the script of Tell Fakhariyeh is archaizing. In fact, I contend that *archaizing is a recognized phenomenon, and Fakhariyeh is a textbook case of archaizing*. Regarding the Northwest Semitic script series, it is readily apparent that it is Phoenician (though the language is Aramaic). Furthermore, I should like to note further that in my opinion there is sufficient evidence within the script itself (heretofore not sufficiently recognized) that is suggestive of the fact that this inscription does not date to the eleventh or tenth centuries. That is, I think the case for archaizing need not be based just on prosopographic or art-historical data. For example, regarding the *waw* of Tell Fakhariyeh, I would note that there are no parallels for this form in the Phoenician script of the eleventh or tenth centuries. Rather, the horizontal base of *waw* in Fakhariyeh reflects substantial typological development from the forms of *waw* attested in the eleventh and tenth centuries (cf. Naveh 1987b, 109). Moreover, the vertical downstroke of the *samek* of Tell Fakhariyeh intersects with the bottom horizontal but not with the top two horizontals. Striking, however, is the fact that during the eleventh and tenth centuries the vertical downstroke begins at (or above) the top horizontal and thus intersects with all three horizontals. At this time, there are no parallels for the Fakhariyeh form in the Phoenician script of the eleventh or tenth centuries B.C.E. Furthermore, this palaeographic evidence dovetails with the orthographic evidence. That is, within the Northwest Semitic text of the Fakhariyeh Inscription (i.e., the Aramaic text), the full-blown system of Aramaic *matres lectionis* ("vowel letters") is used. This is strong evidence against a date in the eleventh or tenth centuries B.C.E. Of course, the prosopographic evidence is also suggestive of a date in the ninth century, but I concur with Cross (1995, 400) about the fact that the prosopographic evidence cannot be considered decisive.

Moreover, from the region of Anatolia, the Phoenician script is also well-attested. Among the most important of these Phoenician inscriptions from the

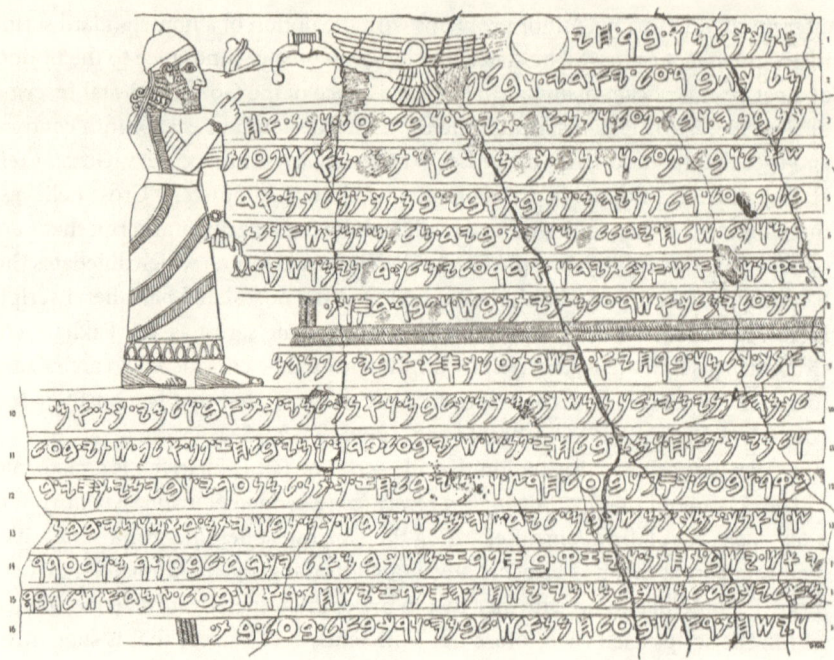

Fig. 2.12. Stele of Kilamuwa, king of Yaudi. From Naveh 1987a, fig. 45.

late-eighth century is the Karatepe Inscription (fig. 2.11). Within this inscription the Anatolian (Neo-Hittite) regent Azatiwada also commissioned a Phoenician inscription, to parallel his native Hittite Hieroglyphic rendition (Röllig 1999). This inscription is among the longest of the Iron Age Phoenician inscriptions.

Regarding other important Phoenician inscriptions, note that the Kilamuwa Inscription from the late-ninth century (fig. 2.12) is written in the Phoenician language rather than the local dialect and arguably the Phoenician script, that is, the prestige script and language of that chronological horizon and region. Also, the Panamuwa I Inscription and the Panamuwa II Incription, both from Sam'al during the eighth century are written in an Aramaic dialect, but employ the Phoenician script. Moreover, the Bar-Rakib Inscription is written in the standard Old Aramaic dialect, but the script continues to be the Phoenician script (see Naveh 1987a, 79–80). The Phoenician script of these later inscriptions all reflect developments that distinguish them from the Phoenician script of the tenth and early-ninth centuries, but the differences are modest (e.g., development of a leg for the *dalet*, consistency of top-left stance of *bet,* consistent strong horizontal stance of *mem* and *nun*, further lengthening of top-right stroke of *taw*, etc). Nevertheless, the script of these inscriptions is definitely the Phoenician script.

Again, this demonstrates that the use of the Phoenician script in Israel during the tenth century and early-ninth century was part of a broader phenomenon, attested not just in Israel, but in various regions.

Finally, the Phoenician script also continued to be used in the Phoenician homeland during these horizons (e.g., Sarepta Inscription) and succeeding ones. Moreover, for subsequent decades and centuries, the typological development of the Phoenician script continued. For example, the Byblian Phoenician lapidary inscription known as the Son of Shipitba'al Inscription (fig. 2.13; Dunand 1937, 31) provides substantial data about script morphology, stance, and ductus of Phoenician of ca. 500 B.C.E. Within this period, the ʾalep now normally consists of a main vertical shaft and two ticks on the right side of the vertical—a remnant of the horizontal crossbars of previous periods; the *mem* consisted of four strokes (sometimes less) and it was a schematized version of the *mem* from previous horizons; the *šin* no longer consisted of four strokes or stroke segments, but of three, and now it looked very similar to the trident-shaped *kap* of previous centuries. In addition, the top-left stroke of the *taw* became vestigial and no longer extended to the left of the top-right stroke. Furthermore, the top-right stroke had elongated substantially (vis-à vis-the early Phoenician script). That is, as time marched on, so also did the typological development of Phoenician (Peckham 1968).

Finally, I should like to stress that although the Phoenician script was used across such wide geographic regions, there is substantial continuity of the Phoenician script during any given chronological horizon regardless of the region from which it hails, or, at times, even the language in which the text was written. I would attribute this to the presence of continued cultural contact and to the nature of the trans-regional Phoenician scribal apparatus.[8]

Fig. 2.13. Son of Shipitba'al. Fragment B.
Drawing by the author.

8. For the scribal apparatus in ancient Israel, see Rollston 2006. The epigraphic evidence suggests that a similar apparatus for scribal education was present for Phoenician.

THE MAJOR "DAUGHTER" SCRIPTS: OLD HEBREW AND ARAMAIC

Based on the preceding discussion it is readily apparent that the Phoenician script flourished in the Levant during the Iron Age. Nevertheless, two major daughter scripts developed from the Phoenician *Mutterschrift* and these became independent national scripts: the Old Hebrew script and the Aramaic script. These script series have been the subject of substantive analyses (Naveh 1970; 1987a; Cross 1961; 1962a; 1962b; Rollston 1999; 2003a; 2006; 2008a; 2008b). For each of these scripts, there are diagnostic features, that is, there are features that distinguish the Hebrew script from the Phoenician and the Aramaic and there are features that distinguish the Aramaic script from the Phoenician and the Old Hebrew.

DISTINCTIVE NATIONAL SCRIPT(S)

OLD HEBREW AND MOABITE

There is sufficient data to state that the Old Hebrew script became a distinct national script during the ninth century B.C.E. The earliest evidence for the Old Hebrew script hails from the region of Moab. This region had been under Israelite hegemony during the ninth century and it can reasonably be postulated that Moabite scribes began to use the fledgling Old Hebrew script during this period of Israelite hegemony. Along these lines, Naveh has written that "strange as it may seem, the first distinctive features of Hebrew writing can be discerned in the scripts of the ninth-century Moabite inscriptions, namely, the stele of Mesha and the fragmentary inscription which mentions Mesha's father Kemošyat." I am in general agreement with Naveh. Of course, the language of the Mesha Stele is Moabite (as Naveh duly notes), but the script is nevertheless Old Hebrew (1987a, 65).

Among the most important of the distinctive features of the fledgling Old Hebrew script is the curvature of the terminal portions of the downstrokes of several letters, namely, *kap*, *mem*, and *nun*. That is, there is a general absence of curvature in these letters in the Phoenician series of the tenth and ninth centuries B.C.E. (e.g., Nora Stone; fig. 2.14), but pronounced curvature is present in the script of the Mesha Stele and the El-Kerak Inscription (i.e., the Kemošyat Inscription; fig. 2.15). Furthermore, this curvature is present in the Old Hebrew inscriptions attested at Kuntillet ʿAjrud dating to the late-ninth or early-eighth centuries B.C.E. and the earliest of the Old Hebrew inscriptions from Samaria.

During succeeding chronological horizons, the Old Hebrew script and the Phoenician script continue to develop along different trajectories. For example,

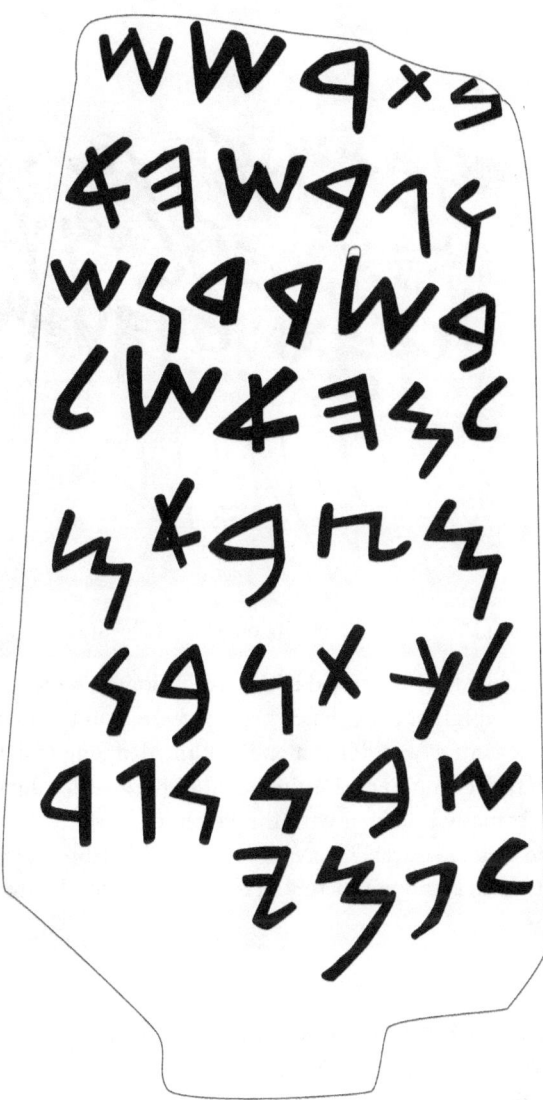

Fig. 2.14. Nora Stone. Drawing by the author.

the stance of certain letters in Old Hebrew is different from that of contemporary Phoenician. Thus, the Old Hebrew *bet* is recumbent (or, in the earliest period, upright), but the standard Phoenician *bet* is top-left (or, in certain cases, upright). Moreover, sometimes it is the general morphology of certain letters that distinguishes the Old Hebrew series from the Phoenician. For example, the Old Hebrew *taw* and the Phoenician *taw* reflect very different morphologies. Thus, within the Phoenician series, a characteristic feature is the lengthening of the top-right stroke, and the (relative) shortening of the top-left stroke. The Old Hebrew *taw* consists of two intersecting strokes, without the extreme reduction of the length of the top-left stroke, in contrast to Phoenician. During most chronological horizons, therefore, there is no difficulty in distinguishing between the Phoenician script and the Old Hebrew script. Of course, this attests to the fact that there was a distinct scribal tradition in ancient Israel.

It is prudent for me to say something about the origins and aegis of the Old Hebrew script. I reiterate the point (discussed above) that there is no evidence for a distinct Old Hebrew national script during the tenth century. Rather, I contend that such a script is first attested only in the ninth century. The late-tenth and early-ninth centuries are the time during which Israel came of age. It is during this horizon

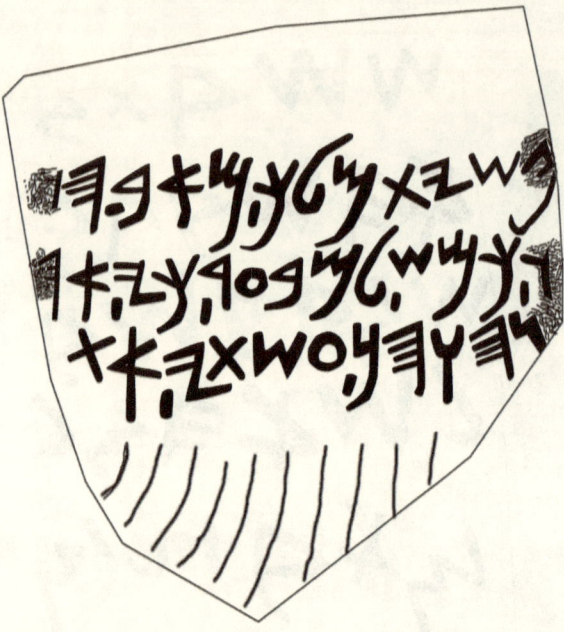

Fig. 2.15. El-Kerak inscription. Drawing by the author.

that monumental Israelite architecture is attested in the archaeological record and it is during this horizon that epigraphic evidence begins to attest to the fledgling power of Israel in the Levantine world. I contend that the fledgling Israelite kindom(s) made a conscious decision to create a national Hebrew script during this time period, thereby formally breaking with the Phoenician *Mutterschrift* that had been used prior to this in Israel. The creation of the Old Hebrew script was, I believe, a nationalistic statement, not merely an evolutionary development.

Aramaic

Although the Phoenician script had been used during preceding horizons to write inscriptions in the Aramaic language, a distinct Aramaic script is attested in Aramaic inscriptions from the late-eighth century B.C.E. (Naveh 1970; 1987a, 80). There are several major features of the Aramaic script that distinguish it from the Phoenician script. For example, the the heads of *bet, dalet,* and *reš* had opened in the Aramaic script and these open-headed forms are regnant from the late-eighth century onward. This is not the case for the Phoenician script. In addition, the *ʿayin* had developed an open-headed form in the Aramaic script during the eighth century B.C.E., but this is not the case for the Phoenician script. Furthermore, the single-barred *ḥet* becomes very common in the Aramaic script of the

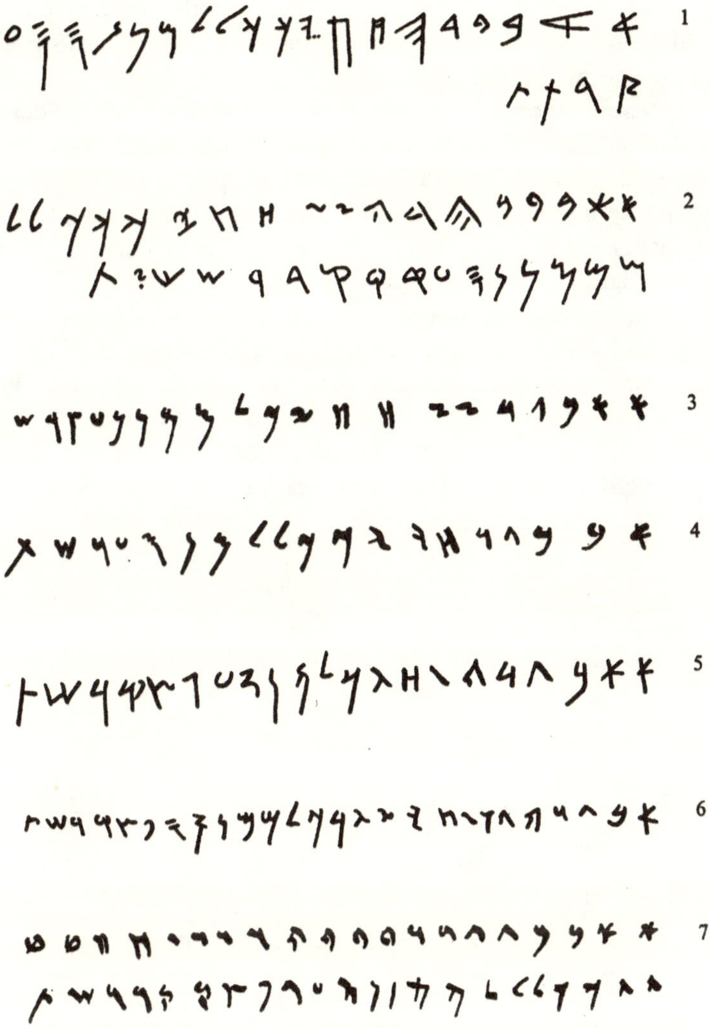

Fig. 2.16. Aramaic script. From Naveh 1970, fig. 2. 1: Hamat bricks (eighth century);
2: lion weights from Nineveh (late-eighth century); 3–4: Nimrud ostracon
(late-eighth century); 5–6: Assur clay tablets (mid-seventh century);
7: Assur ostracon (mid-seventh century).

late-eighth century, but this is not a feature of the Phoenician script at this time.
Thus, it is readily apparent that a distinctive Aramaic cursive script is attested
during the eighth century, a script that is different from the Phoenician *Mutterschrift*. In addition, because the features for Aramaic noted here are not attested

in Old Hebrew either, it is readily apparent that the Aramaic script differs from Old Hebrew as well. The end result is that full-blown national scripts are attested in the Northwest Semitic record.

Basically, then, it can be stated that the alphabet developed during the early-second millennium B.C.E. The early alphabetic script was succeeded by the Phoenician script. From the Phoenician script, the Old Hebrew and Aramaic scripts developed. These three national scripts (Phoenician, Old Hebrew, and Aramaic) and their congeners (Ammonite, Edomite, Moabite) were used in the Levant during various horizons of the Iron Age.

I believe that for each of these national scripts, there was a major scribal apparatus and that scribes were formally educated members of the elite class. In the following chapters, the focus will be upon the Israelite scribal apparatus that produced the lion's share of the Old Hebrew inscriptions. Before turning to this topic, it will be instructive to summarize various types of inscriptions so as to demonstrate something of the diversity of the epigraphic record during the Iron Age.

CHAPTER 3
THE NATURE OF THE NORTHWEST SEMITIC
EPIGRAPHIC RECORD: FORM AND FUNCTION

The corpus of Northwest Semitic inscriptions is diverse in a number of ways. There is variation with regard to the media: stone, papyrus, vellum, metal, and clay are attested. The varied media required different tools. That is, inscriptions made with pen and ink, chisel, and incising tools are all attested. Moreover, there is variation with regard to the function of the epigraphic materials. Some were intended to tout a victory and some were intended to taunt and warn a vanquished enemy. Some were intended as religious displays, and some for the keeping of ephemeral records and missives (e.g., tax receipts and letters). Some were intended to record activities of the elites and some for the purpose of recording "history." Some inscriptions functioned within certain components of the cult. Some may have had mantic function as well. To be sure, many inscriptions will have had multiple functions. That is, the Northwest Semitic epigraphic evidence is broad and deep. In this chapter, the varied forms and functions of the epigraphic record will be discussed so as to provide a window into the nature and function of writing during various horizons of the Iron Age. Attempting to organize these ancient inscriptions into categories is difficult and although the categories I employ are governed by heuristic principles, they should not be considered rigid (see Millard 1972). Still, the diverse epigraphic data remain the best tools for limning the portrait.

I. MONUMENTAL STONE INSCRIPTIONS

The Amman Citadel Inscription (fig. 3.1) is a fine monumental inscription found on the citadel of Amman, ancient Rabbat Amman, the capital of the Ammonite kingdom (Aufrecht 1989, 154–63). It has often been dated to the ninth century on the basis of its script (a lapidary series of the ninth century). Word dividers are used within this inscription. Although this inscription is not complete, and there

Fig. 3.1. Amman Citadel inscription. Photo courtesy of B. Zuckerman and M. Lundberg, West Semitic Research.

is some damage to the surface, sufficient text is preserved for it to be affirmed with some confidence that this inscription is a "monumental dedicatory inscription." For example, at the beginning of the first preserved line, the inscription arguably refers to Ammonite national deity Milkom, a deity also mentioned in the Bible (e.g., 1 Kgs 11:5; Jer 49:3). There is also reference to "building," followed by two words that can be translated as "entrances of the courts." Also present is a formulaic statement about the presence of "peace" (*šlm*). The fact that this inscription is engraved in an elegant hand on a prepared stone is reflective of the fact that this inscription was intended to be permanent.

Although there has been substantial unanimity in the scholarly literature about the fact that this is a dedicatory inscription, there has also been some discussion about the nature of the building that was being dedicated. Some have reasonably suggested that it was a temple. Others have suggested that a royal building, perhaps a palace, was being dedicated. The presence of the divine name "Milkom" cannot be considered decisive evidence for the proposal that this was a temple, because deities were believed to commission and sanction the building of both temples and palaces. For this reason, it can be concluded that this is a dedicatory inscription, but its precise focus must remain a moot point.

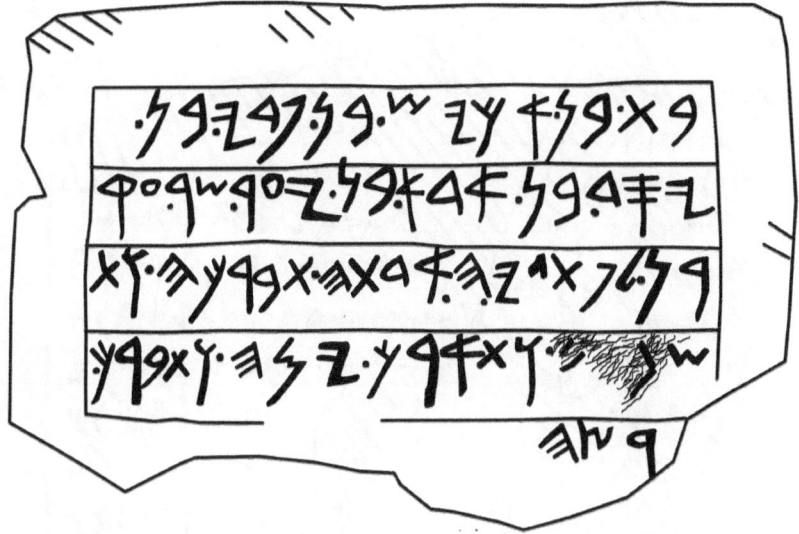

Fig. 3.2. Miqne-Ekron stele inscription. Drawing by the author.

The monumental inscription from Tel Miqne (ancient Ekron; fig. 3.2) consists of five lines of text (Gitin, Dothan, and Naveh 1997). The surface had been prepared with precision and meticulousness, and the script was engraved with substantial attention to detail. Word dividers are used within this inscription. The medium is limestone. Within this inscription the scribe (or stonemason) even chiseled the ceiling line on the stone, demonstrative of rare form and assiduousness. Though scribes of Iron Age Northwest Semitic would sometimes formally "line" the text (with chisel, engraving tool, or ink; e.g., the Honeyman Inscription), it is common for scribes to refrain from doing this. (I would argue that some scribes did not consider it necessary for the production of a "straight" line of text.) Scribes of ancient Northwest Semitic would "hang" the letters from the ceiling line. The placement of the letters of this inscription vis-à-vis the ceiling line is thus the norm.

The archaeological context of the Miqne Stele and the content of the text converge in the most dramatic fashion. The archaeological context is a temple complex and the text of the inscription is that of a royal dedication of a temple. The text can be read as follows: "The son of Achish, the son of Padi, the son of Yasid, the son of Ada, the son of Ya'ir, ruler of Ekron built this temple." Within the inscription there is reference to a divine name (that of a goddess) and then a traditional petition: "May she bless him, and guard him and lengthen his days and may she bless his land." Based on the archaeological context and the histor-

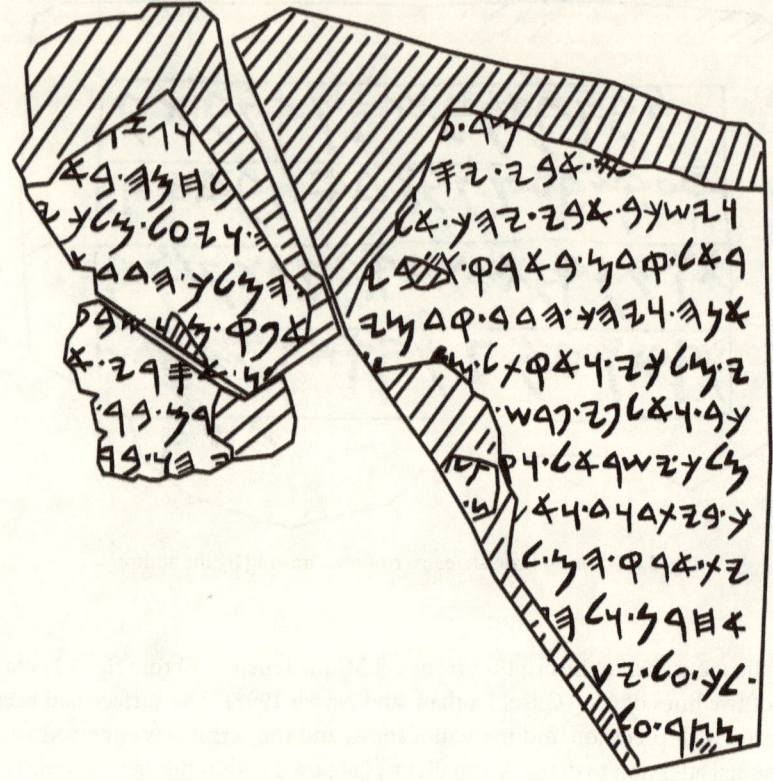

Fig. 3.3. Tel Dan stele. Drawing by the author.

ical content, this inscription can be dated in all likelihood to the seventh century B.C.E.

Some of the personal names on this inscription are of particular interest, among them Padi of Ekron. To be precise, Padi King of Ekron is mentioned in the annals of Sennacherib (Pritchard 1969, 287–88) and from these annals it is stated that the Judean King Hezekiah had, with the complicity of the elites in Ekron, deposed Padi and imprisoned him in Jerusalem. From the context of Sennacherib's discussion, it is readily apparent that Padi had not joined the coalition of Levantine states that had formed against Sennacherib, hence, the ire of various alliance members, including Hezekiah (and thus Padi's imprisonment). Nevertheless, Sennacherib's punitive campaign in 701 B.C.E. was most successful and he was able, among other things, to decimate Judah (he refers to destroying forty-six fortified cities in Judah), kill the elites of Ekron that had surrendered Padi, demand the release of Padi from Jerusalem, and restore Padi to the throne of Ekron (cf. 2 Kgs 18–19; Isa 36–38). In essence, therefore, the Miqne Stele constitutes a fine example of a monumental inscription in a major Philistine city and it also dovetails and augments some of the ancient Near Eastern data regarding the Philistines.

The stele in fig. 3.3 was found during excavations at the site referred to as Tel Dan (Biran and Naveh 1995). Based on the archaeological context and especially the historical content, the inscription can be dated to the ninth century B.C.E. Within this inscription, the "author," that is, the king that commissioned it, states that the kings of Israel and Judah had made incursions into his land during the reign of his father. The text then notes, "Hadad made me king" and "Hadad went before me." This inscription refers to the deity being part and parcel of the selection, coronation, and military success of the Syrian king. The affirmation of divine support is a fairly common motif in ancient texts and it is therefore predictable that various texts of the Hebrew Bible contain similar affirmations about Yahweh's support of an Israelite king (e.g., 1 Sam 9–10 focusing on Yahweh's support of David). The Tel Dan Stele, therefore, as also in the case of the Bible, is simply reflecting ancient assumptions about divine support of a monarch, a standard form of royal apologia.

In any case, at this juncture the Tel Dan Stele states that the new Syrian king engaged the king of Israel (Jehoram son of Ahab) and the king of the House of David (Ahaziah son of Jehorah) in battle, and slew them. The textual evidence points to the Syrian identity of the commissioning king. Hadad, affirmed to be the god that sanctioned his coronation ("Hadad" is the theophoric element in the names of various Syrian kings, such as "Hadadezer," 1 Kgs 11:23), is the Syrian storm god. Moreover, the language of the Tel Dan Stele is Old Aramaic, as indicated, for example, by the direct object marker *yt* (line 10), which is the norm in Aramaic (although often ʾ*yt* is attested), but not Hebrew or Phoenician. Furthermore, the verb *yhk* ("he went" line 3) is Aramaic, not Hebrew or Phoenician, and the independent personal pronoun ʾ*nh* (line 5) is Aramaic, not Hebrew or Phoenician. Furthermore, the word for "land" in the inscription is written ʾ*rq*. In Hebrew and Phoenician *ṣ* was employed to write etymological *ḍ* (and thus in Hebrew and Phoenician the word is written ʾ*rṣ*). Within Old Aramaic, however, *qop* was the grapheme used to write etymological *ḍ*. Thus, a Syrian ("Aramean") king is stating in this inscription that he has made punitive campaign(s) against kings of Israel and Judah and slain them. Based on a constellation of archaeological, epigraphic, and historical data, most argue that the Syrian king who commissioned this inscription was Hazael.

Within the ancient Near Eastern world, it was common for a victor to erect a victory stele. Such texts were often erected on the soil of the vanquished foe,

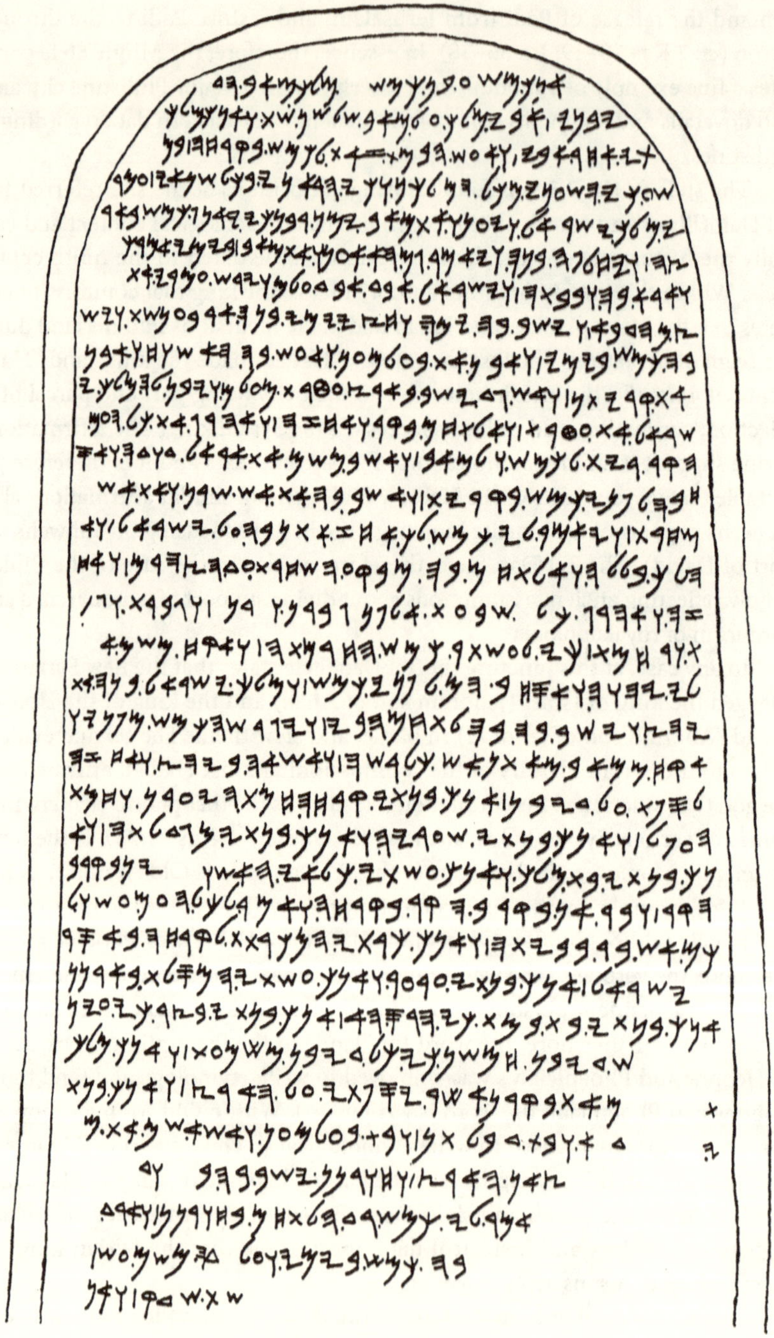

Fig. 3.4. Mesha stele. From Dearman 1989, fig. 1.

narrating the deeds of the victor and serving to suggest to the vanquished that resistance would be futile. Of course, sometimes a stele might also be erected on foreign soil primarily to confirm the hegemony of the figure that commissioned it. However, in the case of the Tel Dan Stele, it is victory that is being acclaimed, not simply hegemony: thus, it is a paradigmatic victory stele that sent a strong signal to the Israelites, even though most Israelites were not capable of reading it.

The biblical account (2 Kgs 9; cf. Hos 1:4–5) states that it was Jehu of Israel (r. 843–815 B.C.E.) who slew Jehoram of Israel and Ahaziah of Judah (i.e., the House of David) in a bloody coup. The Tel Dan Stele, however, attributes this to a Syrian king, most likely Hazael. It may be that Biran and Naveh are correct in stating that there is a "serious contradiction between the Dan inscription and the biblical narrative in 2 Kings 9" (Biran and Naveh 1995, 18). Nevertheless, it is also plausible to suggest that Hazael and Jehu had formed, at one point, a political alliance. After all, Hazael was a usurper who had assassinated Ben Hadad so as to assume the throne of Damascus (2 Kgs 8:7–15) and Jehu was a usurper who wrested the throne of Israel from Jehoram of Israel. In the face of such machinations, one could envision the attractiveness of a political alliance between the usurpers. Some might counter that this is sheer speculation, however, there is a text in the book of Kings that suggests there may have been just such an alliance: "Whoever escapes from the sword of Hazael, Jehu shall kill" (1 Kgs 19:17). I think that it is therefore plausible for Hazael to have claimed to have slain Jehoram of Israel and Ahaziah of Judah by proxy, even if the *coup de grâce* was wielded by his ally Jehu. Some have suggested that this inscription did not hail from the time of Hazael of Syria (Athas 2003), but I continue to consider it most convincing to conclude that the epigraphic and biblical evidence dovetail most nicely with the position that the *Sitz im Leben* were the reigns of Hazael of Damascus and Jehu of Israel. Regardless, the Tel Dan stele contains a scintillating monumental inscription detailing tensions and contact between Syria, Israel, and Judah.

The Mesha Stele (dating to the ninth century B.C.E.; fig. 3.4) is among the most impressive of all Iron Age Northwest Semitic inscriptions (Dearman 1989). Within this inscription, King Mesha of Moab provides his patronymic (son of Kemoshyat) and refers to himself as a "Daibonite." He then states that Kemosh, the national god of Moab (1 Kgs 11:7), had been "angry" with Moab and had allowed it to be subjected to the hegemony of King Omri of Israel. Omri's son and successor (not named in the inscription) had desired to continue with the same "foreign policy." However, Mesha affirms that Kemosh "returned" and assisted Mesha in numerous military campaigns against Israel, resulting in the restoration of much territory to Moab (e.g., Nebo and Yahaṣ). Of course, the Hebrew Bible contains the motif of the anger of Yahweh resulting in foreign hegemony and destruction (e.g., Judg 3–4; 2 Kgs 17; 2 Kgs 23), but also often in restoration. In addition to killing many people, Mesha states that he "took the vessels of Yahweh," the national god of Israel (Smith 2002, 182–99; Rollston 2003b) and "dragged these vessels before Kemosh." Of course, the practice of removing the cult objects of vanquished foes was a common practice in the ancient Near East, attested in various regions (cf. 1 Sam 4–6; 2 Sam 6; Kutsko 2000, 103–23). Naturally, the Mesha Stele also lauds Mesha himself for his many building projects. He claims to have rebuilt gates, restored retaining walls, dug cisterns, and (re)built cities such as Aroer. Of course, this is standard royal rhetoric for ancient inscriptions of this sort.

The genre and function of the Mesha Stele can be distinguished from that of the Tel Dan Stele. The Mesha Stele was erected in traditional Moabite territory and was intended to laud the Moabite King for his victories over Israel. In addition, within the Mesha Stele, there is substantial attention devoted to "public works" projects, something that would be predictable for an inscription that would be intended primarily for the Moabite citizenry. The Mesha Stele, therefore, functions as a paradigmatic memorializing stele.

The script was engraved onto the stele with enormous precision. It is the Old Hebrew script, arguably used here because Israel's hegemony hindered the development of a distinct Moabite script. Word dividers are used in the inscription. There are many similarities between the language of the Moabite Stele and Old Hebrew and Phoenician. For example, etymological (proto-Semitic) $\underline{d}$ is represented by $\underline{s}$, not q or ʿ as in Aramaic. Also, the definite article is prepositive h, not postpositive ʾ as in Aramaic. Moreover, the *nota accusative* is ʾt, not ʾyt or yt as in Aramaic. However, though similar to Hebrew, it is certain that the language of the Mesha Inscription is not Hebrew. Note, for example, that the masculine plural marker is *nun*, not *mem*, as it is in Hebrew and Phoenician. Thus, the Mesha Stele is written in the Moabite language, a language that is similar to, but different from, Phoenician and Old Hebrew.

The material about Mesha detailed in the Mesha Stele parallels some of the material in the Hebrew Bible (2 Kgs 3:4–8). Mesha had been under the hegemony of Israel, but rebelled. There are some putative tensions between the biblical account and the epigraphic account, but they are of modest consequence. According to the Mesha Stele, for example, Mesha rebelled during the reign of Omri's son (i.e., Ahab). However, according to the text of Kings, the rebellion took place after Ahab's death. Someone might suggest that the term "son" (Moabite *bn*, as in Hebrew) could mean "descendent" and thus could refer to Omri's grandson and conclude that there is thus no real tension. This would be a tenable position, but I nevertheless believe that the Mesha Stele contains a nice example of the complementary nature of some of the epigraphic and biblical materials. This monumental inscription also provides priceless data about the Moabite language,

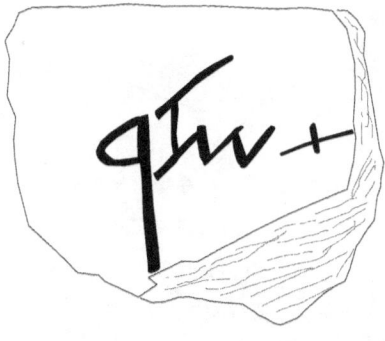

Fig. 3.5. Samaria stele. Drawing by the author.

Fig. 3.6. Ophel stele. Drawing by the author.

as well as about the complex political relationship that existed between Moab and Israel during a segment of the ninth century.

It has sometimes been suggested that there was no tradition of monumental inscriptions in ancient Israel. However, there actually is some evidence to demonstrate that monumental inscriptions were produced in Israel: a remnant of that tradition is the fragmentary Samaria Stele (fig. 3.5; Crowfoot and Crowfoot 1957, pl iv). The surface of the limestone is of high quality. The letters were chiseled with precision, the work of a master. This inscription has been dated to the eighth century, but a date in the ninth century would also be possible. The most fundamental point, though, is that this inscription reflects the same basic features, in terms of medium and quality of script, that are characteristic of monumental script traditions in Phoenicia, Aram, Moab, Ammon, and Philistia and therefore it would be difficult to posit that there was no such tradition in ancient Israel as well.

Moreover, it is reasonable to argue that there was also a monumental tradition in Judah. Although there is again a dearth of evidence, there is not a complete absence of evidence. For example, during excavations at the Ophel in Jerusalem, an inscription with four lines of text was found (fig. 3.6; Ben-Dov 1994). The medium is Jerusalem limestone. The script of this inscription is that of the late-eighth century (or the very-early-seventh century) and reflects some of the finest cursive forms attested in the entire corpus of Iron Age Old Hebrew. Although the text is so fragmentary that attempts to discern the nature of the inscription are precarious, it constitutes evidence that there was also a monumental tradition in Judah.

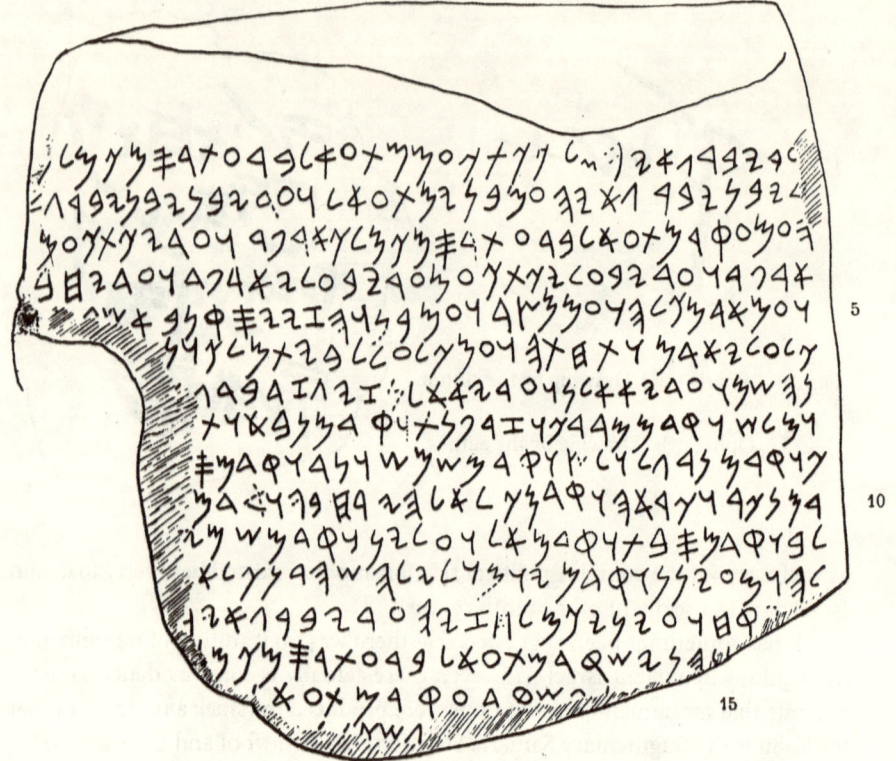

Fig. 3.7. Sefire treaty tablet. From Fitzmyer 1995, pl. 3.

Among the most important of Iron Age Northwest Semitic inscriptions are the international treaty texts from Sefire (fig. 3.7; Fitzmyer 1995). This corpus consists of three stelae, written in Old Aramaic, in a beautiful lapidary script. These stelae are written in *scriptio continua*: that is, there are no word dividers, nor are there spaces between words. Stelae I and II are engraved on several sides (suggestive of a truncated pyramid), but Stele III is flat and engraved on just one side. Because the Sefire Inscriptions were not found *in situ* in a primary archaeological context, and because the stones are broken, there has been some discussion about the sequencing of the three stelae. Regardless of this, because there is so much text preserved, these stelae are invaluable sources of data.

King Mati'el of Arpad, a region in North Syria, is arguably a vassal of King Bar-Ga'yah of a neighboring region. The text of the treaty consists of an introduction, stipulations, list of gods, and curses. Within the introduction, the parties are introduced and the treaty is said to be binding for Bar-Ga'yah and Mati'el and also their sons and grandsons. Within ancient Near Eastern treaties, the gods and goddesses of the parties are named as witnesses and the Sefire Inscriptions are paradigmatic in this regard. The Sefire Inscriptions invoke a number of deities, including Marduk, Nabu, Nergal, Shamash, Kur, Sin, Zarpanit, Nikkar, Hadad of Aleppo, 'El, and 'Elyan.

Stipulations of the suzerain are a fundamental component of a treaty text, and the Sefire Inscriptions contain various pericopes within this domain. There is, for example, reference to the fact that Mati'el must surrender any person that may "utter evil" against Bar-Ga'yah so that he might take appropriate measures. Fugitives that might flee to Mati'el for sanctuary must be surrendered as well. Moreover, any ambassador who might be sent by or to Bar-Ga'yah must be granted safe passage, without exception. Although the treaty discourages Mati'el from becoming involved in problems arising out of succession, there is also a statement that Mati'el must even make a punitive campaign against any of Bar-Ga'yah's relatives ("brothers" or "sons") or high officials who attempt to usurp his throne. Naturally, any attempt by Mati'el to assassinate Bar-Ga'yah is affirmed to be a fundamental breach of the treaty. Indeed, deviation from any of the stipulations is considered to be a demonstration that the vassal is unfaithful (šqr).

Curses are pronounced against Mati'el should he prove unfaithful. Among the curses that are mentioned are things such as the following: "May Mati'el be blinded" and "may his wives be stripped and the wives of his sons and nobles," "may Arpad and her associated cities be burned with fire," and "may Hadad sow them with salt and weeds, and may they not be mentioned again." Moreover, things such as the following are also included: "may seven nurses suckle a young boy, but may he not have his fill," and "though seven mares suckle a colt, may it not be sated," and "may the locust devour Arpad for seven years." Blessings are also present, such as "may the gods keep all evil away from his day and from his house." Curses are also pronounced upon any that might wish to efface or destroy the text of the treaty: "may he and his son die in oppressive torment." Promises such as "if you obey, then I shall not be able to raise a hand against you."

The Sefire Inscriptions can be dated with confidence to the mid-eighth century, based on historical data present in them. The *terminus post quem* cannot be ascertained with absolute certitude, but an Akkadian text records the fact that Mati'el did enter into a treaty with the Assyrian king Aššurnirari V in ca. 754–753 B.C.E. The *terminus ante quem* of the Sefire Inscriptions is ca. 740 B.C.E., the year in which Tiglath-Pileser III made Arpad a formal part of the Assyrian Empire, thus date some time before or after 754–753 B.C.E., but not later than 740 B.C.E. for the inscriptions is likely. Ultimately, the Sefire Inscriptions constitute a superlative exemplar of a treaty text, engraved into stone and displayed in some public space so as to function as a constant reminder of the treaty and its obligations.

Fig. 3.8. Tell Fakhariyeh statue. Photo courtesy of Adam Bean.

II. Inscriptions on Statuary

Modern Tell Fakhariyeh is the site of ancient Sikan, located on the bank of the Habur River in northeastern Syria. Across the Habur is the site of Tell Halaf (ancient Gozan). The Tell Fakhariyeh Statue (fig. 3.8) is a stunning piece of art, standing more than five feet high, of a governor of Gozan named Had-Yith'i. Engraved into the statue is a bilingual inscription, with the long Neo-Assyrian cuneiform text on the front of the statue and the parallel Old Aramaic version on the back of the statue (Abou-Assaf, Bordreuil, and Millard 1982). Within the inscription, Sass-nuri (Shamash-nur) is referred to as the father of Had-Yith'i. Sass-nuri has plausibly been identified with a known Assyrian official of the mid-ninth century B.C.E. The script of the Aramaic text is Phoenician, with numerous typological features that are quite archaic and similar to the script of the late-second millennium, but the Aramaic orthography reflects conventions that are indicative of the first millennium, with final and internal *matres lectionis*. Based on the convergence of a constellation of data, this statue and inscription can be dated with confidence to the ninth century B.C.E. (for additional details regarding the script see above, pp. 37–39).

The Aramaic text, which differs very modestly from the Neo-Assyrian text, begins with the affirmation that the statue is the "likeness of Had-Yit'i" the "king of Gozan." The text continues by stating that the inscribed statue has been placed "before Hadad of Sikanu," affirmed to be the "Great Lord, lord of Had-Yit'i." Hadad of Sikanu is lauded as the "irrigation master of heaven and earth" and the "giver of prosperity and provider of pasture and watering-place for all the lands." He is also affirmed to be the source of "libation vessel, for all the gods, his brothers." Had-Yit'i states that he desires for Hadad-Sikanu to "keep him in good health and to lengthen his life." He also desires for the health and longevity of his family and citizenry, and also that his "prayer may be heard." A curse is pronounced upon any that might efface the inscription on the statue, or on any of the cultic vessels: "may Hadad my lord not accept his food and his water … let him sow but not harvest … and may one hundred cows nurse a calf, but let it not be satisfied, and may one hundred women nurse a child, but let it not be satisfied, and let one hundred women bake bread in an oven, but not fill it … and may Pestilence, the plague of Nergal, not be cut off from his land" (Kaufman 1982).

This inscription is a royal temple dedication. The motifs that are present (e.g., beseeching of various types of blessings) are the standard motifs for a dedicatory inscription (see also the Eqron Stele). Moreover, the presence of curses against those who might wish to efface the inscription are a standard motif in inscriptions of various genres. The inscription also attests to the bilingualism that is often part of the scribal establishment in the ancient Near East.

Fig. 3.9. Amman statue inscription. Photo courtesy of B. Zuckerman and M. Lundberg, West Semitic Research.

The Amman Statue Inscription (fig. 3.9; Aufrecht 1989, 43–109) was discovered several decades ago in the Jordanian city of Amman. Along the front base of this statue is an inscription that has been lightly incised into plaster. Since the time of its discovery, some of the plaster has flaked off. At the time of its discovery, there was debate about the readings, but most have concurred with /Yrhʿzr/, a personal name meaning "the moon god has assisted," followed by a patronymic. Some have argued that the script is Aramaic, but some have suggested it is Ammonite. In any case, this inscribed statue is a superb demonstration of the combination of fine Ammonite artwork and the epigraphic capabilities of Ammonite scribes.

III. Religious Display Text on Plaster

Among the most famous of inscriptions on plaster are the Deir 'Alla Plaster Texts (fig. 3.10). Tell Deir 'Alla is a high tell, located very close to the Jordan River. There has been much discussion about this inscription, which is written in ink, and its importance (Hackett 1980). It has often been assumed that the inscription was originally on an interior wall of a building. However, based on the fact that the edges of the inscription are thinner and curved backward it is more convincing to conclude that a plaster base had been applied to an object (rather than to a wall) and the scribe then penned the ink text onto the plaster (cf. Dan 5).

Two major depositions were found in a small room. The group of fragments found at the base of the wall (Combination II) are believed to have been closest to the floor of the room in antiquity and the group of fragments located furthest from the same wall (Combination I) are believed to have been positioned higher. The assumption is that Combination I was part of the upper portion of the inscription and thus fell further from the wall and Combination II was lower and thus fell close to the base of the wall. But both groups are normally believed to have been part of the same inscription.

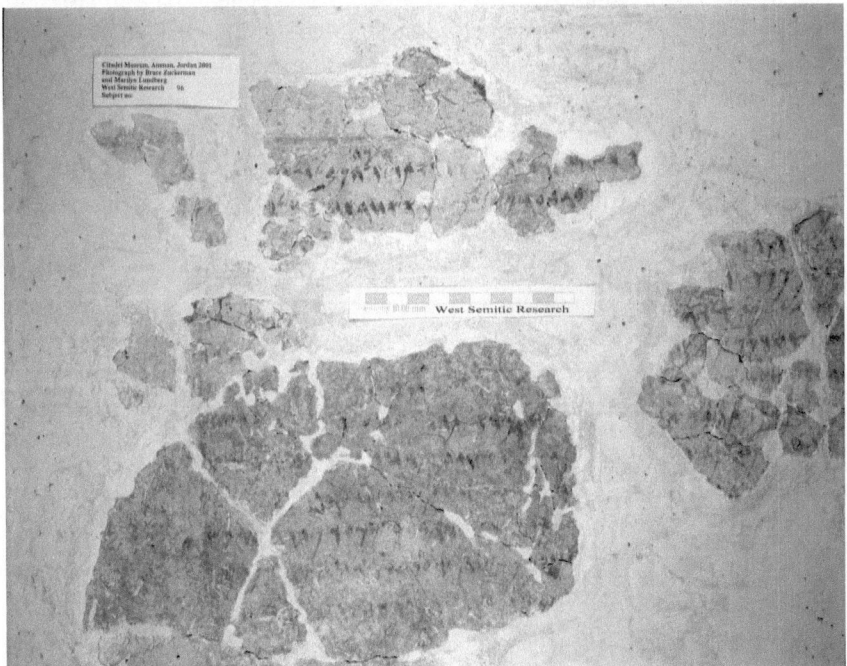

Fig. 3.10. Deir 'Alla plaster text, Combination 1. Photo courtesy of B. Zuckerman and M. Lundberg, West Semitic Research.

Cross has dated the Deir ʿAlla Plaster Texts to ca. 700 B.C.E. and argues that the script is Ammonite (Cross 1973). Joseph Naveh has argued that the script is Aramaic and that it dates to the mid-eighth century (Naveh 1987a, 109). In addition, there has been substantial discussion about the language of the Deir ʿAlla Plaster Texts, with some suggesting that they are written in an Aramaic dialect and some arguing that they are written in a Canaanite dialect. During recent years, John Huehnergard (1989) has proposed that the language is neither a Canaanite dialect nor an Aramaic one, but rather a third branch of Northwest Semitic.

Combination I refers to Balaam son of Beor, a figure attested in biblical literature with the same patronymic (Num 22–24). In Combination I, he is referred to as a "seer of the gods." The gods are reported to have come to him in a night vision. Within this vision, Balaam saw an assembly of the Šaddayyin ("gods of the mountains"; cf. Hebrew ʾEl Shadday, meaning "god of the mountain," not, as used to be supposed, "god almighty") and the decree of this assembly was to "ordain darkness rather than eternal light," "the respected one (now) respects (others) and the one who gave respect is (now) re[spected]. Also, the [foolish] laugh at the wise," "the poor woman prepares myrrh" (rather than the priestess), and "hyenas give heed to chastisement." After this theophany, Balaam fasts and weeps. McCarter (1980) has argued that Combination I consists of a series of reversals of the traditional roles and functions of the world. The second combination contains references to "El's satisfaction," travel to the "House of Eternity," "the house where the traveler does not rise and the bridegroom does not rise," and the "worm from the tomb."

The contents of the complex of rooms (of which the room with the plaster texts were a part) were varied, with many loom weights, pottery, and some inscriptions on stone. It has been described at times as a "sanctuary," but this interpretation seems strained because of the absence of cultic vessels. It has also been described as a "weaving installation." Nonetheless, I would suggest that the Deir ʿAlla plaster texts must have had some function as religious-display texts. Significantly, Millard (1985, 307) has suggested that they comprise a literary text that was part of a scroll that was copied onto the plaster at Deir ʿAlla. Notably, the Hebrew Bible contains references to writing on plaster (Deut 27:2–8; Dan 5).

IV. Inscribed Cultic, Royal, and Prestige Items

A magisterial inscribed incense altar (fig. 3.11) was discovered at the site of Tell Mudeyineh (modern Jordan), a site that is some 20 kilometers southeast of Madaba, in ancient Moab (Dion and Daviau 2000). Among the words of the inscription are the following: "The incense altar which Elishima made." The archaeological context of this inscription has been argued to be ca. 800 B.C.E. Significantly, the script of this inscription is not Phoenician, Aramaic, or Hebrew. Rather it reflects features that are most diagnostic of the Transjordanian script(s), especially Moabite (e.g., the "broad-headed" *mem*, an important typological feature). In my opinion, the script of this inscription can be dated to ca. 800–750 B.C.E. Note that some have suggested that the dating Dion and Daviau have proposed is too high (Routledge 2003, 184–212). Of course, this is precisely the sort of item that could have been used for some time and so discussions about the associated pottery may or may not be relevant for the dating of the inscription (and the same is true for the carbon dates). That is, this altar could have been used for decades after it was made. Regardless, though, this inscribed piece is demonstrative of the sorts of objects that were inscribed in the ancient Near East, including the Trans-Jordanian region of ancient Moab.

Among the most interesting of the early Byblian inscriptions are some inscribed clay pegs (fig. 3.12). The function of these pegs has been the subject of some discussion. Based on parallels from Mesopotamia, I would argue that they served dedicatory and memorializing functions at the time of the completion or renovation of monumental structures such as temples and palaces. They may also have had some sort of protective function. The inscriptions on these cones are often personal names, and it would be plausible to argue that they are the personal names of officials and benefactors. Again, such pieces are reflections of the varied and sundry materials that could be the medium for an inscription.

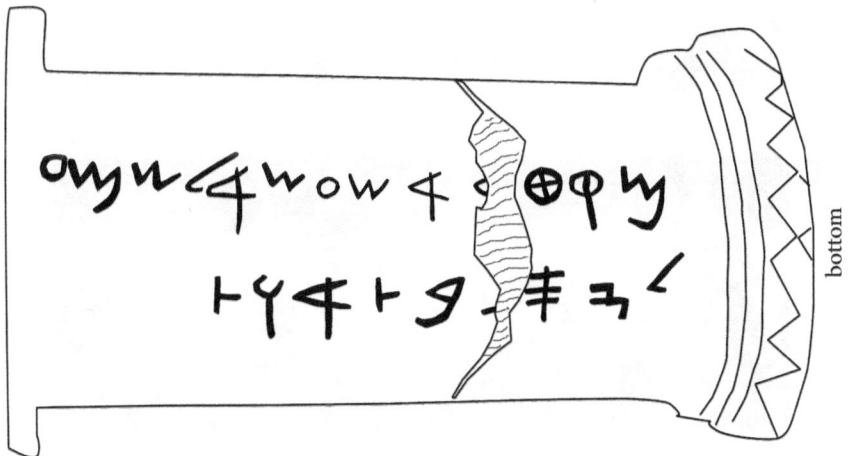

Fig. 3.11. Mudeyineh incense altar inscription. Drawing by the author.

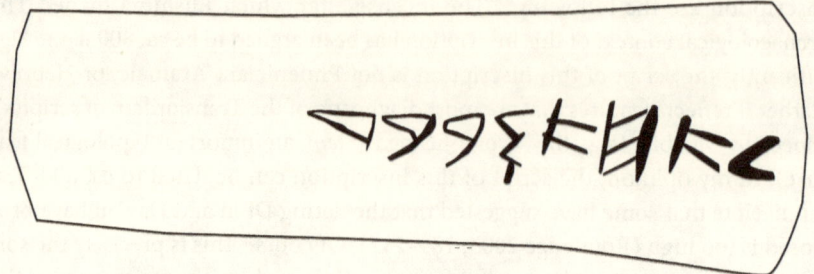

Fig. 3.12. Inscribed peg from Byblos. Drawing by the author.

The Tell Siran bottle is made of bronze and inscribed (fig. 3.13; Aufrecht 1989, 203–11). It was found during a salvage expedition in Amman Jordan. It is quite small (ca. 10 cm long), and at the time of discovery was still sealed with a pin protecting its contents of dried barley and wheat. This inscription consists of eight lines and the letters have all been executed with care. The script is Ammonite as is the language, and it is normally dated to the sixth century. Word dividers are sometimes used in the inscription, but not with absolute consistency (such inconsistency is normal in inscriptions).

The person who commissioned this inscription was "Amminadab king of the Ammonites, the son of Haṣṣal'il king of the Ammonites, the son of Amminadab king of the Ammonites" (note the papponymy, that is, naming a child after a grandfather). This inscription is, of course, royal. The text of this inscribed royal prestige object is very interesting, and is consistent with the sort of memorializing that marks royal inscriptions: "May the produce of Amminadab … the vineyard, and the gardens, and the pit, and cistern cause rejoicing and gladness for many days and distant years." That is, royal inscriptions routinely laud *ad nauseum* the accomplishments of the commissioning monarch. In sum, this

Fig. 3.13. Tell Siran bronze bottle inscription. Photo courtesy of B. Zuckerman and M. Lundberg, West Semitic Research.

inscription is Ammonite, was found in the capital of the Ammonite kingdom, and is a reflection of the fact that the Ammonite scribal apparatus was very capable and sophisticated.

A beautiful but broken bronze bowl from Umm Udeinah is inscribed very lightly along the outer rim, probably with the name of its owner (fig. 3.14; Zayadine and Bordreuil 1986, 146). The inscription was originally read as *l'lšmr [b] n 'lyzn*. However, various readings have been proposed since the *editio princeps*. Based on my collations of this inscription in Amman, and on new photographs, I cautiously read this inscription as *l'lšmr [b]n 'l'zr*, that is, "Belonging to 'Elshamar bin 'Elezer." Based on the script and the archaeological context, I date the inscription on this bowl to the late-seventh or early-sixth century (there is a stunning open-headed *'ayin* in the inscription). Of course, inscribed bowls are a reasonably common commodity, with the Kefar Veradim bowl (fig. 2.6) being a similar fine exemplar.

Late Bronze Age Ugarit has produced some sterling inscribed prestige objects. Among the most impressive are the inscribed adze heads (fig. 3.15). It would be difficult to consider these to have been intended for normal use. Rather, I would suggest that these were prestige objects, probably with an (initial) formulaic function or dedicatory use, perhaps commemorating the work on a temple or palace. That is, this inscribed adze falls into the well-established category of inscribed prestige objects.

During the twentieth century, several arrowheads with archaic inscriptions began to surface, most of them on the antiquities market, but a few from excavations (fig. 3.16). The script of these inscribed arrowheads is often dated to the terminal horizons of the Late Bronze Age and the initial horizons of the Iron Age. Often they will contain the word "arrow" followed by a personal name and a patronymic. There has been substantial discussion about their function. For

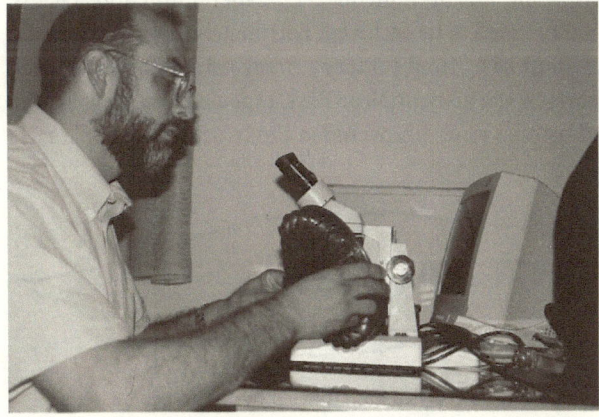

Fig. 3.14. Umm Udeinah inscribed bowl. Photo of author by M. Lundberg.

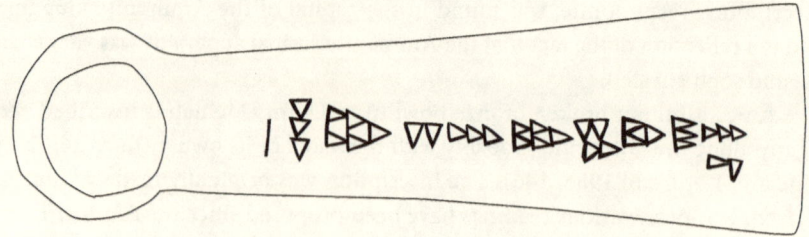

Fig. 3.15. Adze head from Ugarit. Drawing by the author.

example, Cross has suggested that the inscribed arrowheads were used in archery contests (Milik and Cross 2003, 303–8). Thus, according to Cross, because the name of the archer was inscribed on the arrowhead, determinations about winners (and losers) would be facile. McCarter (1996, 79) has suggested that they were actually used in battle and so the presence of the name on an arrowhead served to facilitate the division of plunder (the retrieved arrowhead would identify the person responsible for the kill). Although these are all plausible proposals for the function of the inscribed arrowheads, I suggest that they should be considered inscribed prestige objects. They may have served as display pieces, heirlooms, or funerary items. As such, I do not think that they were used primarily in actual warfare or archery contests. Rather, I suspect that they were primarily "mantel pieces," similar in nature to inscribed adze heads.

V. Ink Ostraca, Ink Jar Inscriptions, and Incised Pottery

The term "ostracon" is used in the narrow sense for an ink inscription written on a broken piece of pottery. Normally, an ostracon was the medium selected for documents that served some sort of immediate, ephemeral function. That is, ostraca were definitely not intended to be archived. Fortunately, however, because of the hardness of the medium (i.e., fired pottery), many ostraca have survived to be found in various parts of the ancient Near East, especially the Levant (fig. 3.17). Some one hundred ostraca were discovered at the Israelite city of Samaria

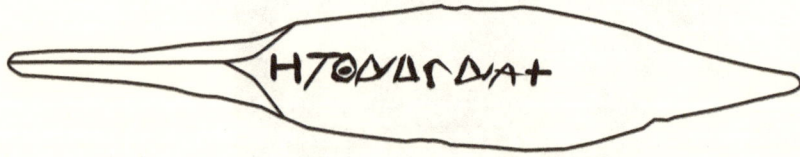

Fig. 3.16. Ø Inscribed arrowhead from el-Khadr. Drawing by Nathaniel E. Greene.

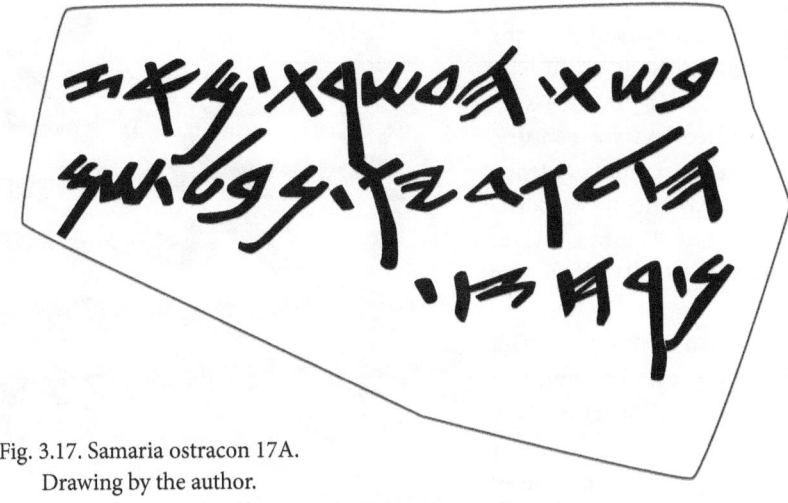

Fig. 3.17. Samaria ostracon 17A.
Drawing by the author.

(Reisner, Fisher, and Lyon 1924). These ostraca from Samaria were, in essence, economic dockets of sorts, recording the receipt of a commodity and a statement about its distribution. For example, Samaria Ostracon 17a reads as follows: "In the tenth year, from Azah, for Gadyaw: a jar of refined olive oil." Based on a constellation of data, including the archaeological context, the "year" reference can be understood with substantial certitude as referring to the tenth regnal year of Jeroboam II of Israel (i.e., ca. 776 B.C.E.). There has been some discussion about the precise function of these ostraca from Samaria. They could be "receipts" for agricultural commodities given to the royal administration at Samaria (e.g., a "tax receipt" of sorts). It is also possible, however, that they are records of dispersements from the crown for those serving the administration in some fashion (i.e., "pay stubs" of sorts). Note that the script of the Samaria Ostraca is Old Hebrew, and reflects a very nice cursive hand of the early-eighth century B.C.E.

Many of the extant ostraca (in various languages) are letters, communicating a variety of messages. This is true of many of the Old Hebrew ostraca from Arad, a number of which are very well preserved (Aharoni 1981). Ancient letters often employed an "epistolary structure," although there is much variation (Pardee 1982). Arad Ostracon 1 (fig. 3.18) contains the name of the addressee, and then uses the transition word "now" (Hebrew 't). At that juncture, there is an order to give the Kittim (often understood to be foreign mercenaries; the term derives from the place name "Kition," a city on Cyprus) various foodstuffs. This constitutes the body of the letter. Arad was the site of a Judean fortress during much of the Iron Age and this letter is arguably an example of some military correspondence. The script is the Old Hebrew script of the terminal horizon of Judean history, that is, the late-seventh and early-sixth century. The palaeographic evidence corresponds nicely with the archaeological context (i.e., Arad Strata VI–VII date to this horizon).

Lachish Ostracon 3 (an Old Hebrew ostracon; fig. 5.9) contains a fuller epistolary form. For example, it begins by referring to both the sender and the addressee: "Your servant Hosha'yahu has sent to tell my lord Ya'ush." Then it contains a greeting: "May Yahweh cause my lord to hear a message of peace." Then, the transition word "and now" is employed and the body of the letter begins. The letter refers to troop movements: "Coniah son of 'Elnathan has gone down into Egypt" and there is also reference to a prophetic warning: "Beware!" The script

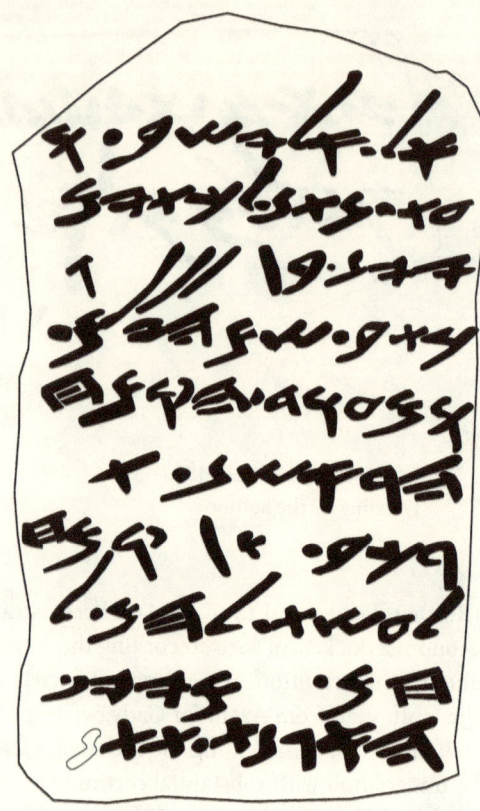

Fig. 3.18. Arad ostracon 1. Drawing by the author.

of the Lachish II corpus (of which Lachish 3 is a part) is the Old Hebrew script of the terminal period of Judean history as well (Tur Sinai 1938). That is, the script reflects the same basic typology as that of the Arad VI–VII Ostraca.

An Old Hebrew letter from Yavneh Yam ("Mesad Hashavyahu"; fig. 3.19) ostensibly contains a plea from a "harvester" to an official (Naveh 1960). From the contents of the letter it can be deduced that a senior supervisor of the harvesting (Hoshaiah the son of Shobay) had seized a harvester's garment. Within the letter, the harvester states that he was completing his tasks as usual, harvesting grain, measuring it, and storing it. The harvester also claims that he has witnesses who can testify to the veracity of his account of things. He then affirms in a very emphatic manner that he is "innocent of guilt." At the conclusion of the letter, he requests that the official listen to his plea and mandate that the garment be returned.

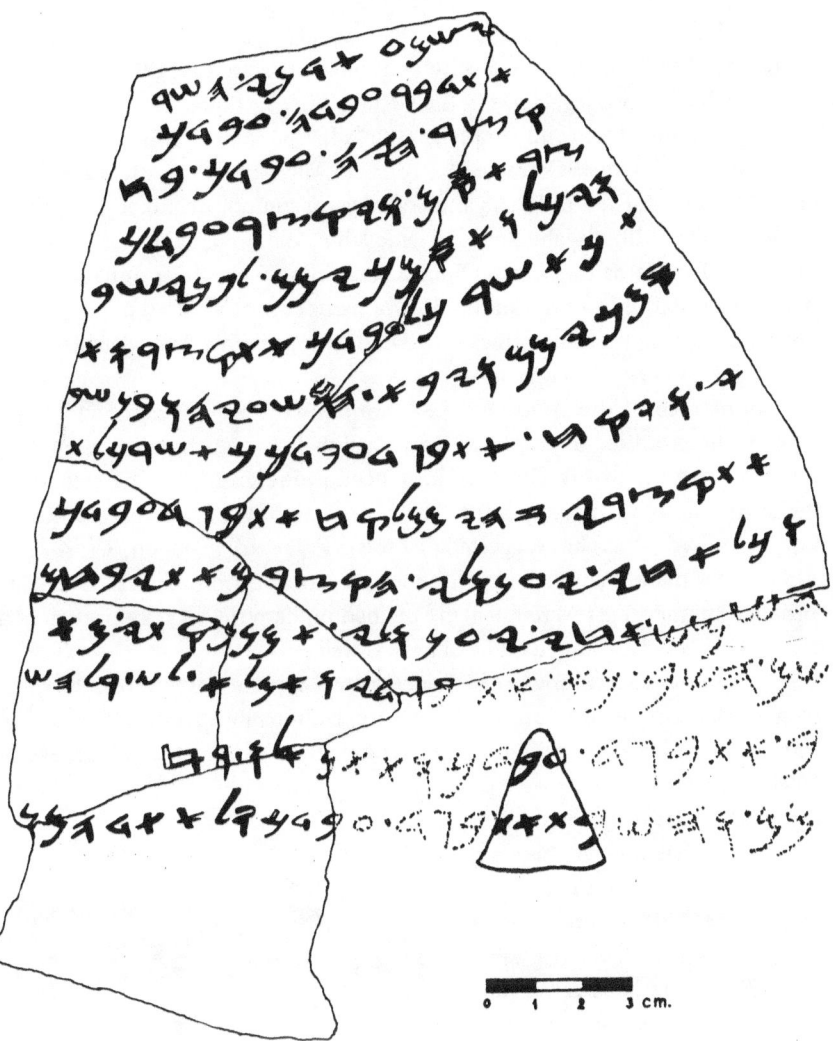

Fig. 3.19. Yavneh Yam letter. From Naveh 1987a, fig. 67.

This letter is important because it can be dated on the basis of the archaeological context and script to the second half of the seventh century and thus is helpful in providing some data about the morphology and ductus of the Old Hebrew script during a horizon when there is not a superabundance of Old Hebrew epigraphic material. Moreover, the petition connects with biblical data focusing on the "taking of a garment in pledge." A text within the Covenant Code, for example, states that "if you take a neighbor's cloak as surety, you must restore it before the setting of the sun" (Exod 22:26; cf. Lev 6:1–7; Deut 24:12–17; Amos 2:8). That is, this letter constitutes a concrete example of the sort of misuse of power that various legal texts in the Hebrew Bible critique.

Sometimes ostraca will simply contain a list of names. This is the case, for example, with Lachish Ostracon 1 (fig. 3.20; Tur Sinai 1938). It reads as follows: "Gemaryahu son of Hiṣṣilyahu; Ya'zanyahu son of Ṭobshillem; Ḥagab son of Ya'zanyahu; Mibṭaḥyahu son of Yirmeyahu; Mattanyahu son of Neriyahu." There is a similar ostracon from Tel Ira containing a small list of names (Beit-Arieh 1999, 403). Moreover, similar lists of names are also found in papyri from Elephantine in Egypt, sometimes associated with accounts. With Lachish 1, the precise function remains opaque.

An ostracon from Arad (fig. 3.21) contains the word "reign" and so can arguably be classified as some sort of a royal ostracon. Although fragmentary, it begins with the words: "I myself have begun to reign in…." The second and the third lines of this inscription refer to "strength of the arm" and the "king of Egypt." Millard (1985) has suggested that this is a "literary ostracon." Cross (2003, 135–37) has made a similar suggestion for an ostracon from Horvat 'Uza. Thus, although literary texts were normally penned on papyrus or vellum, such logia were ostensibly also penned on potsherds as well.

Sometimes inscriptions were penned on complete pottery vessels, rather than on broken pieces of pottery; therefore, technically speaking they are not ostraca. This is the case with the pithoi from Kuntillet 'Ajrud (fig. 3.22; Meshel 1978). These inscriptions were penned on complete (unbroken) vessels. Among the most interesting features of these is the fact that one of them refers to "Yahweh and his Asherah." Old Hebrew inscriptions with similar content have been found at Khirbet el-Qom (Dever 1969–70). There has been a substantial amount of discussion in the secondary literature about the basic import of the phrase "Yahweh and his Asherah". Some have suggested that the "asherah" of this inscription is a cult object, not the deity. Some have suggested that it is indeed a reference to the famed Levantine goddess known as "Asherah" (Dever 2005). McCarter (1987, 137–55) has suggested that the term "asherah" should be understood as a reference to the "culti-

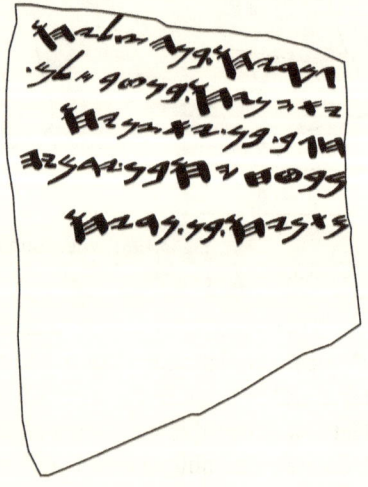

Fig. 3.20. Lachish Ostracon 1. Drawing by the author.

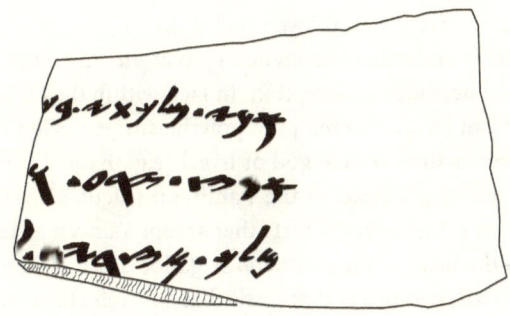

Fig. 3.21. Arad 88. Drawing by the author.

cally available presence." I am most comfortable considering this to be a reference to the goddess herself. Some have objected to this and stated that personal names do not take pronominal suffixes in Hebrew. That is, they argue that because of the word "his" the word "asherah" cannot be a divine name. It must, they suggest, be considered a cult object. However, within Semitic languages, personal names can have pronominal suffixes, and I consider this to be precisely the case with this inscription.

Obviously the inscriptions from Kuntillet 'Ajrud and Khirbet el-Qom are very important and they suggest that Israelite religion was diverse and that some

Fig. 3.22. Kuntillet 'Ajrud pithos inscription. From Meshel 1978, pl. 12.

ancient Israelites believed that Yahweh had a divine feminine consort (Smith 2002; Rollston 2003). Indeed, it is convincing to argue that Israelite religion was certainly not monotheistic at its inception. In fact, within the Hebrew Bible, there are: (1) texts that can be considered pure polytheism (e.g., Gen 6:1–4); (2) texts that accept Yahweh as the national god of Israel (e.g., Exod 20: 1–3), but do not understand him to be the head of the pantheon (Deut 32:8–9, reading with Qumran and the LXX *Vorlage*); (3) texts that accept Yahweh as the national god of Israel and also the head of the pantheon (e.g., Job 1–2); (4) and late texts (i.e., late-seventh and sixth centuries) that posit that Yahweh is not only Israel's god, but also the only god, that is, texts that affirm pure monotheism (Jer 10:5; Isa 44:9–20). Significantly, however, monotheism was a late development, not something that was present in the earliest forms of Israelite religion. The inscriptions from Kuntillet ʿAjrud and Khirbet el-Qom can be understood as reflecting the notion that Yahweh is the national god of Israel, but they certainly also antedate the development of monotheism.

In Ugaritic literature, the goddess associated with the god El (the "head of the pantheon") is Asherah. Although Yahweh's association with Asherah does not necessarily signify a rise in his status, I think it plausible to argue that Yahweh's association with Asherah is a result of the fact that he is now the head of the pantheon and so becomes linked with the goddess associated with the head of the pantheon. That is, because Yahweh became the head of the pantheon, he gets the goddess. Regardless of the precise manner in which the religious content of these inscriptions is understood, they constitute some of the most important religious texts within the Old Hebrew corpus.

Sometimes, rather than writing on pottery with ink and a reed pen, pottery was incised on a pot (or potsherd) after firing. For this type of inscription, a very sharp stylus and a strong hand were required, but even then it was difficult for a scribe to produce the script with fine precision. Nevertheless, inscriptions on fired pottery (sometimes broken, sometimes not) were a common product of the scribal apparatus. A fine example of this is an Old Hebrew inscription referred to as the Barley Letter (fig. 3.23; Crowfoot and Crowfoot 1957). This inscription has been incised into a glazed piece of pottery from the Israelite capital city of Samaria. The script is a stylish (even flamboyant) Old Hebrew cursive and can be dated to the chronological horizon around the time of the Assyrian destruction of Samaria (i.e., ca. 722 B.C.E.). Note that these Old Hebrew inscriptions hail from the terminal period of the Northern Kingdom of Israel, and thus post-date the Reisner Samaria ostraca (Reisner, Fisher, and Lyon 1924).

Sometimes pottery was incised before firing. The scribe (or a potter trained to produce at least a tolerable script) would inscribe the clay when it was leather-hard. This was a more opportune time to inscribe than after firing because of the

Fig. 3.23. Samaria barley letter. Incised after firing. Drawing by the author.

relative ease with which it could be done. Moreover, for the modern palaeographer, these inscriptions sometimes constitute superb samples for determinations regarding ductus (i.e., the number, direction, and order of strokes). For example, an inscription from Tel Ira was inscribed before firing (fig. 3.24; Beit-Arieh 1999, 411). Three letters are preserved in a pristine fashion: *lamed*, *ʿayin*, and *zayin*. The *lamed* was made with a flowing downward stroke. The *ʿayin* was formed with two strokes, something that can also be discerned from many of the exemplars of this letter preserved in ink, but rarely so clearly as in this inscribed sherd. Most striking of all is the fact that the ductus of the *zayin* can be determined with precision: the top horizontal was inscribed first, the vertical stroke was penned second, and the bottom horizontal last. The reason this can be ascertained is because of the damming patterns (the wet clay "wash" pushed into the path of previous strokes) evident in the strokes.

Although it is most common for inscriptions in fired pottery, whether broken or not, to be incised with a sharp stylus, there are also some inscriptions that were chiseled into fired pottery. On a superb, though fragmentary, example from the Judean site of Tel Ira (fig. 3.25; Beit Arieh 1999, 409), each chisel mark of the two preserved letters, *pe* and *lamed*, is visible.

Sometimes jar handles would be inscribed. Numerous inscribed jar handles were excavated at Gibeon, often referred to by its Arabic name el-Jib (Pritchard

Fig. 3.24. Tel Ira inscription. Drawing by the author.

1959; 1960). The majority of these were found in a cistern, that is, in a secondary context. Based on the script of these inscriptions, some have dated these inscriptions to the terminal period of Judean history (ca. 587 B.C.E.); however, I have argued that the script of the Gibeon inscribed jar handles suggests that they were produced during the late-eighth or early-seventh century (Rollston 2006). Many of these inscriptions contain the word Gibeon and then the letters *Gdr* (though some have read *Gdd*). Although there are several tenable proposals for understanding the meaning of these letters, I suggest that *gdr* (a low stone fence or stone wall) is a very attractive reading. Thus, *gbʿn gdr* would refer to walled vineyards in the vicinity of Gibeon. Note that a personal name is also normally present (e.g., Azariah, Amariah), arguably the name of a vintner or manager. Significantly, some of the Gibeon inscribed jar handles were inscribed before firing, and this fact has been of considerable usefulness in determining the ductus of the letters. For example, the jar handle drawn in fig. 3.26 is number 14. It was inscribed before firing and substantial data are discernable regarding the ductus of the letters based on patterns of damming.

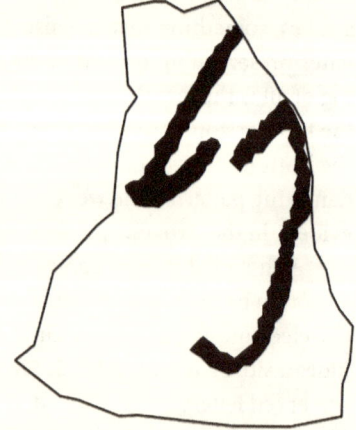

VI. Papyri, Seals, and Bullae

Papyrus was used widely in the ancient Levant as a medium for writing documents, especially those that were intended to be

Fig. 3.25. Tel Ira inscription. Chiseled after firing. Drawing by the author.

Fig. 3.26. Gibeon inscribed jar handle. Drawing by the author.

permanent. Thus, contracts, deeds of purchase, marriage licenses, divorce certificates, and literature were often written on papyri. The Hebrew Bible contains references to papyrus (and vellum). For example, the book of Jeremiah refers to the fact that King Jehoiakim of Judah listened to an official read three or four columns (*dltwt*) of a papyrus scroll containing Jeremiah's oracles. He then periodically took a penknife, cut off portions of the scroll, and threw the severed columns of text into a temple fireplace (Jer 36:20–23). Of course, even without the vindictiveness of an angry monarch, papyrus documents from Iron Age Syria-Palestine have rarely survived into the modern period. One of the documents that has survived, however, is an Old Hebrew document referred to as the Murabbaʿat Papyrus (Milik 1961, 93–100). This papyrus fragment is a palimpsest, that is, there was an initial text that was penned on this papyrus, but then at some later point, someone attempted to remove (by scraping) the original text so as to reuse the papyrus to write a different text. To be sure, the "underwriting" (i.e., the first text) is faded and abraded. The "upper-writing" (i.e., the second text) is a crude list of names. Cross has argued that both date to the first half of the seventh century B.C.E. (2003, 116–24). Obviously, this papyrus constitutes a nice example of the reuse of a writing surface.

Although Iron Age Levantine papyri have rarely survived, associated bullae (and the seals used to produce the bullae) often have survived. In essence, ancient papyri documents were written and then rolled. A string was then wrapped around the rolled papyrus scroll and a small, rounded piece of soft clay would be placed on the string (the impressions from the strings are consistently visible on the reverse side of bullae). Then the seal(s) of one (or more) of those indi-

Fig. 3.27. Umm Udeinah seal J14653.

Fig. 3.29. Umayri seal J19332.

Fig. 3.28. Umayri seal J16685, inscribed on both sides.

Photos by
B. Zuckerman and
M. Lundberg, West
Semitic Research.

Fig. 3.30. *La-melek* jar handle.

viduals who were part of the agreement would be pressed into the wet clay. The term "bulla" (plural: bullae) is used for the clay impressed by a seal. The sealed documents would then be stored in some fashion (e.g., in a personal archive or temple archive). Of course, these documents would remain sealed until such a time as there was a need to ascertain the contents. Naturally, sometimes sealed documents would never have been opened.

Within the biblical text, there are multiple references to seals. For example, Judah is said to have given his seal (among other things) to a woman that he believed to be a prostitute (Gen 38:18). Queen Jezebel is reported to have used Ahab's seal to authorize documents resulting in the death of Naboth (1 Kgs 21:8). The book of Jeremiah contains a wonderful synopsis of the process of signing and sealing legal documents (Jer 32:9–15). Within this pericope, there is reference to the fact that Jeremiah signed the deed of purchase with its terms and conditions, paid the agreed sum, and sealed the document. Significantly, this pericope refers not just to the "sealed copy," but also to an "open copy." Naturally, the production of two copies, one sealed and one open, would have been common. The sealed copy would be stored in a secure place (e.g., a temple, palace, or scribal home) and was the one that would be consulted in a legal case as the seals were proof that there had been no tampering with the document. The open copy would have been used for easy reference.

During Shiloh's excavations in the City of David (Jerusalem), some fifty-three bullae were discovered, many of them burnt and most at least partially legible (Shoham 2000, 29–57). These bullae date to the late-seventh or early-sixth centuries B.C.E. The papyrus documents to which they were attached were destroyed in the very conflagration that preserved the bullae. These documents had probably been part of an archive of some sort. Most of the bullae consist, of course, of a personal name and a patronymic (i.e., a name and then the father's name). Sometimes, however, a title will be given. For example, a bulla from the City of David contains reference to "[Tobšillem] son of Zakar, the physician" (Shoham 2000, 35 no. 6). Excavations at Lachish produced a jar with a number of bullae inside (Aharoni 1975, 19–22). In this case, someone in antiquity had opened sealed documents and placed the bullae that had sealed the documents in a jar. It should be noted that on the rarest of occasions, papyri will be discovered with the clay sealing(s) still in place. For example, some of the Elephantine papyri (Porten and Yardeni 1989) and Samaria papyri (Gropp 2001) have been discovered still sealed. It is reasonable to posit that the royal records of ancient Israel would have been archived on papyri. Predictably, however, none of these survived antiquity.

The seals used in the ancient Levantine world (including Israel) are often among the most beautiful objects from antiquity. Stamp seals (to be contrasted with the cylinder seals that are often found in Mesopotamia) are normally very small, about the size of a fingernail or thumbnail. They are normally carved out of precious stones. Note that some seals contain just an inscription. Some contain just iconography, but no inscription (that is, they are anepigraphic). Some contain both an inscription and iconography. Iron Age stamp seals have been found throughout much of the Levantine world. Note that seals are inscribed in mirror image, so that, when they are impressed in clay, the stance of the letters and the direction of writing is "correct."

The beautiful seal (J14653) in fig. 3.27 was found replete with the "ring" (Abu Taleb 1985). Of course, seals normally have holes in them for rings (or strings), but it is rare actually to find the ring. This one, however, comes from a tomb, hence, the fine preservation of both seal and ring. Some astrological iconography adorns the top of this seal. Two clear personal names inscribed on the seal, namely, "Palatiy, ben Ma'as." Significantly, a title, the "Mazkir," (presumably referring to Palatiy) is given as well; it is a title that is also attested in biblical literature, and often rendered "the herald" (e.g., 2 Sam 8:16; 20:24; 1 Kgs 4:3). The tombs where this seal was found are securely dated, based on the archaeological materials found in them, to the eighth through mid-sixth centuries. Based on the script of this seal, I date it to the eighth or early-seventh century.

A seal from the Tell Umayri excavation (modern Jordan; fig. 3.28) is inscribed on two sides and both sides have some iconography, the obverse with a bird, and the reverse with a ram (Herr 1998, 323–30). The inscription on the obverse reads "Belonging to Il-Amuṣ, son of Tamik-'il." The inscription on the reverse reads simply "belonging to Il-Amuṣ." Although many seals are inscribed on just one side, some, like this one, are inscribed on both. Note that the name "Il-Amuṣ" means essentially "Il is strong," and Tamak-'il means essentially "Il sustains." This seal has been dated to the seventh century, and I concur with this dating. The script is, of course, Ammonite.

The seal in fig. 3.29 consists of two clear registers. It has been drilled. The top register reads "*l 'zn bn*" and the bottom register reads "*brk'il.*" That is "belonging to 'Ozen ben Barak-il." This seal demonstrates that although iconography is common, some seals do not have any iconography (that is, they are aniconic).

During the late-eighth century, large storage jars associated with the Judean crown in some fashion were impressed with "*lmlk* seals," that is, seals that contained the words "belonging to the king" (fig. 3.30; Vaughn 1999) These inscriptions would routinely have a place name on them as well. During the middle of the twentieth century, scholars often dated the "La-melek Jar Handles" to the late-seventh and early-sixth century. However, during the final decades of the twentieth century, a strong consensus, resulting from the cogent arguments of Ussishkin 1978), developed that these jar handles are to be dated to the late-eighth and early-seventh century. The La-melek Jar Handles are often associated with the reign of the Judean king Hezekiah (ca. 715–687 B.C.E.). To date, more than one thousand have been found.

VII. Funerary Inscriptions

Funerary inscriptions are a relatively common type of inscription. Moreover, certain motifs are also quite standard. The Royal Steward Inscription (fig. 3. 31) was found in a tomb in Silwan, near Jerusalem (Ussishkin 1993, 247–54). The inscription reads: "This is [the sepulcher of …]yahu who is 'Over the House.' There is no silver and gold, but rather [his bones] and the bones of his female servant with him. Accursed is the man who might open this!" This inscription is written in a very nice Old Hebrew cursive script of the late-eighth century. Note that the theophoric element is "-yahu." This is a standard southern Hebrew Yahwistic theophoric (the northern Hebrew Yahwistic theophoric was "-yaw").

The Ahiram Sarcophagus Inscription (fig 2.2; Dussaud 1924) constitutes a fine example of a funerary inscription in Phoenician. It can be read as follows:

> The Sarcophagus that [Itto]ba'l son of Ahiram king of Byblos made for Ahiram his father when he placed him in eternity. And to a king among kings or a governor among governors, or ruler of camps who may come up against Byblos, and uncover this sarcophagus, may his scepter be overturned, and may the throne of his kingdom be overthrown, and may peace flee from Byblos. And as for him may his writing be effaced from Byblos.

The content of this inscription is fairly standard, replete with a curse language pronounced upon any that might campaign against Byblos and upon any that might disturb the corpse. It should be noted in this connection that there has been much debate about the ending of the Ahiram Inscription. During my collations of the Ahiram Sarcophagus Inscription in Beirut, it was immediately apparent that the stone at the terminal portion of the inscription was severely

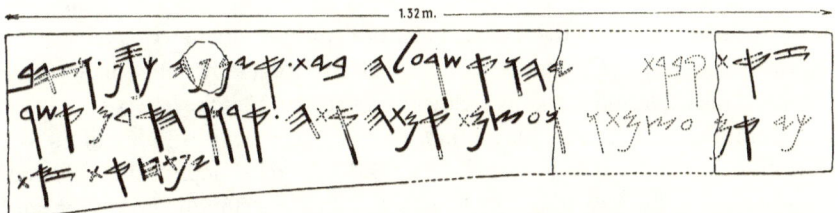

Fig. 3.31. Royal Steward Inscription. Drawing by Avigad 1953, fig. 4.

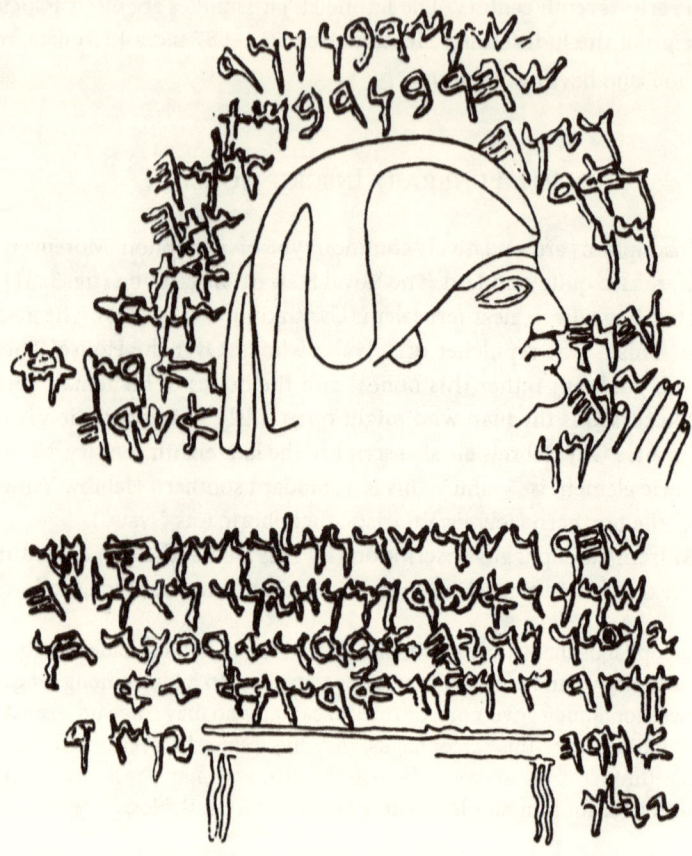

Fig. 3.32. Stele 1 from Narab. From Naveh 1987a, fig. 76.

chipped. Moreover, the terminal portion of the inscription (especially the letters *gbl*, i.e., Byblos) is written in a different "hand." I believe that the inscription
was inscribed and then this portion of the sarcophagus was accidently chipped,
resulting in the loss of several letters, including *gbl*. At that juncture, a different
hand (without the skill of the first scribe or stonemason) attempted to replace the
damaged word "Byblos," but was not able to do so particularly well. This scenario
is entirely plausible and accounts for the different "hand" of the letters *gbl*.

During the late-nineteenth century, an inscribed relief was found in the village of Nerab, a village near Aleppo (fig. 3.32). The relief depicts the deceased,
a priest named Sîn-zēra-ibni. The language of this inscription is Aramaic, and
it is often dated to the seventh century. The name of the late priest is Akkadian

and means "[the Moon God] Sin has produced an heir." The inscription makes a specific reference to the incised image of the deceased: "this is his image and his grave." A traditional curse is present: "Whoever you are who may remove this image and grave from its place, may Sahar and Shamash and Nikkal and Nusk remove your name and your place from life, and may they make you die a miserable death and may they destroy your seed." A corresponding blessing is also present: "But if you protect this image and grave, may that of yours be protected."

In sum, tomb inscriptions are reasonably common in the ancient Near Eastern world. Sometimes they will contain reference to the fact that no precious metals are present (note that tomb robbers were often elites, hence, a written warning). Sometimes tomb inscriptions will contain some sort of blessings or curses, or both, often associated with some reference to the fact that the tomb and its remains are not to be disturbed. In short, the burial inscriptions referenced here are fairly typical of the genre.

VIII. WEIGHTS

Weights were an important part of ancient economies (i.e., the weighing out of commodities that were being bought or sold). Normally, they were made of stone and they bore some sort of mark that indicated the amount of the weight. Often the weights were very small, but sometimes they were larger. The Hebrew Bible contains a number of references to weights, and especially references to the fact that the use of "improper" weights was morally wrong (e.g., Prov 20:23; Micah 6:11; Deut 25:13; Lev 19:36). The large stone weight drawn in fig. 3.33 is from the site of Deir 'Alla and is inscribed with the word "stone."

CONCLUSIONS

Although not all of the different types of Northwest Semitic epigraphic texts have been discussed, it should be readily apparent at this juncture that the epigraphic record is broad and diverse. Inscriptions on various media, with various types of content, from various social and religious

Fig. 3.33. Deir 'Alla weight. Drawing by the author.

contexts, and with multiple functions, have been considered. Now I will focus on the segment of society that produced the lion's share of these inscriptions, namely, the elites of the ancient Levant.

PART 2

THE SCRIBE AND LITERACY

Chapter 4

The Status of the Scribe and
the Tools of the Trade

Within the ancient Near East, the scribe was a respected member of the elite class. Texts from Egypt and Mesopotamia laud the scribal profession, proclaim the distinction and status of the scribe, the freedom from manual labor that he enjoyed, and his enduring legacy (Rollston 2001). Most of these texts are considered school texts. That is, they were copied within the schools of ancient Mesopotamia and Egypt and were designed to assist in the recruitment and retention of scribal students. After all, scribal training required a substantial commitment of time; therefore, to emphasize (even to the point of hyperbole) the most beneficial aspects of the scribal profession must have seemed prudent. Significantly, there are texts within the Hebrew Bible that reflect the fact that the Israelite scribe was part of elite circles as well. Moreover, during the Second Temple period, the high status of the scribe persisted. The picture that emerges of the scribe in the ancient Near East, therefore, is that of an elite member of society, often present in powerful circles.

Egyptian Texts Lauding the Scribal Profession

Egyptian school texts sometimes brandished the power and prestige associated with the scribal profession. For example, the Satire of the Trades inaugurates its paean to the scribe by noting the place of importance to which the scribe rapidly ascends. "Barely grown, still a child, he is greeted, sent on errands, hardly returned he wears a gown" (Lichtheim 1973, 186). Papyrus Lansing also extols the scribal profession by affirming that the scribe "makes friends with those greater than he.... You will be advanced by your superiors. You will be sent on a mission" (Lichtheim 1976, 168). It continues this theme by urging that the student persist in training and become a scribe so that "you may become one whom the king trusts; to make you gain entrance to treasury and granary.... To make you issue the offerings on feast days" (171). In addition, Papyrus Lansing notes that the scribe will have an entourage of those willing to assist him, "You call for one; a thousand answer you" (171). Naturally, an individual of such distinction would have a lasting reputation. Therefore, Papyrus Chester Beatty IV declares: "Man decays, his corpse is dust, all his kind have perished; But a book makes him remembered.... Better is a book than a well-built house, than tomb-chapels in the west" (177).

One of the most beneficial aspects of the scribal profession was that it did not require "manual labor." In the Satire of the Trades, therefore, Duauf's son Khety, while bringing his son, Pepi, to school, reminds him of the freedom from manual labor which the scribe enjoys: "I have seen many beatings; set your heart on books! I have watched those seized for labor; there's nothing better than books!" (Lichtheim 1973, 185). Papyrus Anastasi II contains an even more explicit statement about this: "Be a scribe. It saves you from toil and protects you from all manner of work. It spares you bearing hoe and mattock, so that you do not carry a basket. It sunders you from plying the oar and spares you torment, as you are not under many lords and numerous masters" (Caminos 1954, 51). Papyrus Lansing also alludes to the scribe's freedom from manual labor: "Set your sight on being a scribe.... You will not be like a hired ox" (Lichtheim 1976, 171).

MESOPOTAMIAN TEXTS LAUDING THE SCRIBAL PROFESSION

Similar statements are made about the scribal profession in Mesopotamian texts.[1] A bilingual cuneiform text known as Examination Text D states that "the scribal art is the mother of orators, the father of masters" (Sjöberg 1972, 127). It continues, affirming that "the scribal art is delightful, it never satiates you." Obviously, becoming proficient in Mesopotamian cuneiform (both Sumerian and Akkadian) was rigorous and this text concedes this "the scribal art is not (easily) learned," but then emphasizes that "he who has learned it need no longer be anxious about it." Furthermore, there is an emphasis upon the fact that wealth accompanies the practice of the scribal art. Thus, the text states "strive to (master) the scribal art and it will enrich you, be industrious in the scribal art and it will provide you with wealth and abundance." The text then continues and states "Do not be careless concerning the scribal art, do not neglect it, the scribal art is a 'house of richness,' the secret of Amanki, work ceaselessly with the scribal art and it will reveal its secret to you." However, there is also a warning for those students who are not diligent in pursuing this elite vocation, namely, "if you neglect it, they will

---

1. For similar texts to the following, see Sjöberg 1973, 105–69; 1975, 137–76; Civil 1985, 67–78; Vanstiphout 1997, 588–93.

make malicious remarks about you" (Sjöberg 1972, 126–31).Obviously, therefore, Mesopotamian school texts vaunted the scribal profession.

Egyptian Texts Denigrating the Trades and Lauding the Scribes

Within the corpus of Mesopotamian school texts, there is a dearth of material that compares and contrasts the life of the scribe with the life of artisans. However, within the corpus of Egyptian school texts, this motif is present. For example, in the Satire of the Trades various professions are denigrated, as the following selections indicate:

> I have seen the smith at work, at the opening of his furnace, with fingers like the claws of a crocodile, he stinks more than fish roe…. The jewel-maker bores with his chisel in hard stone of all kinds; When he has finished the inlay of the eye, his arms are spent, he's weary…. The potter is under the soil, though as yet among the living, he grubs in the mud more than a pig, in order to fire his pots…. The farmer wails more than the guinea fowl, his voice is louder than a raven's; his fingers are swollen and stink to excess." (Lichtheim 1973, 186–88).

Immediately after relating these woes, the Satire of the Trades concludes this component of the text by stating that:

> There's no profession without a boss, except for a scribe; he is the boss. Hence if you know writing, it will do better for you than those professions I've set before you, each more wretched than the other….The day in school will profit you, its works are forever (189–90).

Papyrus Lansing contains components that not only aggrandize the scribal profession, but also defame other professions:

> See for yourself with your own eye. The occupations lie before you. The washerman's day is going up, going down. All his limbs are weak, from whitening his neighbors' clothes…. The maker of pots is smeared with soil, like one whose relations have died…. The carpenter who is in the shipyard carries the timber and stacks it. If he gives today the output of yesterday, woe to his limbs! … Come, let me tell you the woes of the soldier, and how many are his superiors…. He is hungry … he is dead while yet alive (Lichtheim 1976, 169–70, 172).

Papyrus Sallier I contains a letter to a scribal student who has withdrawn from the school and has begun farming. He is reminded of the miseries of the farmer:

> Do you not recall the condition of the cultivator faced with the registration of the harvest-tax after the worm has carried off half of the corn and the hippopotamus has eaten up the rest? The mice abound in the field, the locust descends, the cattle devour. The sparrows bring want upon the cultivator. The remainder that is on the threshing-platform is almost at an end, and is for the thieves.... But a scribe, he is at the head of everybody's work" (Caminos 1954, 315–16, but with "worm" for "snake," following Hans-W. Fischer-Elfert, personal communication).

Obviously, it is necessary to factor in the presence of hyperbole in these texts. Nevertheless, I am confident that scribes in both Mesopotamia and Egypt believed that the scribal vocation was a superb one. That is, the life of the scribe may have required arduous training, but the rewards were argued to be many, in terms of wealth and prestige.

THE HIGH STATUS OF THE SCRIBE IN THE HEBREW BIBLE

To date, there are no extant epigraphic texts in Old Hebrew that laud the scribal profession in the same manner as the Egyptian and Mesopotamian texts. However, there is sufficient evidence in the canonical Hebrew corpus from the eras of the First and Second Temple to discern that the scribe was an esteemed member of elite society. Note, for example, that the majority of the biblical references refer to scribes associated with the palace and temple. For example, the term *sōpēr ham-melek*, "scribe of the king," and "royal scribe" (2 Kgs 12:11; 2 Chr 24:11; cf. Esth 3:12; 8:9) suggest the close association of certain scribes with the palace (and thus in a position of power and status). There is also a reference to a *šĕkat sōpēr*, "scribal chamber" located within the royal palace (Jer 36:12), and the "house of Nathan the scribe" was under royal auspices (Jer 37:15, 20). Producing and maintaining royal records such as "the chronicles of the kings of Israel," "the chronicles of the kings of Judah," and "the chronicles of Solomon" were certainly among the responsibilities fulfilled by royal scribes (1 Kgs 11:41; 14:19, 29). Recording decrees and taking dictation were probably among the duties of scribes (Jer 36:32; Esth 1:19; 8:9–14; Dan 6:8). Furthermore, the epigraphic record demonstrates that scribes were also responsible for maintaining certain economic dockets (e.g., Reisner Samaria Ostraca). Within the Hebrew Bible, the term *sōpēr śar has-sābā'*, "scribe of the commander of the army" (2 Kgs 25:19; Jer 52:25) suggests that certain scribes were responsible for aspects of the military (e.g., mustering the troops, ordering rations, and so on), another indication of the royal affiliation of certain scribes. Naturally, scribes would be included among the śārîm, "officials," as also demonstrated by the presence of scribes in lists of officials (e.g., 2 Sam 8:17; 20:25; 2 Kgs 12:11; Jer 36:12). Because of the royal scribe's status as a literate high official, certain responsibilities connected with the temple sometimes devolved to the royal scribe (e.g., 2 Kgs 12:11; 22:3). The fact that a scribe was present, along with additional officials, during negotiations with Sennacherib's delegation, is also indicative of the power and prominence sometimes attained by a royal scribe (2 Kgs 18:18). The scribe Baruch (associated with Jeremiah) was known in royal circles (Jer 36:11–20). The Deuteronomistic text of Kings reflects the assumption that the Judean officials during the reign of Hezekiah (r. ca. 715–687 B.C.E.), including the royal scribe, were bilingual (2 Kgs 18:26), something that can be considered significant in antiquity (Gass and Selinker 2008). For various reasons (e.g., diplomacy, copying and transmission of texts), bilingualism was a reasonably common phenomenon in the ancient Near East, but the fact remains that it was often confined to elite circles. Nevertheless, someone might counter that some scribes in ancient Israel would have functioned in a number of non-royal and non-sacerdotal capacities, including producing deeds of purchase, sale, marriage, divorce, and so on. Obviously, this would have been the case, but I would argue that even in these capacities, the scribe would have been considered an educated member of elite society and that these roles were still reflective of high status.

A SECOND TEMPLE SCRIBE ON THE STATUS OF HIS VOCATION

Among the scribes of the canonical corpus during the Second Temple period, Ezra seems to have functioned in various capacities. Indeed, he is described as both a "scribe of the law of God" and "a priest" (Ezr 7:6; 7:11; Neh 8:4; 8:9; 8:13; 12:26; 12:36). The book of Ben Sira, however, is the book that contains the most detailed discussion of the scribal profession. The pericope about the scribal profession in Ben Sira was intended as a tool of recruitment and retention and from this text it is readily apparent that the scribe was considered to be a member of elite society. For example, Ben Sira wrote the following: "Scribal wisdom increases wisdom; whoever is free from toil can become wise" (Sira 38:24). With those laudatory remarks, Ben Sira begins his pericope about the superlative aspects of the professional pursuit and dissemination of wisdom, that is, the scribal profession (Sir 38:24–39:11). To paint the picture more graphically, he first describes the lives of the artisans: The farmer does not have the luxury of acquiring wisdom because "his objective is to complete the fattening (of the cattle) and his attention is turned toward the fields" (Sir 38:26). The "seal maker" (note: the seal maker is distinguished here from the scribe) does not acquire wisdom because the exigencies of his craft require that he "make a great variety" of seals (Sir 38:27), that is, seals with different personal names and iconography. Similarly, the smith "contends with the heat of the furnace," "sears his flesh," and "deafens his ears," so that he can "complete the projects" (Sir 38:28). Likewise the potter toils endlessly at the wheel, employing both hands and feet, because he is compelled to "finish his work" (Sir 38:29). In short, Ben Sira affirms that the demands of an artisan's life stifle the possibilities for the acquisition of wisdom. He does acknowledge the value and necessity of such trades: "All these are skilled with their hands ... without them a city is not habitable, and wherever they stay, they do not hunger" (Sir 38:31, 32). Nevertheless he observes that artisans, in contrast to the scribes, "are not sought for the council of the people, are not prominent in the assembly," and they "do not deliberate about judicial regulations or expound on discipline and justice" (Sir 38:32, 33). The scribe, Ben Sira continues, "seeks out the wisdom of all the ancients," "is in the midst of the great," "travels in the land of foreign peoples," and "many praise his understanding" (Sir 39:1,4,9). Clearly according to Ben Sira, the life of the scribe is far superior to that of the populace (Rollston 2001; Tov 2004), a view that accounts for the fact that he himself was the head of a school located in Jerusalem (Sir 51:23).

The scribe was an esteemed member of society who often operated in powerful circles. He was capable of performing functions that most people simply could not, as literacy levels were low in antiquity. What distinguished the scribe from the majority of the population and allowed him to perform such functions was the receipt of a formal, standardized education.

CHAPTER 5

SCRIBAL EDUCATION IN ANCIENT ISRAEL:
THE OLD HEBREW EPIGRAPHIC EVIDENCE

INTRODUCTION TO THE PROBLEM

The evidence for "schools" in ancient Israel (i.e., Iron Age Israel and Judah) has been analyzed by numerous specialists, but with no consensus achieved. Some have affirmed that schools were present in ancient Israel (Hermisson 1968; Lemaire 1981). Others have concluded that the data (biblical, epigraphic, and comparative ancient Near Eastern) supporting the existence of schools are inconclusive at best. For example, regarding the fact that there is no reference to "schools" in the Hebrew Bible, Golka has stated that "the best explanation for the fact that no schools are mentioned is still that there were none!" (1993, 4–15). After discussing the epigraphic and biblical evidence, Weeks affirmed that "there is neither any strong evidence for schools nor any convincing reason to suppose that they would have existed" (1994, 156). Jamieson-Drake theorizes that "schools would be located in Jerusalem, if schools even existed." (1991, 156). Whybray conceded that there may have been some sort of modest scribal education, but he also asserted that it was confined to a small number of "scribal families" and that these were sufficient for "transact[ing] the business, both public and private, of the entire nation." (1974, 38). Of course, Lemaire attempted to make a sustained argument for pervasive education in ancient Israel based on epigraphic and biblical evidence, but his work has been the object of substantial criticism because his broad conclusions are often based on tenuous interpretations of the evidence (Crenshaw 1985; 1998). At this juncture, the field continues to be at an impasse (Carr 2005, 112–16; cf. Schniedewind 2004, 59).

I am convinced that the Old Hebrew epigraphic evidence demonstrates that there was formal, standardized scribal education in ancient Israel. The focus of this chapter will be on Old Hebrew epigraphic evidence, specifically palaeography, orthography, and hieratic numerals. I will also make reference to the nature and function of abecedaries and the formulaic nature of the epistolary epigraphs.

In addition, I will give some attention to the rapid pace at which some scholars have assumed an ancient alphabetic writing system could be learned. Ultimately, I will argue that the Old Hebrew epigraphic record reflects depth, sophistication, and consistency in the production of written materials, and that the Old Hebrew data are most consistent with the presence of a mechanism for the formal, standardized education of scribal elites in ancient Israel.

SUPPOSITIONS ABOUT THE PACE OF LEARNING THE OLD HEBREW WRITING SYSTEM

The writing systems developed and employed in ancient Mesopotamia and Egypt were complex non-alphabetic systems, with large inventories of signs. Scholars have argued that, for even the most assiduous students, developing substantial facility in these writing systems required years of arduous training (George 2005, 127–37; McDowell 1999). Conversely, it has normally been argued that the mastery of the linear alphabetic Northwest Semitic was facile, requiring just days or weeks of training to master. Regarding the Old Hebrew alphabet, for example, Albright stated that "since the forms of the letters are very simple, the twenty-two-letter alphabet could be learned in a day or two by a bright student and in a week or two by the dullest." He proceeded to affirm that he did "not doubt for a moment that there were many urchins in various parts of Palestine who could read and write as early as the time of the Judges" (1960, 123). Jamieson-Drake has opined that the Old Hebrew alphabet was "simple enough that functional knowledge of it could be passed on from one person to another in a comparatively short time" and that "schools would hardly have been necessary" (1991, 154–56). Weeks states that "the Phoenician alphabet adopted and then adapted in Israel is neither complicated nor arcane, and it is not necessary to suppose that lengthy schooling and a course in reading literature was necessary for a good grasp of the essentials" (1994, 151). Crenshaw has stated that "as for training to read and write Hebrew, its simplicity would have enabled students to acquire the necessary skills in a short time" (1998, 107).

Ultimately, however, I contend that assumptions such as these about the simplicity of the Old Hebrew writing system, and the rapidity of the pace at which proficiency could have been achieved, are much too sanguine. Rather than positing rapid proficiency in alphabetic writing, recent empirical studies for modern languages have delineated developmental phases ("stages") in the process of word reading and word spelling. Ehri summarizes these stages in broad terms as follows: (1) Prealphabetic; (2) Partial alphabetic; (3) Full alphabetic; (4) Consolidated alphabetic. The first stage applies to "prereaders who operate with

nonalphabetic information because they know little about the alphabetic system."
The second stage applies to "novice beginners who operate with rudimentary
knowledge of some letter-sound relations." The third level applies to students
who "possess more complete knowledge involving grapheme-phoneme units and
how these units form words." The fourth level "applies to more advanced students
who have knowledge of letter patterns as well as grapheme-phoneme units" (Ehri
1997, 240, 253–56). Moreover, it has been argued on the basis of these empirical studies that for children to become proficient in a modern writing system
(i.e., their first writing system) a few years are normally required, not a few days
or weeks (Ehri 2002, 7–28; Henderson 1985). Of course, it is readily apparent
that emergent writing is often attested within "initial" periods of instruction, but
proficiency (e.g., capacity to produce "documents" with minimal orthographic
errors, and with the letters reflecting accurate morphology and stance as well as
standard relative size) requires substantial time.

Naturally, some alphabetic writing systems are more difficult to master. For
example, modern languages with a deep orthography (e.g., English and French
in which there is not a "simple correspondence" between letters and sounds,
and in which irregularities are quite common) arguably require more time for
the achievement of proficiency than languages with a shallow(er) orthography
(e.g., German). However, the fact remains that, regardless of the orthography,
any suggestion that proficiency in one's *first* alphabetic writing system (ancient
or modern) can be achieved in a few days or weeks must be considered most
problematic.

Of course, because of the dominance of consonants in the ancient Hebrew
writing system, some might suggest that proficiency was accomplished with
particular ease and at a rapid pace. Some studies of proficiency in the modern
Hebrew writing system have been produced that are among the most relevant
of all the studies of the development of proficiency in modern writing systems.
Levin (personal communication) has summarized the progression of facility in
the modern Hebrew writing system as follows: (1) Israeli children begin writing
words phonetically at around five years of age. (2) Training in the basic features of orthography, including Masoretic pointing, continues for most children
through the age of eight. (3) Most spelling errors disappear by around the age
of ten, but some (e.g., the usage of *yod* and *waw* as *matres lectionis*) persist into
adulthood even among literate adults (see also Share and Levin 1999, 89–111). In
short, multiple years are normally necessary for proficiency. Of course, there are
certain aspects of modern Hebrew phonology and orthography that differ from
ancient Hebrew, but I do not believe that this factor would result in grossly dis-
proportionate differences in the time required for proficiency. Naturally, some
might retort that adult Olim can learn to reproduce the script in a matter of hours

and that this is demonstrative of the fact that the Hebrew script is so simple that almost no instruction is needed (either in antiquity or in the modern period). The problem with this analogy is that adult Olim (immigrants to Israel) already have the cognitive building blocks and the manual dexterity (i.e., for the physical act of writing) in place, established previously when they learned their first writing system. For this reason (among others), any comparison between modern adult Olim and ancient Israelites learning their first writing system is fundamentally flawed.

Furthermore, with regard to the teaching and learning of the modern Arabic writing system, Assaad Skaff and Helen Sader have noted (personal communication) that the short vowels and the long vowels are learned at the same time, along with the consonants and that this training begins in earnest during the first grade (although parents often begin instruction in the home at an earlier age). During the succeeding years, proficiency begins to develop, and by the ninth grade ("brevet" according to French nomenclature) students are very capable of writing Arabic with substantial proficiency. Thus, the learning of the Arabic writing system parallels, in many respects, the pace of learning the modern Hebrew writing system in Israel. The point is that learning one's first writing system is hardly a facile enterprise and this is the case even for alphabetic writing systems.

The Problematic Term "School"

The definition and delimitation of "Israelite schools" have sometimes been problematic components of the discussion of education in ancient Israel. For example, Whybray proposed to define a school as an "institution" that "existed for the purpose of giving specialized training" in "organized classes comprising a number of pupils, whose teachers were 'professional' in the sense that they were not the parents, or relations, or even tribal heads, of the pupils." Furthermore, he affirmed that the teaching was to be "given on a regular basis and occupied a substantial part, though not necessarily the whole, of their time" (1974, 35). Crenshaw has articulated a definition of "school" that has garnered much support: "By school is meant professional education, which involved both reading and writing, at a specific location to which young people came and for which fees were paid to a teacher" (1985, 602; 1998, 113). Note that Crenshaw desires to make a strong distinction between "schools" and "guilds." Because scholarship has often used the term "school" in broad senses (e.g., "Deuteronomic School," "Wisdom School," "Isaianic School"), it was necessary for Whybray and Crenshaw to propose more precise definitions. Nevertheless, the definitions Whybray and Crenshaw have articulated are arguably rather rigid. That is, to state that to be a "school" the teacher cannot be related to a pupil (or even a "tribal head") and that teaching must occupy the majority of the teacher's time is problematic. Moreover, to affirm that class size must be part of the equation is quite prescriptive, as is also the notion that there must of necessity have been some sort of tuition. To be sure, even some modern schools would not meet some of these criteria. After all, teachers are sometimes related to a pupil or pupils, teachers can teach part-time, and classes can be very small. Ultimately, because of the sometimes broad and sometimes narrow definitions of school that have been propounded, I believe that the term school has become polarizing. For this reason, I have avoided using it, preferring the term "formal, standardized education."

Lemaire (1981) has argued that there were numerous schools throughout much of Israel and Judah in the Iron Age with a broad curriculum and many students. Subsequent discussions of the problem have sometimes revolved around the pervasiveness of schools. Reacting to Lemaire's thesis, Crenshaw concluded that "nothing seems to require the existence of public schools, supported by taxpayers and open to everyone" (1985, 113). Weeks has argued that "the biblical and epigraphic evidence adduced for schools in Israel seems very weak indeed, and can certainly not support any hypothesis of a large, integrated school system" (1994, 153). Lemaire's decision to propose such a pervasive system of education was an "Achilles Heel," because the evidence could not carry the load with which he saddled it. Therefore, as an *Ausgangspunkt*, I emphasize that I am arguing that there was a mechanism in ancient Israel (defined broadly) that facilitated formal, standardized scribal education. I am not arguing for an educational system serving the non-elite masses.

PALAEOGRAPHIC ANALYSIS OF OLD HEBREW INSCRIPTIONS: AN INTRODUCTION

It has sometimes been said that the synchronic variation and diachronic development of the Old Hebrew cursive script is poorly attested and poorly understood. For this reason, palaeographic analyses of Old Hebrew are said to be very tenuous. However, the fact of the matter is that the number (and quality) of Old Hebrew inscriptions (of the eighth through early-sixth centuries) is substantial and many of these are datable on the basis of non-palaeograpic criteria. For example, the Kuntillet 'Ajrud inscriptions (fig. 3.22) can be dated to the very-early-eighth century. Moreover, there are scores of legible cursives from Samaria (fig. 3.17) that can be dated reliably (based on a constellation of data) to the early-eighth century. Also from the eighth century are the Khirbet el-Qom cursives (primarily carved in stone) and the Beth She'an Ostraca. From the late-eighth century are the Samaria Joint Expedition cursive inscriptions (fig. 3.23) and from the same basic horizon is the Royal Steward Inscription (fig. 3.31). Note that, cumulatively, these epigraphs come from various regions, north and south, on various media. Moreover, there is also a substantial amount of data for the Old Hebrew script series of the terminal period of the seventh century and the early-sixth century. For example, scores of the Lachish Ostraca (fig. 3.20) and Arad Ostraca (figs. 3.18 and 3.21) can be dated to this period, and the Horvat 'Uza Ostraca also hail from this horizon. Cursive inscriptions from the very-late-eighth century to the mid-seventh century are also attested (e.g., Arad IX–VIII; Gibeon; fig. 3.26), as are some from the second half of the seventh century (e.g., Mesad Hashavyahu; fig. 3.19). Finally, it should also be noted that some Old Hebrew inscriptions can be dated to the ninth century, but these are often very fragmentary (for detailed references and arguments for dates for all of these inscriptions, see Rollston 2003a; 2006).

Comparative analysis of these Old Hebrew inscriptions (normally using non-epigraphic data as a control for the dating) demonstrates that there are diagnostic features that distinguish the major various horizons (e.g., early-eighth century, mid- to late-eighth century, very-late-eighth to mid-seventh century, very-late-seventh to early-sixth century), regardless of the site at which they were found and the distance between them, or the media. Naturally, new discoveries of provenanced inscriptions from this script series will augment, refine, and nuance script typologies, but the data for the Old Hebrew script series of the eighth through early-sixth centuries are not negligible.

Weeks has asserted that "it is simply a fallacy to suppose that it [the Iron Age Hebrew script] was uniform: it went through periods of very rapid development, and different styles certainly existed side by side" (1994, 152). The fact of the matter is that no trained palaeographer would suggest that there was some sort of "uniformity without development or variation" during the course of some two centuries. That is, Weeks is arguing against a straw man. Trained palaeographers argue, based on analyses of the actual epigraphic evidence, that the Old Hebrew script reflects diachronic development and synchronic consistency, with synchronic variations restricted to perimeters that can be described in an empirical fashion.

Also of fundamental importance are the following factors: For the Old Hebrew script there is basic uniformity between the semi-formal cursive script employed on ostraca (i.e., ink on pottery) and that of the cursive script employed on stone or inscribed in pottery. The script of Old Hebrew seals is normally a formal cursive script. Although there is also substantial continuity between the semi-formal cursive script (e.g., of ostraca and various sorts of incised inscriptions), it is clear that the formal cursive script of seals (though these are incised, of course, as well) does exhibit certain differences from the semi-formal cursive. For this reason, the palaeographic dating of Old Hebrew seals is complicated, and the plus and minus range must be larger than for the Old Hebrew semi-formal cursive. Again, future discoveries will augment current typologies of the Old Hebrew script series (cursive, formal cursive, and lapidary); however, the fact remains that the quality and quantity of the provenanced, datable data are good. Moreover, this evidence derives from many different sites, in different regions, and from various chronological horizons.

Furthermore, this evidence is consistent in revealing definite chronological development. The Old Hebrew script, therefore, is neither poorly attested nor poorly known. At this juncture, I will provide a synthesis of certain aspects of the Old Hebrew script so as to delineate the basic morphology, development, and variation within this script series. The purpose of this is to reveal in a fairly precise nature the features of the Old Hebrew script through time so as to demonstrate that there were strictures in place that mandated precisely features such as morphology, stance, and letter environment.[1]

OLD HEBREW PALAEOGRAPHY: DIACHRONIC DEVELOPMENT WITH SYNCHRONIC CONSISTENCY

ʾAlep. Among the earliest exemplars of the cursive Old Hebrew ʾalep (fig. 5.1) are those of the Kuntillet ʿAjrud inscriptions (ca. 800 B.C.E.; fig. 3.22) and the Reisner Samaria Ostraca (ca. 777–770 B.C.E.). The hallmark feature of the eighth-century Old Hebrew ʾalep is the dramatic increase in the length of the vertical shaft (e.g., compared with the classical tenth century Phoenician forms such as Ahiram, fig. 2.2); for this reason, the vertical shaft is consistently longer—normally substantially so—than the top horizontal crossbar (e.g., Sa17a.1.'1). This feature is also present in the Khirbet el-Qom epigraphs from the eighth century, the Siloam Tunnel Inscription (very-late-eighth century), and the City of David Inscription 2. Some of the fragmentary ostraca from Beth Sheʾan reflect this feature as well. Another important early feature found in (some of) the Reisner Samaria Ostraca is the presence of a cursive reflex (i.e., "tick") at the right terminus of

---

1. Throughout this section of the article, a system of abbreviations is employed. Ad = Arad; Gn = Gibeon; Lh = Lachish; Mh = Mesad Hashavyahu; Sa = Reisner Samaria Ostraca; Sa.JE.BL = Samaria Joint Expedition Barley Letter. In addition to identifying the site, this system also contains information that indicates the precise letter of the precise inscription to which there is reference. Thus, the abbreviation Sa17a.1.'1 signifies Ostracon 17a from Samaria, the first line, and the first ʾalep of that line.

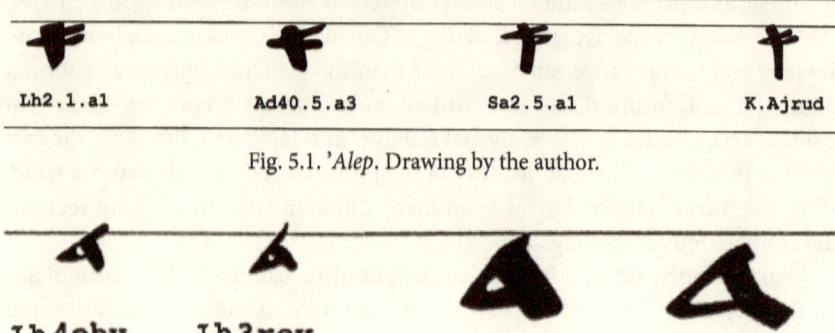

Fig. 5.1. *'Alep*. Drawing by the author.

Fig. 5.2. *Dalet*. Drawing by the author.

the bottom horizontal, which descends leftward at an oblique angle (e.g., Sa2.5.'1; Sa24.1.'1; Sa51.3.'1). This morphological feature is also present in the *'alep* of the Royal Steward Inscription (late-eighth century; (fig. 3.31), Samaria Joint Expedition Ostracon 1142, and a variant of it is attested in the corpus of the Gibeon Jar Handles (e.g., Gn.17, 21, 22), suggesting a floruit for the tick that was rather wide, though confined to the eighth and perhaps early-seventh centuries. The cursive tick is not present in the corpus of epigraphs from Arad VIII (very-late-eighth to early-seventh centuries) or Mesad Hashavyahu (ca. mid- to late-seventh century). Moreover, the evidence from these two sites (Mesad Hashavyahu and Arad) demonstrates that during the seventh century the relative length of the vertical shaft decreases, with the vertical consistently shorter than the top horizontal crossbar (e.g., Ad1.1.'1), often substantially so. Moreover, this trend (i.e., the shorter vertical shaft) persists during the late-seventh and early-sixth centuries B.C.E., as demonstrated by epigraphs from Arad VI–VII, Lachish II, and Horvat 'Uza. The point is that there are consistent diagnostic features that distinguish the eighth century Old Hebrew *'alep* from the late-seventh and early-sixth century *'alep*. Moreover, the late-eighth century and early-seventh century Old Hebrew *'alep* reflects intermediate development. Ultimately, the evidence demonstrates that there are distinct diagnostic features for the chronological horizons of Old Hebrew.

Dalet. The morphology of the Iron Age cursive Hebrew *dalet* is very well-established on the basis of provenanced inscriptions (fig. 5.2). The diachronic evolution of *dalet* can be summarized as follows: During the early-eighth century, *dalet* was "delta shaped," but normally with a short leg and a minute "overlap"

| Lh3obv.1.h1 | Ad1.8.h1 | Sa6.2.h1 | K. Ajrud |

Fig. 5.3. *He*. Drawing by the author.

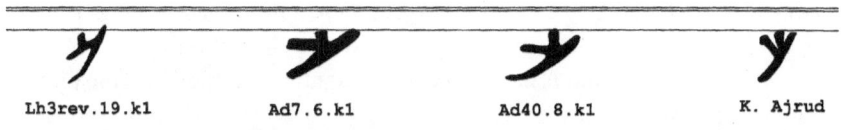

| Lh3rev.19.k1 | Ad7.6.k1 | Ad40.8.k1 | K. Ajrud |

Fig. 5.4. *Kap*. Drawing by the author.

on the right side of the head (Sa6.2.d1; Sa17a.2.d1; Sa40.1.d1; Sa57.2.d1). During the late-eighth and early-seventh centuries, the leg sometimes lengthens moderately, and there is a small increase in the length of the head's overlap (Ad40.10. d1; Ad52.1.d1). During the mid- to late-seventh century, these features persist (Mh1.1.d1; Mh1.2.d1; Mh1.2.d2). During the late-seventh and early-sixth centuries, the length of the leg is sometimes slightly greater, and the head's overlap also increases slightly (e.g., Ad1.5.d1; Ad18obv.1.d1; Lh4obv.5.d1). Rarely, the head's overlap can be quite pronounced (Lh3rev.19.d1). In any case, the long "overlap" is a feature attested in the late-seventh century and the early-sixth century, not earlier. That is, the length of the head's overlap is a diagnostic feature of the Old Hebrew script.

Het. The eighth-century Old Hebrew *he* consists of a vertical stroke and three horizontals (e.g., Kuntillet ʿAjrud and Reisner Samaria Ostraca; fig. 5.3). The rightward extension ("overlap") of the top horizontal stroke is of typological significance. That is, it is routinely absent at Kuntillet ʿAjrud, is absent at Beth Sheʾan, and is normally slight in the Reisner Samaria Ostraca (e.g., Sa6.2.h1; Sa17a.2.h1; 51.3.h1; 55.1.h1); however, it is normally more substantial in the late-seventh and early-sixth centuries, for example, in Arad VI–VII and Lachish II (e.g. Ad1.8.h1; Ad17rev.9.h1; Lh3obv.1.h1). Exemplars from the late-eighth and early-seventh centuries often reflect intermediate development (e.g., SaJE.Bl; Ad60.4.h1; Ad40.4.h1). Rarely, an archaic form will appear in a corpus from the late period (e.g., Lh1.5.h1).

Kap. There is a substantial amount of information about the synchronic variation and diachronic evolution of the Old Hebrew cursive *kap* (fig. 5.4). The salient components of its morphology and development can readily be summa-rized. During the early-eighth century, this letter consists of a main shaft and two oblique strokes that are both "penned into" the main shaft. The top oblique stroke is often at an angle of eighty to ninety degrees, and the angle of the bottom oblique is normally forty to fifty degrees above "absolute horizontal" (Kuntillet 'Ajrud; Sa44.1.k1). During the late-eighth and early-seventh centuries, the angle of the bottom oblique decreases (sometimes approaching absolute horizon-tal); the top oblique continues normally to be penned directly into the vertical shaft (Ad40.8.k1; Ad44.2.k1; Ad49.4.k1). For some mid- to late-seventh century epigraphs, the top oblique is normally penned into the bottom oblique (rather than the main shaft), and it has migrated substantially leftward on the bottom oblique (e.g., Mesad Hashavyahu). During the late-seventh and early-sixth centuries, the angle of the bottom oblique is routinely near, or at, absolute hori-zontal (Ad18obv.3.k1; Ad24rev.17.k1) or even below it (Lh2.3.k1; Lh3rev19.k1). Moreover, the tendency for the top oblique to migrate leftward (on the bottom oblique) continues.

Mem. The Iron Age Hebrew *mem* (and *nun*) evolved in various ways during the eighth through sixth centuries (fig. 5.5). The angle of the main vertical shaft of the Iron Age Hebrew *mem* is one diagnostic component of this letter (the morphology of the head is another). During the early-eighth century, the vertical shaft was normally penned at angles ranging from fifty to sixty degrees (Sa10.1.m1; Sa17a.1.m1; Sa20.2.m1; Sa27.2.m1; Sa48.2.m1; Sa55.2.m1). However, during the late-seventh and early-sixth centuries, the letter's stance had shifted radically in most exemplars of the cursive script, and the vertical shaft was nor-mally penned at angles ranging from twenty to thirty-five degrees (Ad1.5.m1; Ad17obv.6.m1; Lh1.5.m1; Lh2.3.m4). Provenanced Old Hebrew epigraphs from the late-eighth and early-seventh centuries reflect intermediate develop-ment (Ad60.4.m1; Ad49.11.m1), ranging from approximately forty to fifty-five degrees. With regard to the angle of the shaft, rarely a harbinger form will occur (Ad60.4.m1), as will also an archaic form (e.g., Mesad Hashavyahu).

Samek. The standard Old Hebrew *samek* consists of a vertical shaft and three horizontal strokes (fig. 5.6). The horizontal strokes are consistently penned with strokes that are dextrograde. During the early-eighth century, the upper two horizontals are sometimes penned above the vertical shaft (i.e., without intersect-ing it), while the bottom horizontal is penned across the top of the vertical shaft (Kuntillet 'Ajrud). Sometimes the middle horizontal does intersect with the verti-cal shaft (Sa29.3.s1). The vertical shaft is normally very long at this period, and is penned at an angle of ca. 80 to 85 degrees (top left stance). Ticks are present on the right side of the horizontals, although those on the top two horizontals can be very small. Note that the early incised exemplars from Arad X have a tick on the

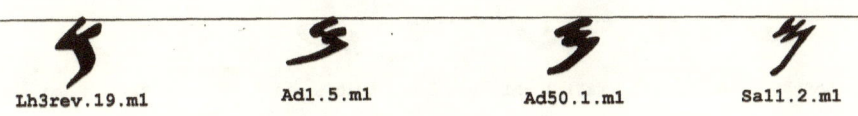

Lh3rev.19.m1   Ad1.5.m1   Ad50.1.m1   Sa11.2.m1

Fig. 5.5. *Mem*. Drawing by the author.

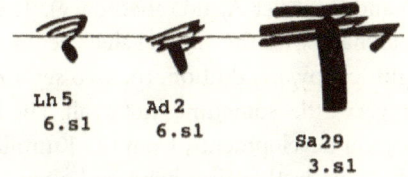

Lh 5
6.s1

Ad 2
6.s1

Sa 29
3.s1

Fig. 5.6. *Samek*. Drawing by the author.

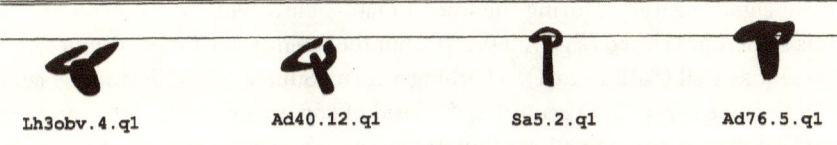

Lh3obv.4.q1   Ad40.12.q1   Sa5.2.q1   Ad76.5.q1

Fig. 5.7. *Qop*. Drawing by the author.

bottom horizontal, but none on the top two horizontals (Ad98.1.s1). *Samek* of the late-seventh century and early-sixth (e.g., Arad IV–VII and Lachish II) consists of three horizontals and a vertical shaft, although the junction between the bottom horizontal and the top of the vertical shaft is sometimes created via the tick (e.g., Ad16.8.s1; Lh4rev.9.s1), rather than the bottom horizontal. Ticks (often quite substantial) are consistently present on all three horizontals in this period. Moreover, the stance of the vertical shaft of the Lachish II Ostraca ranges from 60 to 75 degrees, and that of the Arad VI–VII ostraca ranges from 70 to 80 degrees, demonstrating that there is a subtle change of stance through time. It is also readily apparent that the relative length of the vertical shaft has experienced diminution by this period when compared to the relative length of the early-eighth century exemplars. The *samek* of the Ophel Stele demonstrates that the shaft can have substantial curvature and space considerations can be determinative for the presence of ticks (note that ticks are a cursive feature deriving from writing with ink).

Qop. The Old Hebrew *qop* was consistently made with three strokes during Iron II: two semi-circular downstrokes that formed the head, and a vertical shaft (fig. 5.7). The earliest good evidence for the Old Hebrew *qop* derives from

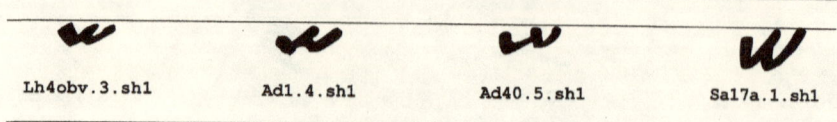

| Lh4obv.3.sh1 | Ad1.4.sh1 | Ad40.5.sh1 | Sa17a.1.sh1 |

Fig. 5.8. *Šin*. Drawing by the author.

Arad (Ad76.5.q1) and Kuntillet ʿAjrud (abecedary). The exemplars of *qop* from these corpora are archaic, with the vertical shaft beginning at or near the top of a closed head. Significantly, in addition, the two semi-circular strokes forming the head are offset very little, sometimes not at all. The Reisner Samaria Ostraca exhibit two typological developments, from the Kuntillet ʿAjrud and early Arad exemplars, namely, a modestly offset head and a vertical shaft that no longer begins at the top of the head; the top of the head, however, still remains closed. Note that the angle of the vertical shaft ranges from 80 to 90 degrees during the early-eighth century. During the mid- to late-eighth century, the head of *qop* was sometimes closed (e.g., Ad60.4.q1), but the open-headed type is sometimes present as well (SaJE.Bl.2.q1), a harbinger form. Subsequently, during the late-eighth and early-seventh centuries, the head of *qop* is consistently open, and the vertical shaft is now sometimes (but not always) showing a tendency to become more oblique (e.g., SaJe.Bl.2.q1). Exemplars from the late-seventh century have an open head as well (e.g., Mh1.4.q1; Mh1.10.q1; Mh1.11.q1). During the late-seventh and early-sixth centuries, the head is normally open (e.g., Lh3obv.4.q1; Lh4obv.6.q1; Ad1.5.q1), although there is evidence that the closed head persisted sometimes in the more formal cursive (e.g., Ad24rev.15.q1). The stance of the majority of exemplars from the late-seventh and early-sixth centuries is normally more oblique, ranging from 50 to 75 degrees, and thus, with obvious typological significance. Note that the vertical stroke of this letter was often the final stroke.

Šin. The Old Hebrew cursive *šin* was often formed with four separate (down) strokes, analogous to /W/ (fig. 5.8). The normal angle of the left external stroke of the early-eighth century (Kuntillet ʿAjrud; Sa17a.1.š1) was approximately 80 to 90 degrees (top left), with some exemplars actually exhibiting a top-right stance (Sa21.1.š1; Sa30.1.š2). The normal angle of the right external stroke was approximately 55 to 65 degrees (top right).[2] During the late-seventh and early-sixth centuries (Arad VI–VII; Lachish II), the normal angle of the left external stroke ranges from 35 to 60 degrees, and that of the right external stroke from 30 to 45 (Ad1.1.š1). Significantly, the angles of the exemplars from the late-

---

2. The angle of the internal strokes is also important, but I will not provide these details in this volume.

eighth and early- to mid-seventh centuries are intermediate (e.g., Ad40.2.š1; Ad40.5.š1). The best exemplars of the large Mesad Hashavyahu ostracon reflect angles that fall within the same basic range as the Arad VI–VII and Lachish II (e.g., Mh1.5.š1; Mh1.8.š1). The essential point is that the data from provenanced cursive exemplars demonstrate that the angles of the external strokes are typologically significant.

The locus of the junction of the two internal strokes descends through time. Of course, the fact that the script exemplars from the ninth and early-eighth centuries (e.g., Mesha; el-Kerak; Kition Bowl) have very high junctions (i.e., at the upper terminus of both strokes) is predictable. This feature is present (to some extent) in some exemplars from Kuntillet 'Ajrud, but gradual descent is noticeable here as well. The Reisner Samaria Ostraca (e.g., Sa30.1.š2; Sa17a.1.š1) reflect a similar trend (i.e., descent of junction point). This development continues during the seventh and early-sixth centuries, with many junctions being very low (e.g., Ad1.4.š1; Lh4obv3.š1). There is a general tendency for the internal strokes to become more vestigial through time. Forms with almost completely vestigial left internal strokes (e.g., Ad10.1.š1; Ad11.1.š1) must not be construed as a *šin* with high junctions. Rather, it is readily apparent that substantial morphological evolution is present within these forms, so much so that the left external stroke is non-existent, something that ultimately leads to a trident-shaped *šin*.

In sum, the Old Hebrew script reflects clear developments during the eighth through sixth centuries, and these developments can be discerned and described in an empirical manner. Moreover, the Old Hebrew script of a specific chronological horizon also reflects synchronic consistency. The fact that the Old Hebrew epigraphic record reflects synchronic consistency *and* diachronic development is significant because it necessitates a mechanism, namely, formal, standardized scribal education.

Case Study of Letter Environment: *Samek-Pe* Sequence

Letter morphology, stance, and ductus are critical aspects of palaeographic analysis. Nevertheless, letter environment is also of fundamental importance. That is, ancient scribes of a script series were also trained to know conventional practices regarding relative spatial relationship of letters: letters were certainly not conceived of as being some sort of isolated entity. That is, it was not enough for a writer to be able to write a letter in the conventional form during a particular horizon, but rather he also needed to know the relative position of each letter vis à vis the letters that preceded and followed it. The *samek-pe* sequence constitutes a superb case study of this aspect of palaeographic analysis.

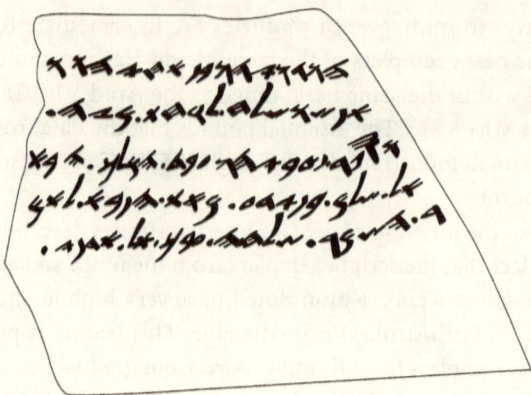

Fig. 5.9. Lachish 3 (reverse). Drawing by the author.

Based on the attested exemplars in the corpus of provenanced Old Hebrew inscriptions from the eighth through early-sixth centuries, it is readily apparent that the head of the Old Hebrew *samek* was consistently initiated above the "ceiling line." Moreover, there are a number of examples of the sequence *samek-pe* in provenanced Old Hebrew inscriptions; therefore, it is possible to analyze with precision the relative heights of *samek* and *pe* when they are in sequence, a particularly useful tool to compare relative size, stance, and relative height. Note, therefore, the *samek-pe* sequence in the following Old Hebrew inscriptions from various periods and sites: Kuntillet ʿAjrud (abecedary), Samaria (Sa29.3.s1), Royal Steward Inscription (fig. 3.31), Mesad Hashavyahu (Mh7.2.s1), Arad (Ad3obv7. s1; Ad16.8.s1), Lachish (Lh3obv.5.s1; Lh3obv.9.s1; Lh3obv.10.s1; Lh3rev.19.s1 [fig. 5.9]; Lh5.6.s1; Lh6.4.s1; Lh6.14.s1; Lh11.4.s1; Lh18.1.s1). Within every single case, *samek* is substantially higher than the *pe* that follows, and normally the *samek* simply towers over *pe*. That is, Old Hebrew scribes were meticulous about the morphology and stance of the letters they penned, but they were also meticulous about maintaining precise conventional spatial relationships of letters. I contend that this sort of consistent precision must be the result of specialized curricular training in script production.[3]

---

3. I first articulated this feature of Old Hebrew palaeography in presentations at the Annual Meeting of the Society of Biblical Literature in 2000 and 2002 and published my findings in Rollston 2003a, an article on modern epigraphic forgeries, in which I argued that the forger of the Moussaieff Ostraca and the Jehoash Inscription was ignorant of this feature of Old Hebrew palaeography.

Ancillary Data: Selected National Script Diagnostics

The Old Hebrew and Aramaic scripts evolved from the Phoenician *Mutter-schrift*. Based on comparative analyses of the Phoenician script and the earliest Old Hebrew and Aramaic inscriptions, a consensus has developed that the Old Hebrew script became an independent national script during the ninth century B.C.E. and that the Aramaic script separated from the "prestige" Phoenician script at some point during the eighth century B.C.E. These alphabetic national script series (i.e., Phoenician, Old Hebrew, and Aramaic) are dominant in the first millennium. The critical point, though, is this: *there are discernible diagnostic differences between the Old Hebrew, Phoenician, and Aramaic scripts.* That is, script heterographs are present. For the purposes of demonstrating the point, I will summarize some macro differences, based on standard exemplars of two letters of the target script series.[4]

Bet. The Kition Bowl (fig. 2.10) typifies the standard Iron Age cursive and lapidary Phoenician *bet* (fig. 5.10). The head of the *bet* is consistently closed. Regarding stance, the Phoenician *bet* is often upright (e.g., the Old Byblian), but also often top-left (e.g., Kition Bowl). The early Aramaic *bet* has similar morphological features, including the closed head and the top-left stance (e.g., Amman Citadel, Zakir Stele, Sefire). Significantly, the head of the Aramaic cursive *bet* begins to open in the eighth century, as demonstrated by the morphology of certain exemplars on the Hamath Bricks and the Nimrud Ostracon (see fig. 2.16). The open-headed *bet* becomes regnant in the Aramaic cursive during the seventh century (e.g., Saqqarah Papyrus, Assur Ostracon). The standard Old Hebrew *bet* (e.g., Kuntillet 'Ajrud; Reisner Samaria Ostraca; Beth She'an; City of David Inscription 2; Royal Steward; Arad; Lachish), however, consistently has a closed head. Regarding stance, the Old Hebrew *bet* is consistently top-right, and becomes progressively more so during the course of the eighth through sixth centuries. The stance and morphology of the head are diagnostic national features: the Old Hebrew *bet* is distinct, differing from the Phoenician and Aramaic script series.

Dalet. The tenth century Phoenician *dalet* (fig. 5.10) is delta-shaped (e.g., Yehimilk), but the Phoenician Kition Bowl reflects the fact that the right downstroke begins to lengthen during the late-ninth and early-eighth centuries (forming a "leg"). This basic morphology persists in the Phoenician series during the Iron Age. The early period of the Aramaic series reflects the same basic morphology present in the Phoenician series (e.g., the Kition Bowl). However, during

---

4. For detailed bibliographic data, see Rollston 2006.

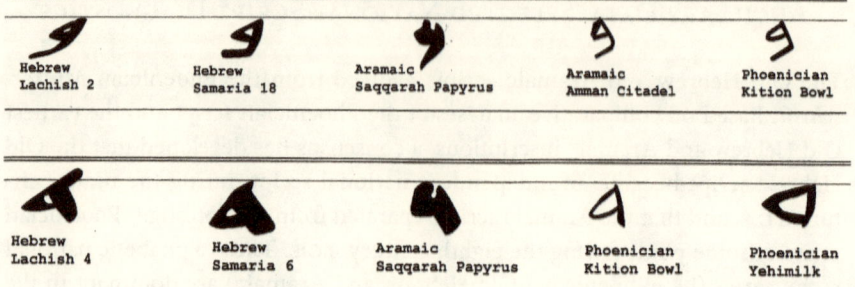

Fig. 5.10. Selections from National Scripts. Top: *bet*; bottom: *dalet*. Drawing by the author.

the eighth century, the head of the cursive *dalet* opens (e.g., Nimrud Ostracon), and this development is regnant in the seventh-century Aramaic cursives (e.g., Assur clay tablets; Assur Ostracon; Saqqarah Papyrus), and persists in the Aramaic series for centuries and becomes the basis for further developments. Significantly, the head of the Old Hebrew *dalet* of the eighth through sixth centuries (from Kuntillet 'Ajrud and the Reisner Samaria Ostraca to the Lachish II Ostraca) is consistently closed, in spite of the dominance of the Aramaic script in the Near East during this period with its open-headed *bet*. That is, the morphology of the Old Hebrew *dalet* of the eighth through sixth centuries differs markedly from the Aramaic series of the same period. Similar morphological differences are present between the Aramaic cursive 'ayin and *reš*, with the open-headed forms being the norm for Aramaic, but with Old Hebrew consistently retaining the closed-headed forms.

This sort of analysis could be done for all the letters of the Old Hebrew, Phoenician, and Aramaic scripts. In any case, the point is that the Old Hebrew script was a distinct national script, differing from the Phoenician and Aramaic series and reflecting independent developments. There must have been, I contend, a mechanism for the development, use, and retention of a distinct Old Hebrew national script.

Of course, Jamieson-Drake has argued that the alphabetic script is "simple enough that functional knowledge of it could be passed on from one person to another in a comparatively short time." He states further that "schools would hardly have been necessary, unless other skills that demanded an educational setting were being taught alongside literacy" (Jamieson-Drake 1991, 154). To be sure, many biblical scholars have concurred with this sort of assessment. However, the fact of the matter is that the Old Hebrew epigraphic record attests, not to some "functional knowledge" of the Old Hebrew script, but to a sophisticated and consistent production of letter morphology and stance considered standard during specific horizons. Moreover, the Old Hebrew script also reflects the fact that Old Hebrew scribes adhered to certain strict curricular conventions about the relative positions of certain sequential letters (e.g., *samek-pe*). Furthermore, the Old Hebrew scribes were such meticulous tradents that the Old Hebrew script can be readily distinguished from Phoenician and Aramaic as a distinct national script. Of necessity, it must be affirmed that the lion's share of the Old Hebrew epigraphic record does not reflect "functional knowledge" of the script. It reflects the sophisticated knowledge of trained professionals.

OLD HEBREW ORTHOGRAPHY: DIACHRONIC DEVELOPMENT AND SYCHRONIC CONSISTENCY

The Old Hebrew script was a distinct script series, with diagnostic differences distinguishing it from Phoenician and Aramaic, and reflecting both diachronic development and synchronic consistency. Similarly, the orthographic practices used for Old Hebrew differ from those of Phoenician. Moreover, the development of certain orthographic conventions in Old Hebrew (namely, internal *matres lectionis* "vowel letters") occurred later in Old Hebrew than in Aramaic. In addition, the orthographic conventions employed within the Old Hebrew writing system also reflect diachronic development and synchronic consistency.[5] Nevertheless, these facts are not widely known and for this reason the Old Hebrew orthographic practices are sometimes misunderstood.

For example, some have argued that there is *some* consistency in Old Hebrew orthography, but they have stated that the primary reason for the consistency is that there were no real orthographic options for the Old Hebrew writing system. Thus, Weeks has argued that "the general uniformity of orthography is explained simply by the nature of the script: it is really quite hard to come up with alternative spellings of a word when the alphabet offers little or no choice of characters to represent a given sound." He goes on to affirm that "it was only with the widespread use of the more ambiguous vowel letters, in a later period, that great variation was able to occur" (1994, 152). Similarly, Crenshaw states that "the Hebrew alphabet offers little option in spelling, at least until the use of vowel letters" (1998: 106). With all due respect, however, it is readily apparent that these statements are problematic.

---

5. The best analyses of these orthographic systems continue to be those of Cross and Freedman 1952; Garr 1985, and now Rollston 2006. Although often useful, both Zevit 1980 and Gogel 1998 must be used with some caution.

Regarding the time period for the presence of *matres lectionis* in Old Hebrew inscriptions, the fact of the matter is that *matres lectionis* actually occur not simply "in a later period," but in the early Old Hebrew inscriptions. Thus, final *matres lectionis* occur in Old Hebrew inscriptions from the time of the early Old Hebrew inscriptions (late-ninth and early-eighth centuries), and this usage persists for the succeeding chronological horizons of the Iron Age. Moreover, internal *matres lectionis* begin to be used in an incipient fashion during the late-eighth and very-early-seventh centuries in Judah, and they become reasonably common in the late-seventh and early-sixth centuries. Furthermore, regarding the presence of "options" for a writer of Old Hebrew, the fact of the matter is that comparative analysis of the orthography of Iron Age Phoenician, Old Hebrew, and Aramaic serves to elucidate the complexities and nuances of the orthographies of these writing systems (including diachronic developments) and also to demonstrate that "alternative spellings" were indeed real options for Iron Age Levantine writers of Phoneician, Hebrew, and Aramaic, in spite of the fact that they were employing the same twenty-two-letter alphabet (for demonstration of this, see Rollston 2006, 61–65).

Regarding the consistency of the Old Hebrew orthographic system, Weeks ultimately concedes that if there were "consistency" in the Old Hebrew orthographic system, there would be some "force in this argument" that "schooling must be hypothesized." However, he then states that "the use of *matres lectionis* is far from consistent" (1994, 151–52). Nevertheless, Weeks is wrong. The Old Hebrew orthographic conventions reflect synchronic consistency and diachronic development. Here are the data: (1) During the ninth and early-eighth centuries, Hebrew orthography employed a system of final *matres lectionis*: final /$\bar{\imath}$/ was represented by *yod*; final /$\bar{u}$/ was represented by *waw*; final /$\bar{a}$/ was represented by *he*; final /$\bar{e}$/ was represented by *he*; final /$\bar{o}$/ was represented by *he*. There is a general absence of the internal *matres lectionis* throughout the lion's share of the eighth century. (2) During the terminal period of the eighth century and the beginning of the seventh century, final *matres lectionis* continued to be used, with final /$\bar{\imath}$/ represented by *yod*, final /$\bar{u}$/ represented by *waw*, final /$\bar{a}$/ represented by *he*, final /$\bar{e}$/ represented by *he*, and final /$\bar{o}$/ represented by *he*. In addition, there is Old Hebrew evidence for incipient usage of internal *matres lectionis*, with *waw* serving as a *mater lectionis* for internal /$\bar{u}$/, and *yod* serving as a *mater lectionis* for the internal /$\bar{\imath}$/. (3) During the second half of the seventh century and the beginning of the sixth century, final *matres lectionis* continued to be used, with final /$\bar{\imath}$/ represented by *yod*, final /$\bar{u}$/ represented by *waw*, final /$\bar{a}$/ represented by *he*, final /$\bar{e}$/ represented by *he*, and final /$\bar{o}$/ represented by *he*. In addition, there is growing usage of internal *matres lectionis*, with *waw* serving as a *mater lectionis* for internal /$\bar{u}$/ and *yod* serving as a *mater lectionis* for the internal /$\bar{\imath}$/.

Finally, I would argue that certain additional strictures regarding usage within Old Hebrew are also of some import. For example, although *he* could serve as a *mater lectionis* for final /ē/ and final /ō/, it was never used as an internal *mater lectionis* in Old Hebrew for any vowel. Moreover, although medial /ī/ and /ū/ could be marked with *yod* and *waw*, medial /ā/ was never marked with a *mater lectionis*, not even with *he*. Of course, Weeks might concede that synchronic consistency is present, but counter that diachronic development is incompatible with the presence of formal, standardized education. However, descriptive and prescriptive grammarians concur that orthographic development can and does occur in living alphabetic writing systems, even though formal, standardized education is present.

In any case, it is readily apparent that Weeks is not *au courante* with regard to Old Hebrew orthographic data in the Old Hebrew epigraphic corpus and he speaks in generalities. The fact of the matter is that there is synchronic consistency (and also diachronic development, which makes synchronic consistency even more stunning). Moreover, there were orthographic options for the writers of Old Hebrew, as comparison with Phoenician and Aramaic demonstrates. For these reasons, I contend that there must have been a mechanism for this consistency: namely, formal, standardized education in the orthographic conventions of the day.

Dialectal Differences in Old Hebrew

Two dialects of Hebrew are attested in Old Hebrew inscriptions, northern ("Israelite") and southern ("Judean"). For example, within the southern dialect (as reflected in biblical Hebrew) the word for "year" was *šnh* /*šanāh/. Significantly, the northern dialect is consistent in using *št* /*šat(t)/ for "year" (Reisner Samaria Ostraca, *passim*). Moreover, within the southern dialect, dipthongs do not contract (*pace* Zevit 1980, *passim*), while, within the northern dialect, dipthongs do contract. For example, within the southern dialect the word for wine is spelled *yyn* /*yayn/ (Ad1.3, 9) but in the northern dialect, the dipthong has contracted and the word is spelled *yn* /*yên/ (Reisner Samaria Ostraca, *passim*). Moreover, within the southern dialect the dipthong *aw* has not contracted. For example, the word /*ham-mawṣaʾ/ ("the source") is spelled *hmwṣ*ʾ (Siloam Tunnel, line 5), and the word /*baʿawd/ ("while yet") is spelled *bʿwd* (Siloam Tunnel, line 1). That is, the dipthong *aw* has not contracted. Although the evidence is modest, it has been argued that this dipthong does contract in northern Israelite. To be sure, two dialects of Hebrew are reflected in the Old Hebrew epigraphic record, but random dialect variation does not occur. Rather, consistency is the norm.

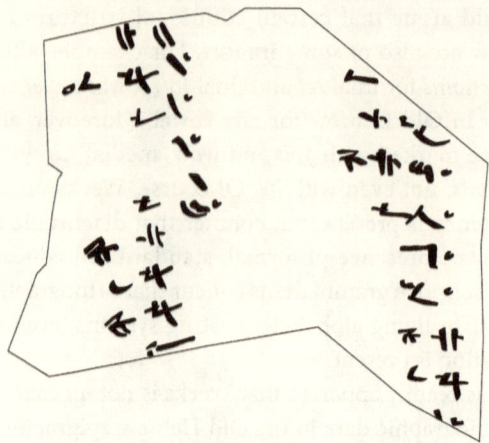

Fig. 5.11. Arad 34. Drawing by the author.

COMPLICATED SCRIBAL CONVENTIONS: HIERATIC NUMERALS

Egyptian hieratic numerals are attested at several different Iron Age Israelite and Judean sites, spanning from the ninth to early-sixth centuries. For example, hieratic numerals and Old Hebrew script are both present on an ostracon from Arad XI (Ad76). Moreover, the Reisner Samaria Ostraca frequently use hieratic numerals (e.g., Sa22, Sa27; Sa28; Sa34, Sa58, 61). Hieratic numerals are also attested for Arad IX (e.g., Ad60; Ad65) and Arad VIII (e.g., Ad42; cf. Ad46). Several of the Arad VI–VII Hebrew ostraca use hieratic numerals and symbols (e.g., Ad2; cf. Ad22; Ad31; Ad33), and one ostracon consists solely of hieratic numerals (Ad34; fig. 5.11). Hieratic numerals were also found at Lachish (e.g., Lachish weights) and also arguably at Mesad Hashavyahu (cf. Mh3; Mh4). The use of hieratic numerals at Kadesh-Barnea is particularly significant, because among the Old Hebrew ostraca were several with hieratic numerals, including one that was an ostracon that originally consisted of hieratic numerical data spanning, in numeric order, from one to ten thousand. This ostracon also contained at least the beginning of another similar listing of the numbers. Based on the epigraphic evidence, it is demonstrable that Israelite scribes during the course of the ninth through sixth centuries, at disparate sites in Israel and Judah, were capable of using a complicated, originally foreign numeric system. Developing some proficiency in the writing of hieratic numerals would not have been facile. For this reason, I believe that it is convincing to argue that learning hieratic numerals reflects formal, standardized scribal training.

COMPLEMENTARY NOTATIONS

A. ABECEDARIES AND EXERCISE TABLETS

Of course, abecedaries have been discovered at various sites in Israel and Judah, as well as in various other parts of the Levant (including Ugarit). It has often been argued that abecedaries are the product of an educational context. For example, Puech has affirmed that "Il ne fait aucun doute que la plupart des abecedaries relevant de l'apprentissage de l'art d'écrire" (Puech 1988, 189). However, Haran has argued that there is no necessary connection between many of the abecedaries and schools (1988, 85–91). To be sure, Lemaire has drawn some broad conclusions from the presence of abecedaries at various sites (i.e., the presence of an abecedary at a site was indicative of a school at that site), and he has also considered certain brief fragmentary inscriptions (e.g., qr at Aroer) to be probable abecedaries, even though these could be read as word fragments (1981, 7–33). For these sorts of reasons, his work has been subjected to severe criticism. Of course, some have actually suggested that abecedaries were perceived as having some sort of mantic function in ancient societies, and not educational (Weeks 1994, 150–51). However, I am not convinced that abecedaries functioned as talismans or were perceived as having actual mantic functions. Naturally, though, I would not argue that the presence of an abecedary at a site must necessarily be indicative of a school at the site (e.g., it might be indicative of the presence of a student at a site). Nevertheless, I would affirm that it would be difficult to suggest that none of the abecedaries is to be associated with curricular activities.

B. GENERAL CONTENTS: EPISTOLARY DOCUMENTS

Within the corpus of Old Hebrew inscriptions are a number of letters (Pardee 1982; Lindenberger 2003). These documents will normally begin with some reference to the recipient and often contain some sort of greeting (e.g., "May Yahweh cause my lord to hear a message of peace and good things"; cf. Lh2; Lh3; Lh4; Lh5; Lh6; Ad16; Ad21; Ad40). Sometimes the name of the sender is also provided (e.g., Lh 3; Ad 16; Ad21; Ad40), but this is not a dominant component of Old Hebrew letters. Normally, Old Hebrew letters reflect a clear transition from the traditional greetings to the body of the letter. The word w't ("and now") is a very common mode of transition, although sometimes different transitional formulae can be used. After the transitional component of the letter, the body of the letter was penned. Closing formula, such as signature, list of gods, and witnesses, are not a traditional component of Old Hebrew letters. It would not be tenable to argue that learning the basic features of Old Hebrew epistolary formulae is a complex procedure; however, the presence of a certain common structure within the epistolary corpus cannot be dismissed as being of no curricular import.

THE SPECIALIZED TOOLS OF A TRAINED PROFESSIONAL

Because Iron Age Israelite scribes were specialized elites, there were certain "tools of the trade" that they would have used.

Reed pen and associated items. Biblical Hebrew ʿēt, as demonstrated by the term ʿēt sōperîm, "scribal pen" (Jer 8:8), referred to a scribal writing implement. Moreover, the fact that the Septuagint translators could render Hebrew ʿēt with the Greek word κάλαμος, "reed" (Ps 45:1) confirms that the term ʿēt referred, at least sometimes, to a reed pen. Reed pens, of course, necessitated the use of ink, biblical Hebrew děyô (Jer 36:18; cf. 3 Macc 4:20; 2 John 12; 3 John 13). Although wet ink could be washed off (cf. Num 5:23), it becomes durable after drying. The color of the ink was normally black, but sometimes red was used (e.g., at Deir ʿAlla, as a rubric).

Pen case and knife. The scribe using a reed pen also used, and wore at the waist, a qeset hassōperîm, a "scribal palette" or "scribal pen case" (Ezek 9:2, 3, 11). Various items would have been included in this case, including a taʿar hassōperîm, scribal knife (Jer 36:23), that is, the penknife used to cut parchment and papyrus (e.g., for sizing). It was probably also the instrument used to trim the end of a reed at a desired angle. The Hebrew word gillāyôn is used to refer to a papyrus roll (that would need to be cut), but could (by extension) denote various writing surfaces (cf. Isa 8:1; 30:8).

Chisel. Iron Age Hebrew inscriptions were sometimes inscribed with a hammer and chisel. For some such inscriptions, the individual chisel marks are readily apparent (fig. 3.25).

Stylus. Many Iron Age Hebrew inscriptions were inscribed with some type of stylus. For clay vessels, note that the incising with the stylus was sometimes done before firing (fig. 3.24), but more frequently after firing (fig. 3.23). In the Hebrew Bible, the term ʿēt barzel, "iron pen" referred to a metal stylus, but may have also been used to refer to a chisel (Jer 17:1; Job 19:24). The biblical Hebrew word ḥereṭ certainly refers to some type of writing implement (Isa 8:1), but the precise nature of this implement and the medium upon which it was used is difficult to ascertain.

CONCLUSIONS

Old Hebrew scribes were trained to be meticulous about the morphology and stance of the letters they penned. In addition, they were also trained to be meticulous about maintaining precise conventional spatial relationships of letters (e.g., *samek* and *pe*). Furthermore, the script of Old Hebrew inscriptions can be distinguished from the Phoenician and Aramaic script series: that is, there are Old Hebrew script heterographs. Moreover, the orthographic conventions of Old Hebrew also reflect synchronic consistency (and diachronic development). Some have supposed that the reason for orthographic consistency is the fact that the twenty-two-letter alphabet permitted no real orthographic options; however, comparative orthographic analysis of Phoenician, Aramaic, and Old Hebrew has demonstrated that there were indeed orthographic options, thus the consistency of Old Hebrew orthography cannot be dismissed. Numerous Old Hebrew inscriptions from the ninth through sixth centuries B.C.E. (and from Israelite and Judean sites) contain hieratic numerals, a complicated numeric system. Such things were, I contend, fundamental curricular foci in ancient Israel. Of course, some have argued that becoming proficient in an alphabetic writing system is facile, and so no formal education would be required. However, modern studies of the time required for proficiency in an alphabetic writing system demonstrate that learning an alphabetic system is not facile. Rather, substantial time is required even for the most gifted students. Moreover, learning a complicated numeric system would require even more time. It is simply not convincing to attempt to account for the Old Hebrew epigraphic data without positing some sort of formal, standardized education. After all, the production of formal, standardized, and sophisticated epigraphs necessitates the presence of formal, standardized scribal education.

Thus, Israelite scribes were the recipients of formal, standardized education. Furthermore, in terms of aegis, I believe that the mechanism most responsible for the standardized education of professional scribes was the state. Note that many of the Old Hebrew inscriptions are to be associated in some fashion with statecraft (e.g., administrative economic dockets from a capital, missives from military outposts, royal stamped jar handles, and so on). I am confident that there were also scribes who often functioned predominantly within the private sphere; however, these scribes would also have marketed themselves as professionals proficient in the production of Old Hebrew texts in the standard script of the period, the standard orthography of the period, the capability of using a dominant numeric system, and the capability of employing a standard format (e.g., for letters, deeds, and so on). I contend that those capable of conveying the necessary data to the Old Hebrew scribal students would have been a scribal teacher associated with the national Old Hebrew apparatus.

CHAPTER 6
MONUMENTAL BUILDINGS FOR EDUCATION, SCRIBAL PRACTICE TEXTS, AND PRINT EXPOSURE IN THE SCRIBAL HOME

I have argued that there was formal, standardized scribal education in ancient Israel. The data that have been marshaled are epigraphic in nature. Nevertheless, someone might retort that such education in ancient Israel would have required a monumental building that could be identified on the basis of its contents as a "school" building. Based on the fact that no such monumental building has been discovered to date, therefore, they might posit that there was no formal, standardized education. Prima facie, because large portions of Jerusalem have not been excavated, this is not a particularly persuasive argument. Nevertheless, at least as problematic, is the fact that this assumption itself may be anachronistic, that is, based on modern assumptions more than on ancient evidence.

ASSUMPTIONS ABOUT THE NEED FOR MONUMENTAL SCHOOL BUILDINGS

George has argued that for Mesopotamia "already in the Old Babylonian period much scribal training was a small-scale activity." He states further that scribal teachers "may have taught only two or three boys at a time, their own sons and other young relatives and maybe also the sons of colleagues" (2005, 131; see also Black, Cunningham, Robson, and Zólyomi 2004). Furthermore, Veldhuis has stated that "Old Babylonian schools are found in domestic areas. They are not monumental buildings; in fact they may be rather small." He then goes on to say that "from this it has been concluded that no school could have had much more than 10 pupils. A class with more than 4 was probably large" (1996, 13). Regarding Egypt, Janssen, and Janssen have argued that scribal education often occurred in the home or some sort of scribal workshop. Discussing education during the New Kingdom in the Valley of the Kings, they state that "nowhere has a structure been excavated that was clearly used as a school. Most Egyptian life took place in the open air, as will have been the case with the classes ... the phrase 'house of instruction', the equivalent of our 'school,' therefore rather indicates the institution" (1990, 76–77; see also McDowell 1996, 602 *et passim*; 2000, 222–23 *et passim*). I contend, therefore, that it is problematic for someone to assume that monumental school buildings must be found in Iron II Israel prior to accepting the proposal that there was formal standardized education in ancient Israel. Rather, my assumption, based on the comparative evidence, is that Israelite scribal education would have been located, for the most part, in a domestic context, such as the home of a scribe.

STUDENT PRACTICE TEXTS: MESOPOTAMIA AND EGYPT

Education in Mesopotamia has been the subject of a number of studies. Among the most recent and authoritative are those of Vanstiphout (1995), Tinney (1998; 1999), Veldhuis (1997; 2003; 2004), and George (2005), building on the seminal research of scholars such as Sjöberg (1972; 1975) and Civil (1985). Similarly, education in ancient Egypt has been the subject of intense research, with the studies of several recent scholars such as Janssen and Janssen (1990), McDowell (1999), and Gasse (2005). Although the research of Brunner (1957) remains foundational, McDowell's convincing critiques (1996; 2000) now nuance and correct significant components of Brunner's discussions of education in ancient Egypt. It is not my intent to focus on the broad subject of education in ancient Mesopotamia and Egypt, but rather to refer to certain specific data regarding scribal education in Mesopotamia and Egypt: (1) writing exercises that consist of a teacher's "model text" and a student's copying of that text; (2) the presence of a remedial hand in some of the student texts; and (3) a teacher's (rare) correction of a student's work.

Regarding the cuneiform tablets, Tinney has argued that it is certainly possible to discern different hands in the Old Babylonian period and sometimes it is possible to discern the hands of "beginners." He also states that these can be identified on the basis of the "often poorly written learner's parts" (1999, 160–61). Veldhuis has made similar arguments, based upon the cuneiform materials from Nippur. Of particular importance are certain exercise tablets. These are divided into two basic registers. The left register (i.e., left side) contains a school text written by the teacher. The right side was the place on the tablet upon which "the teacher's example was copied by a pupil." Velduis does note that "few examples survive where the pupil's copy or copies are still extant." He argues that the reason for this is that "the regular procedure was that the pupil's side was erased, so that he could recopy his teacher's model. This process could be repeated several times."

Evidence for this includes the fact that "the right side of the obverse of a Type II tablet is usually blank, and much thinner than the left side (1997, 31–32; see also Tinney 1999). In sum, from Mesopotamia, there is evidence for student writing exercises consisting of a text on the left written by the teacher, and a text on the right written by the scribal student. There is also evidence for the presence of a "beginner's hand."

From Egypt, numerous epigraphs are considered student copies and hail from multiple cities (e.g., Memphis and Thebes). The epigraphs from the site of Deir el-Medina are now among the most important sources of data regarding scribal practices and scribal education (Janssen and Janssen 1990, 67–89; McDowell 1996, 601–8; 1999, 128–30). For example, there is an ostracon from Deir el-Medina upon which a teacher wrote in black and red ink the names of King Amenophis I. On the reverse, the student attempted to copy them, but in a remedial and clumsy hand. Janssen and Janssen state that "he was clearly still a beginner." Moreover, they also note that in the student's attempt to copy the names, he rotated the stance of the signs in the right-hand cartouche (Janssen and Janssen 1990, 87–88; see also McDowell 1996, 602). It should be emphasized that in this case the teacher's text was short and consisted of the writing of the names of a royal figure. Also attested are multiple copies of the book *Kemit* (used in Egyptian education) that are written in an "untrained hand" (Janssen and Janssen 1990, 80). Significantly, sometimes the epigraphs from Deir el-Medina contain "student colophons" as well, a rich source of varied data (McDowell 1999, 128; 2000, 217–33). Although it seems that it was "advanced students" who wrote much of the student material found at Deir el-Medina (McDowell 1999, 128),[1] recently it has been reasonably suggested that there is, nevertheless, some evidence at Deir el-Medina for a "master" correcting a student's text. To be precise, it has been argued that such corrections are present in some of the New Kingdom hieratic literary texts from Deir el-Medina (Gasse 2005, 1, 37–38). From Egypt, therefore, there is evidence for texts that were "writing exercises" and contain the hand of the teacher and the student's hand attempting to copy the teacher's text. In addition, the student's copy was sometimes in a remedial (clumsy) hand, and problems of stance are attested. Moreover, there is also evidence that some texts contain the student's copy and the teacher's corrections of that copy.

---

1. Brunner (1957, 66, 87) and Erman (1925, 23) had suggested that the student exercises from Deir el-Medina were the work of elementary students and that the Late Egyptian Miscellanies were the work of secondary (i.e., more advanced) students. However, McDowell (1996; 2000) rejects this proposal. Rather, based on a constellation of evidence, she argues convincingly that the "student exercises from Deir el-Medina represent the same secondary stage of education as the Late Egyptian Miscellanies and cannot be used to reconstruct the elementary school curriculum and teaching methods" (2000, 223).

GRECO-ROMAN TEXTS: THE TEACHER'S TEXT
AND THE STUDENT'S COPY

Significantly, there are also some student-writing exercises in Greek (Pestman 1990; Cribiore 1996). Among the most important of these is a wooden tablet filled with wax and inscribed with six lines of Greek uncial text (Turner 1971, 32, no. 4 and plate), dating to the second century C.E., and hailing from Egypt.[2] The first two lines of text are written in a refined hand, on the line, replete with consistent spacing. These two lines are those of the teacher. After them, there is a large space and then four lines of text. These four lines consist of the teacher's two-line text written twice. The letters of these four lines are written in a rather remedial hand and are those of the student. Note also that the letters are written between two lines rather than simply on a line, as with the two lines the teacher wrote. That is, there are four ruled sets of parallel lines, a common feature of Greek writing exercises. Significantly, the margin of the wooden tablet has been drilled, reflecting the fact that it had been part of a student's notebook. Similarly, a writing exercise entitled the "Song of Boatmen on the Nile" contains a Greek lyric that has been copied in a large, clumsy hand, with uneven size and spacing, and the correction of some malformed letters. It has been dated to the second or third century C.E. Turner argues that these features demonstrate its status as a writing exercise of a student (1971, 32 no. 5 and plate). Thus, from the Greco-Roman world, there is evidence for texts that were writing exercises and consist of a teacher's text and a student's copy of that text. In addition, the student's copy is recognizable because of its remedial quality (see also Eshel, Puech, and Kloner 2007). And corrections of the student text are present at times.[3]

THE ARCHAEOLOGICAL CONTEXT OF THE
CITY OF DAVID INSCRIBED STONE

The consensus view is that similar data (i.e., "student texts" with the corrections of teachers) are simply not present in the Old Hebrew epigraphic record. To be sure, some scholars have posited that certain texts can be understood as student practice texts; however, it is often difficult to posit in a definitive manner that any of these contains the corrections of a teacher. Sometimes this has been understood as

---

2. This writing table is in the British Museum and is labeled B.M. Add. Ms 34186 (I).

3. The Greek exemplars (with the teacher's text and the student's copy) are considerably shorter than the standard Mesopotamian ones. Of course, the ostracon from Egypt with the names of Amenophis I demonstrate that in Egypt a writing assignment might be very short.

a fundamental problem for those who believe there must have been some sort of educational apparatus in ancient Israel. For example, Crenshaw discusses the purported student exercise texts and then writes the following: "A problem surfaces immediately.... Why do these student exercises lack any corrections by the hands of teachers? Similar texts from Egypt and Mesopotamia show clear corrections, thus indicating circumstances of actual pedagogy. If the Palestinian inscriptions had similar corrections, the evidence for schools would be much more compelling" (1998, 106). Crenshaw's point is well taken. I would reply that are tens of thousands of epigraphs from Mesopotamia and Egypt and the percentage of such documents in a student's hand with a teacher's correction is miniscule. Bracketing the seals and seal impressions, the number of inscriptions from ancient Israel is in the hundreds. For this reason, there should be no assumption that the extant Old Hebrew epigraphic corpus would contain anything approximating the numbers from Mesopotamia and Egypt. Having said that, a tantalizing inscription was discovered during excavations in Jerusalem during the late-twentieth century that definitely is the work of two hands. I believe that it is plausible to suggest, albeit with caution, that it is a product of scribal education.

The stone in fig. 6.1 was found in Locus 790 of Yigal Shiloh's Area G in the City of David excavations which he attributed to Stratum X (the destruction level marking the end of the Iron Age II, in ca 587 B.C.E.). Locus 790 represents the excavation of stone collapse found in the middle room of the four-room House of Ahiel. In his preliminary report, Shiloh stated that "the stone bearing the inscription, which was slightly better dressed than the other stones, may have been fixed in one of the walls of the structure" (1984, 34 n. 73). In a personal communication, Jane Cahill has stated that the inscribed stone was discovered on June 27, 1980, when paving stones initially revealed during the previous 1979 season of excavation were removed so that excavation could continue beneath L. 790. The fact that the stone bore an inscription was not noticed until it had been removed from the floor. While it is possible that the stone fell from one of the surrounding walls as suggested by Shiloh, since L. 790's floor surface had been thoroughly cleaned during the 1979 season, she believes that it is more likely that when the House of Ahiel was destroyed at the end of the Iron Age II, c. 587 B.C.E., the inscribed stone was in secondary use as a stone paver in the north half of the central courtyard. In any case, the occupation of this stratum was seventh century and early-sixth century. Significantly, the House of Bullae was also located in area G and in Stratum X (Shoham 1994, 55–61; 2000, 29–57). Because the many bullae found in this domestic building arguably represent the remains of a significant archive of some sort, it is likely that Area G of Stratum X was a place of substantial epigraphic activity.

OLD HEBREW EPIGRAPHIC EVIDENCE:
A TRAINED HAND AND A REMEDIAL HAND

Most Old Hebrew inscriptions were written by trained scribes and so the attested Old Hebrew script is normally a good "cursive" or "formal cursive" (Rollston 2006). To be sure, though, there is some evidence for remedial hands in some Old Hebrew epigraphs. For example, a stone bowl from Arad (Aharoni 1981, 112 [= Arad 99]) was inscribed in archaic letters in a remedial hand, replete with problems of letter morphology and stance. Also, an incised inscription on a jar handle from Arad reflects a remedial hand as well (Aharoni 1981, 109 [= Arad 97]). Moreover, an Old Hebrew seal from Arad reflects the capabilities of a seal maker of remedial or modest training (Aharoni 1981, 121 [=Arad 109]). That is, sometimes inscriptions of modest quality, reflecting the hand of a beginner, are attested in the epigraphic record. Nevertheless, the great majority of Old Hebrew inscriptions are written in a trained and refined hand. The inscribed stone from the City of David (fig. 6.1) is of particular significance because both a trained hand and a remedial hand are attested on the same inscription, and both are of the same personal name. Based on the script, I would date the stone to the seventh century B.C.E.

Note that the name *Blṭh* is written twice (fig. 6.2), both times preceded by a *lamed* (meaning: "belonging to," or "for," etc). The first time the personal name and the preceding *lamed* are written in a good cursive hand of a trained scribe. The letters reflect fine morphology, and they also reflect the standard stance and spacing. However, the second occurrence of the name (i.e., in the remedial hand) is very different. (1) The *bet* is poorly formed, without a horizontal base. (2) Notice also the stance of the *lamed* that follows the *bet*. Within Old Hebrew, the top of a *lamed* is normally top-right. This is not the case with this *lamed*, how-

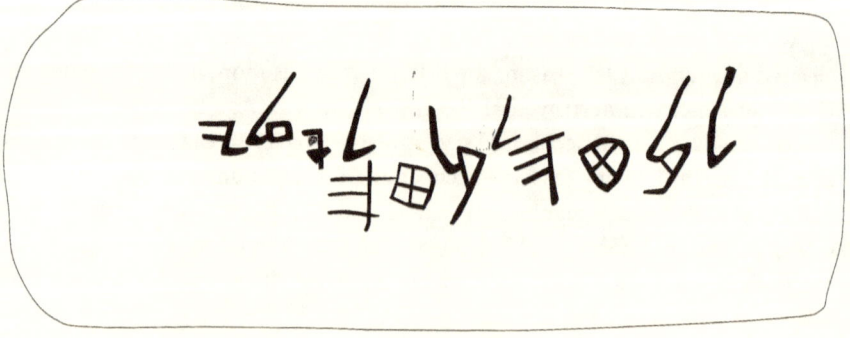

Fig. 6.1. City of David Inscription. Drawing by the author.

remedial hand   trained hand

Fig. 6.2. Trained hand and remedial hand. Drawing by the author.

ever. (3) The morphology of *ṭet* is acceptable, but most of the time in Old Hebrew the two internal strokes will be written as an /x/, not as a /+/ (e.g., City of David Bullae B4 and B5 [Shoham 2000, 34]; Lachish 1.2.ṭ1; Lachish 4.2.ṭ1 [Tur-Sinai, Harding, Lewis, and Starkey 1938, 20, 76]). (4) The *he* is a very crude form. The main vertical stroke protrudes through the top horizontal rather substantially. Moreover, the bottom of this stroke does not extend down as far as is the norm. Visually, this letter has the appearance of having been written by a very clumsy hand. That is, the first hand is a trained and confident hand, but the second hand is clumsy with regard to morphology and stance. Ultimately, based on the Old Hebrew palaeographic data as well as the comparative ancient Near Eastern data, I believe that it is plausible to suggest that the trained hand is that of a scribe and the remedial hand is that of a student. Note the *lamed* that precedes the personal name. It is written high on the line and there does not seem to have been sufficient space for it. Note, however, that the stance and morphology are both quite good. Based on the fact that there was no real space for this letter between the *he* and *bet*, I would suggest that it was written after the student copied the personal name (i.e., the student forgot it). Moreover, because its stance and morphology are superior to those of the student's hand, I would suggest that this is the teacher's correction (i.e., the teacher's addition of the omitted letter).

The remaining portion of the inscription consists of the letters *l{y}ʿly*. Certain features of this segment of the inscription merit reference. Notice that the line with the repeated personal name descends from right to left. The letters *l{y}ʿly* are not part of the same line as the one with the repeated personal name. That is, these letters constitute a separate line. The first *lamed* of this portion of the inscription reflects good morphology and stance. The strokes present between the *lamed* and ʿ*ayin* are probably disparate strokes (similar to those that were made just above the student's *bet*). However, it may also have been an aborted *yod* (perhaps aborted because the stone seems to have chipped badly during the chiseling process). The ʿ*ayin* is very nicely formed. The second *lamed* of this portion of the inscription also reflects good morphology and stance, as does the *yod*. Many forms similar to this are attested in the corpus of bullae from the City of David (Shoham 2000, *passim*). Because of the general quality of the writing of this line, I do not think that it is the product of the remedial hand.[4]

In sum, I am suggesting that this stone may have been inscribed as part of some curricular activities. It has been suggested that it might have been a stone weight on which a designation of ownership was inscribed (Eran 1996, 221–22); however, this fails to account for the fact that the name *Blṭh* was written not once, but twice. Furthermore, this proposal fails to account for the dramatic difference in the quality of the two writings of the personal name *Blṭh*. Clearly the same person did not write the first and second occurrence of *Blṭh*. This much *is* certain. Of course, someone might propose that a trained scribe had inscribed the name *Blṭh* on the stone and then subsequently an illiterate person (not a student) simply happened along and attempted to copy the personal name. Naturally, this proposal cannot be completely ruled out.

Ultimately, however, I find it most plausible to suggest a curricular context for this composition. This stone consists of a trained hand inscribing the personal name *Blṭh* followed by a remedial hand inscribing the same personal name. Texts that consist of a teacher's text and a student's copy are attested in the ancient Near East. Among the features that form the basis for the assumption that an ancient Near Eastern text might be a teacher-student text is the presence of a text written twice, first in a trained hand and then in a remedial "clumsy" hand.[5] Sometimes these texts are long, but sometimes they can consist of a few lines, or even a few words (e.g., the names of Amenophis I on the ostracon), as with the City of David inscribed stone.

PRINT EXPOSURE IN THE HOME AND SCRIBAL FAMILIES

I have argued in this chapter that scribal education in ancient Israel need not have been conducted in a designated monumental education building. In fact, comparative evidence from Mesopotamia and Egypt reflects the fact that even in these cultural centers, education often occurred in non-monumental contexts. Furthermore, I have argued that an inscription from Jerusalem contains the hand of a

---

4. Because of the difficulty in determining whether the letter between the *lamed* and ʿ*ayin* is an aborted *yod* or simply some extraneous marks, it is difficult to discern the personal name. Obviously, though, it is either ʿ*ly* preceded by a *lamed* or *y*ʿ*ly* preceded by a *lamed*.

5. In addition, in Mesopotamia (for example) we do have the thinning of the clay on the student's side of a tablet, which indicative of scraping and reuse, but obviously this cannot be expected on a stone such as the City of David inscribed stone.

teacher and the hand of a student, something that can be construed as a small, but important, line of evidence for training in writing. At this juncture, and as a precursor to the content of the succeeding chapter, I would like to focus on the putative implications of print exposure in the ancient scribal home.

It seems to me that it is a rational *a priori* assumption that there would have been some "scribal families" in the ancient Near East, including Israel. After all, in antiquity, as in the modern period, a responsible father and a mother would have been concerned about the vocational success of a child for any number of reasons, not the least of which is the capability of caring for the parents during old age. Because of parental concerns about the vocation of a child, it would stand to reason that a father would often teach a son the trade that he (the father) knew best, namely, his own. Similarly, note the Talmudic dictate that "a father is obligated to teach his son .... a trade (Kiddushin 29a). A correlative of this is that within an ancient society a son would often have spent substantial time with his father, on occasion assisting him in his vocational duties—depending on the nature of his vocation, to be sure. For this reason, a son would often learn the rudiments of a trade in a most natural manner during his youth and thus have a predisposed aptitude for the vocation of his father.

Within the corpus of ancient Near Eastern literature, there is evidence for "family vocations." For example, from the workmen's village at Deir el-Medina in Egypt there is reference in multiple hieratic ostraca to a draughtsman named Pay. Based on colophons in some of the ostraca, McDowell states that three of his sons, Neb-Re, Pre-hotep, and Pre-em-heb "were to follow him in his profession" (McDowell 2000, 224). The fact that a son would work in the same profession as his father is predictable. Therefore, it is not at all surprising that this would be the case with the scribal profession. For example, the colophon on one ostracon from Deir el-Medina refers to "the scribe Huy, his son the scribe Baki" (McDowell 2000, 225; 1999, 129). That is, both the father and the son were scribes.[6] Porten and Yardeni have analyzed the prosopographic evidence for the Aramaic documents from the Jewish colony at Elephantine in Egypt. From these data, it can be concluded that a scribe named Nathan son of Ananiah fathered two sons who also became scribes, namely Ahio son of Nathan son of Anani and Mauziah son of Nathan (Porten and Yardeni 1989, 188–89). Furthermore, the textual evidence from the Neo-Babylonian Ebabbar Temple at Sippar also attests to a scribal family. For example, a scribe named Erība-Marduk had at least two sons who were scribes, namely, Kī-Bel and Kī-Nabû (Bongenaar 1997, 58, 444). From the same

---

6. Although the term "son" could be a means of referring to a "student," McDowell considers these to be statements about actual family relationships, based on the data present in the various colophons.

archive, there is reference to a scribe named Nabû-šum-lîšir, all five of whose sons became scribes, including the one named Bêl-uballiṭ. In addition, Bêl-uballiṭ's son, Murânu, became a scribe (Bongenaar 1997, 445). Thus, within the ancient Near East there is sufficient evidence to posit that a son of a scribe would some-times follow in the vocational steps of his father. At this juncture, it seems prudent to turn to some of the modern theoretical studies about literacy in the modern period so as to elucidate certain sociological aspects of scribalism in antiquity. Specifically, there has been some significant research on the subject of literacy, print exposure, and the home that I believe has ramifications for understanding scribal families in the ancient Near East.

Based on a substantial amount of empirical data it has been argued in a cogent manner that "home experiences" have a formative impact upon such fundamental aspects of literacy as phonological awareness and knowledge of letters. There are a number of variables, but among the most important contributors is the practice of reading in the home, parental attempts at instruction in reading and writing, parental emphasis on the importance of literacy, and even the nature of general conversations in the home (Baker, Fernandez-Fein, Scher, Williams 1998; Phillips and Lonigan 2005). Similarly, some studies have focused on "repetitive and cumulative actions" such as the constant presence of print (in the home and in society in general) that can serve to galvanize interest and success in reading and writing. That is, children with rather constant higher levels of print exposure will achieve literacy at a more rapid rate (Cunningham and Stanovich 1998). Naturally, socio-economic factors are an important component of this equation (Duncan and Seymour 2000). Thus, students from homes with low-literate parents, poor home language, and more modest amounts of cultural and educational opportunities have poor(er) literacy outcomes. Students from homes with literate parents who emphasize the importance of literacy and attempt to provide contexts for the fostering of literacy will have rich(er) literacy outcomes. There is, therefore, a "generational component" to literacy in a family: literacy begets literacy (Wasik, Dobbins, and Herrmann 2002). Conversely, illiteracy begets illiteracy. Nevertheless, there are exceptions. That is, sometimes a lower income family will emphasize literacy strongly and higher literacy levels will be attested for children. Of cognate interest is the fact that families of more modest means often are not able to travel as widely and this could have indirect (negative) implications for levels and types of literacy (Teale 1986). In addition, some recent studies have also argued that genetics are part of the nexus of factors contributing to literacy development. That is, nurture and nature are both factors that impact levels of literacy (Olson and Gayan 2002; Evans and Seymour 1997).

The amount of print exposure in modern society is much higher than in ancient society. Some monumental inscriptions were on display in urban centers in various parts of the ancient Near East, but these sorts of inscriptions would have provided just a modicum of print exposure, often to a segmented component of society, and thus is very different from the pervasive nature of modern print that is available in public places. Moreover, the amount of print exposure in a modern home is much higher than the amount of print exposure in most homes in antiquity. After all, many people within antiquity were agriculturists and pastoralists and most would have found no reason for numerous printed documents in the home. Naturally, agriculturalists and pastoralists might have sometimes had contracts stored in the home, deeds of purchase, deeds of sale, perhaps a marriage contract. Nonetheless, it is likely these would have been stored, not displayed. Someone might argue that ancient artisans had some reason for certain documents. I do not doubt this, but am confident that this was the exception rather than the rule. In sum, since Gutenberg's invention of the printing press, print exposure has risen exponentially, but during antiquity the printed word was a rare commodity indeed. After all, the production of written documents required trained specialists, was labor intensive, and, therefore, expensive. Thus, I contend that written documents would have been a rarity in the homes of non-elites.

The lives of the sons and daughters of scribes, however, would have been much different. After all, they would have seen their fathers working on documents at home. Witnesses would have sometimes gathered at the scribe's home to sign certain documents. Longer projects could have sometimes been lying out for longer periods of time and would have been a fertile educational fields for the young son or daughter of a scribe. Similar statements can be made for the children of military and religious officials, courtiers, and high(er) level military commanders. That is, the children of the agriculturist would have been accustomed to seeing, and working with, the implements and activities associated with agriculture. The children of pastoralists would have been accustomed to the activities and implements associated with pastoralism. The children of the blacksmith would have been familiar with the implements and techniques associated with metalworking. And the child of scribes would have been accustomed to seeing the activities and implements associated with the production of epigraphs. Based on the modern data regarding print exposure and literacy, I contend that the children of scribes and officials would have been environmentally predisposed to have higher degrees of literacy. Therefore, it should come as no surprise that the scribal profession was sometimes the "family business." Indeed, this is a rather predictable phenomenon. For this reason, it should come as no surprise that a biblical text should refer to "the families of the scribes that dwell at Jabez: the Tirathites, the Shimeathites, and the Sucathites" (1 Chr 2:55). Moreover, although from a later period, it comes as no surprise that there were

Masoretic scribal families such as the Ben Asher family and the Ben Naphtali family of Tiberius. Again, this phenomenon is predictable.

Finally, it should be noted in this connection that although most scribes in the ancient Near East were male, there are some references to female scribes. For example, Enheduanna was a female scribe and author (she was a daughter of Sargon the Great). Nevertheless, this sort of thing was the exception, rather than the rule.

Chapter 7
The Extent of Literacy in Ancient Israel

Definitions

The definition of literacy for antiquity (and modernity) is the subject of substantial debate. Some might suggest that in "oral cultures" the capacity to use language (i.e., the spoken word) in a functional or sophisticated manner constitutes literacy. However, some would argue that literacy is a term that is to be understood as referring to the ability to read and write texts. Occasionally, there are those who propose that functional literacy could be defined as just the capacity to write one's name. The United Nations Educational Scientific and Cultural Organization (UNESCO) has recently employed the following definition: "Literacy is the ability to read and write with understanding a simple statement related to one's daily life. It involves a continuum of reading and writing skills, and often includes also basic arithmetic skills (numeracy)" (UNESCO). The bibliography for the subject of literacy in antiquity (and modernity) is vast and varied (Treiman and Kessler 2005; Seymour 2005; Byrne 2005; Frost 2005; Niditch 1996; Schniedewind 2004; Carr 2005; Rollston 2008a).

For the southern Levant during antiquity, I would propose as a working description of literacy the possession of substantial facility in a writing system, that is, the ability to write and read, using and understanding a standard script, a standard orthography, a standard numeric system, conventional formatting and terminology, and with minimal errors of composition or comprehension. Moreover, I would affirm that the capacity to scrawl one's name on a contract, but without the ability to write or read anything else is not literacy, not even some sort of "functional literacy." Rather, those with this level of eptitude should be classed as illiterate. However, I would also argue that there were some in ancient Israel who should be classed as semi-literates. That is, there were ostensibly those who were capable of reading the most remedial of texts with at least some modest level of comprehension and often the ability to pen some of the most common and simplest of words. Naturally, I would also posit that there was much variation within each of these categories, but precise penetration into the nature of such variation is not something that the data (ancient or modern) can accomplish.

CAVEATS REGARDING THE CONNECTION BETWEEN LITERACY AND THE ALPHABET

The data do not support the contention that a high rate of literacy is a necessary corollary of a society with an alphabetic writing system. Greek is an alphabetic script (derived from the Phoenician script), but there is no decisive evidence that literacy of the populace in ancient Greece was the norm. Latin also uses an alphabetic script, but there is no decisive evidence that literacy was the norm for the populace in ancient Italy. The evidence suggests that the vast majority of the population was not literate.[1] Similar statements can be made for the European world of the Middle Ages. Furthermore, some societies or regions with complex non-alphabetic writing systems have very high literacy rates, but some with alphabetic writing systems have low literacy rates. Obviously, this is the case for China and Japan. I am not suggesting that there is no relationship between the complexity of a writing system and literacy rates. Rather, I am suggesting that there were multiple variables and the nature of the writing system is simply one of these variables and it is not even the most determinative variable (Harris 1989, 12–24). Ultimately, writing systems and literacy rates are related but independent variables.

LITERACY AND BROADER OFFICIALDOM

Professional scribes of Old Hebrew were among the most learned practitioners of writing and reading. Scribes were often part of the royal administration. The majority of the extant Old Hebrew inscriptions are administrative in nature. The Lachish II Ostraca hail from the terminal period of Judean history and revolve around the activities of the Southern Kingdom's military apparatus, an important component of the royal administration (Tur-Sinai, Harding, Lewis, and Starkey 1938). Many of the Arad ostraca hail from chronological horizons of the eighth through sixth centuries B.C.E. (Aharoni 1981). Most of these ostraca are adminis-

---

1. W. Harris (1989, 22, 114, 267) has suggested that literacy rates in Attica were probably about 5 to 10 percent and those in Italy were probably below 15 percent. Within this volume (*passim*), Harris has cogently critiqued those that have proposed high(er) rates of literacy for the populace.

trative in nature, revolving around military activities at the Arad fortress. Within the Hebrew Bible, there is reference to the "scribe of the army commander" (2 Kgs 25:19; Jer 52:25) and it is possible that the scribes producing the majority of the ostraca from Arad and Lachish were commissioned as "military scribes." The Reisner Samaria Ostraca (Reisner, Fisher, and Lyon 1924) are essentially economic dockets produced as part of the Northern Kingdom's accountancy during the early-eighth century. Although very brief, they contain references to commodities and often regnal years. The scribes of all of these corpora wrote in elegant hands, even though the medium was a potsherd and these texts were to serve an ephemeral administrative function. Moreover, the orthography is consistent and hieratic numerals are attested on multiple ostraca. Those who penned the Reisner Samaria Ostraca were trained scribes. Furthermore, the massive corpus of *la-melek* jar handles is to be classified as administrative in nature (Vaughn 1999, 185–219). The seals used to make these impressions reflect enormous skill and care (even if those using the seals to make impressions failed to be as careful). Indeed, it is cogent to argue that most of the extant Old Hebrew inscriptions are the product of trained scribal professionals and this is definitely the case for these major corpora. Ultimately, I have argued that nothing else can account for the quality and consistency of these Old Hebrew epigraphs: formal, standardized scribal education is the most rational means of accounting for the quality of the Old Hebrew epigraphic materials. *Nevertheless, I do not believe that those functioning as scribes were the only literate elites.* Rather, I believe that at least some of the royal and temple officials would also have been literate.

For example, I would contend that Lachish Letter 3 is reflective of the literacy of a broader officialdom (i.e., not just scribes) in Old Hebrew, in this case the literacy of a military officer. Within this letter Hosha'yahu writes to his superior officer, a certain Ya'osh. In the body of the letter, he describes that fact that he was chagrinned by Ya'osh's suggestion (in a letter the preceding day) that he (Hosha'yahu) should summon a scribe because he (Hosha'yahu) had not understood a previous missive. Hosha'yahu replies (in Lachish 3) that he has never required the services of a professional scribe (from whom he clearly distinguishes himself) and that he would not pay any scribe who might come to him. Rather than suggesting that this letter is indicative of the growth of literacy among the populace (i.e., "even a lowly soldier could write"), I would note that this is arguably an officer, a member of the military elite. Hosha'yahu was not a member of the "populace." After all, the content of the letter is hardly the casual conversation of two ordinary Judean citizens. Rather, within the body of the letter, Hosha'yahu provides important military information: Konyahu son of Elnathan (the commander of the army) has gone done into Egypt and Konyahu has requested that Hodavyahu son of Ahiyahu and his men leave Judah to go down to Egypt as well.

Also, Hosha'yahu reports that he has also sent to Ya'osh the letter of Tobyahu the servant of the king, which had been transmitted to Shallum son of Yaddua at the behest of the prophet with the prophetic message "Beware." This is a military missive with critical military information. Ultimately, this letter is reflective of the fact that those who desired to pursue positions of responsibility and author- ity within elite circles would also have found it beneficial to have some formal, standardized education in the Old Hebrew writing system as well. That is, non- scribal professionals would have found it sage to have some facility in the Old Hebrew writing system. Lachish Ostracon 3 is, therefore, reflective of the pres- ence of at least some literacy in circles that were associated with the Judean administration. Note that Cross has suggested that the person writing Lachish Ostracon 3 was an army scribe, not Hosha'yahu (Cross 2003, 129–32). Based on Hosha'yahu's statement that he had "never called a scribe" and that he "would not pay" any scribe who might come to him it seems likely Hosha'yahu himself penned Lachish Ostracon 3. Regardless, though, I would be disinclined to use this letter as definitive evidence of non-elite literacy (Rollston 2008a; but cf. also Schniedewind 2000).

Yavneh Yam (Mesad Hashavyahu) Ostracon 1 (Naveh 1960) has sometimes been referred to in discussions of the literacy of the populace, with affirma- tions that this ostracon testifies to "the spread of writing and literacy in the late Judean monarchy" (Hess 2002, 93; Schniedewind 2004, 103). Significantly, the script of this ostracon is a fine cursive Old Hebrew script of the mid- to late- seventh century. The orthography of this inscription is the standard orthography of this period. Naveh has suggested that this letter was penned by a scribe, who employed the traditional opening formula, but that the body of the letter may be the *ipsissima verba* of the non-elite reaper (Naveh 1960, 136). Note that some of the remaining inscriptions from Yavneh Yam contain references to units of money and employ hieratic numbers (Naveh 1962, 27–32). Because Yavneh Yam was a Judean fortress, we may posit that the scribe was an army scribe who penned the letter for the reaper. Conversely, it is also plausible to posit that this plea is not from a peasant reaper at all, but from an administrative official charged with the supervising of reaping, measuring, and storage—that is, this letter was from an official and modern scholarship has misconstrued the social status of the complainant. Nevertheless, the main point is that arguments for the literacy of the populace on the basis of this letter are laden with assumptions.

It has also been suggested that the presence of non-administrative epigraphs from ancient Israel is reflective of the presence of literacy outside the confines of a royal administration. Millard, for example, implies this in reference to the inscriptions from Kuntillet 'Ajrud (1995, 211). Similarly, Hess has argued that there is "no evidence" that the writing of the Old Hebrew alphabet was "restricted to one class and not available to another level of society" and "there is no evidence from epigraphy to assume that members of any class could not learn how to read and write." Within his article, he refers to the writers of the inscriptions from Kuntillet ʿAjrud simply as "travelers" (2002, 92, 95).

The inscriptions from Kuntillet ʿAjrud (Meshel 1978) are certainly not administrative in nature; they contain few or no references to commodities received, rations dispensed, military movements, and so on. For this reason, I would not wish to posit that these inscriptions were produced by royal scribes. Moreover, those who penned the Old Hebrew texts could have been "travelers" of some sort. However, it would be most difficult to argue on the basis of these assumptions that these "travelers" must have perforce been non-elites. After all, elites traveled at least as much as non-elites! In addition, the quality of the writing from Kuntillet ʿAjrud is high and the orthography is consistent and standard for the period. In addition, I would argue that it is plausible to propose that, although not written by royal scribes, they were written by members of the cultic or prophetic elite (Van der Toorn 2007, 75–108). Furthermore, even if one were to concede the point that the travelers were non-elites (something I am not willing to concede, based on the epigraphic evidence), it would still be naïve to assume that said non-elites could not have hired scribes to have produced these inscriptions. At the end of the day, I contend that there are no absolutely compelling reasons for assuming that non-elites wrote these inscriptions themselves. However, I would argue that there are epigraphic reasons (e.g., script, orthography) to affirm that those with formal, standardized training produced these inscriptions. In any case, to base an argument for widespread literacy on the inscriptions from Kuntillet ʿAjrud is tenuous indeed. Dramatic conclusions, such as the literacy of the non-elite populace, require dramatic evidence.

The Gibeon Inscribed Jar Handles have sometimes been a component of discussions of literacy in ancient Israel. I would concur that these jar handles are not reflective of the finest scribal hand (quite the contrary), but for some time now, I have argued that it is plausible to suggest that these jar handles were inscribed by functionalists who desired for the words to be legible, but had no interest in attempting to inscribe letters on the handle of a jar that would be representative of their best work. Perhaps these handles are the work of state functionaries with more modest amounts of education in the Old Hebrew writing system. Perhaps, though, they are the work of trained scribes, the quality of whose work reflects the fact that they had many inscriptions to write and a difficult surface on which to work. To be sure, Naveh has stated that these inscriptions are to be regarded as representative of his "vulgar cursive," that is, the hand of the lower middle class (Naveh 1968, 68–74) I would, however, be disinclined to attempt to draw precise conclusions about socio-economic and educational status on the basis of these jar handles. The evidence is just too problematic.

Some have suggested that Old Hebrew graffiti are evidence for non-elite literacy. For example, an inscription from Khirbet el-Qom has been used to posit this. The inscription begins with the statement that "'Uriyahu the rich wrote (commissioned) it." Then, in line four, the inscription contains the letters *l'nyhw*. Of course, the *lamed* is simply the preposition and the succeeding letters constitute the personal name 'Oniyahu. Dever had suggested that this personal name was actually the signature of the writer of the inscription, that is, the "executor of the inscription" (1969–70, 162). Based on Dever's suggestion, Schniedewind refers to Khirbet el-Qom and writes that "what is of interest here is the social class of the person who inscribes the graffiti ... in the case of the Khirbet el-Qom graffiti, the author identifies himself as the tomb cutter" (2004, 104). Nevertheless, the inscription itself *does not refer to the social class or vocation of the inscriber of the text*. Also, it is tenable to propose that some stone masons were formally trained in the same fashion as were scribes that wrote upon papyrus, vellum, and potsherds. Ultimately, the perennial problem is that arguments from silence about the non-elite status of the writers of an inscription are tenuous.

Literacy and the Populace

Professional scribes were certainly among the literati in ancient Israel. Based on the caliber of the Old Hebrew epigraphs, I argue that scribes with formal, standardized training in the Old Hebrew writing system were responsible for the majority of the Old Hebrew epigraphic corpus. However, there are some epigraphs that were written by those not serving as professional scribes, but rather as officials in the royal administration. Lachish Letter 3 is an example of this. Nevertheless, I would argue that these officials were subjected to some of the same formal, standardized training as were the scribes (hence, the general quality of these inscriptions). This formal training was ostensibly conducted under the auspices of the state. Of course, a small number of the extant corpus of Old Hebrew inscriptions may have been produced by those with minimal amounts of training. However, when this is the case, it is normally dreadfully apparent.[2]

Some have affirmed that substantial segments of the populace in ancient Israel were literate (Barkay 1992, 349; Albright 1960, 123; Millard 1972, 98–111; 1985, 301–12; 1995, 207–17). After all, it had been assumed that learning to write

---

2. For example, Arad 99 is the product of a very poor hand (see Naveh 1968, 68–74).

and read a Semitic alphabet was quite facile and so the presence of an alphabetic script perforce resulted in high(er) rates of literacy. However, the theoretical and comparative literature focusing on various periods demonstrates these assumptions are not accurate. Rather, the fact of the matter is that alphabetic writing systems are not that simple and the presence of an alphabetic writing system in a society does not necessarily raise the literacy rates among the populace. Moreover, the Old Hebrew and epigraphic data are reflective of rigorous formal education.

Some have countered that because there are several hundred Old Hebrew inscriptions, from several different horizons, and from disparate geographic regions, it is necessary to postulate the presence of substantial literacy among the common folk. Moreover, it is often noted that there are more Old Hebrew inscriptions from the seventh through sixth centuries than there are from the eighth and ninth centuries, which is seen as evidence that literacy was spreading among the populace. I would point out in response that a small coterie of professional scribes during any chronological horizon could produce very large numbers of inscriptions without much difficulty. Moreover, scribes are hardly to be assumed to be anchored always to a site or region. That is, scribes did travel and, quite frankly, so did the inscriptions they wrote. Furthermore, the reason for the increase in numbers of inscriptions during the seventh and sixth centuries could be attributable to the growth of the administrative apparatus during these horizons. Of course, site selection, excavation techniques, and preservation issues can account for the data as well: that is, the sample-size arguments are operative components of the discussion. In essence, the "spatial distribution" argument is very tenuous.

Sometimes scholars will refer to the number of times "reading" and "writing" is mentioned in the Hebrew Bible and assume that this demonstrates that elites and non-elites could read and write. However, I would contend that the Hebrew Bible was primarily a corpus written by elites to elites. That is, it would be difficult to suggest that statements in the Hebrew Bible could be used as a basis for assuming the literacy of non-elites. Significantly, in this connection, Young wrote two seminal articles on the subject of literacy in ancient Israel. Among the most important of his findings is the fact that those referred to in the Hebrew Bible as writing and reading were primarily scribes, royal officials, kings, priests, and prophets. Some skilled craftsmen may have also been able to write and read (Young 1998a; 1998b). Ultimately, Young's analysis demonstrates in a convincing manner that the Hebrew Bible itself attests to literacy of elites, not the non-elite populace. Young's conclusions about "writing in the Hebrew Bible" dovetail with the Old Hebrew epigraphic record quite nicely: elites wrote and read, non-elites did not.

Mesopotamian cuneiform and Egyptian (hieroglyphic, hieratic, or demotic) were difficult to master. For this reason, it is also plausible to posit that the rates of literacy among the populace were higher in ancient Levantine societies with an alphabetic writing system than in Mesopotamia or Egypt. I will concede this point. Of course, literacy rates in ancient Mesopotamia and Egypt are estimated to be very low, with some studies suggesting that the rate is in the low single digits.[3] Therefore, even if it is plausible to posit higher rates of literacy for those living in ancient Israel than for those living in Mesopotamia or Egypt, this does not lead to the conclusion that the non-elite populace was literate. Ultimately, I would contend that the Old Hebrew epigraphic data and the biblical data align and reveal that trained elites were literate and there is a distinct dearth of evidence suggesting that non-elites could write and read. Those wishing to argue for substantial amounts of non-elite literacy can do so, but it is a perilous argument without much ancient or modern support.

Context for the Origins of Israelite Literature

Finally, lest my arguments about literacy in ancient Israel be misconstrued, I should like to emphasize the obvious: the epigraphic evidence demonstrates that elites in ancient Israel were writing during Iron IIA (900–800 b.c.e.), Iron IIB (800–722 b.c.e.), and Iron IIC (722–586 b.c.e.). Thompson has written that "we cannot seek an origin of literature in Palestine prior to the eighth, or perhaps even better the seventh-century" (1992, 391). With all due respect to Thompson, I must state that his position is in direct conflict with the epigraphic evidence and I do not consider his position to be at all defensible. After all, southern Levantine states are producing monumental inscriptions (e.g., the Mesha Stela, the Amman Citadel Inscription, the Tel Dan Inscription). Moreover, there is a distinct Old Hebrew national script that is already attested during the ninth century. Finally, this script is even used in a foreign region, by a foreign monarch, to inscribe a monumental text in a foreign language (Mesha Stela). It would be most difficult to argue that a culture capable of developing and employing a distinct national script with a developed scribal culture did not have the capacity to write texts of various sorts.

Someone might retort that the Israelites were capable of writing during Iron IIA, but not capable of writing "literature." Naturally, however, this would be a

---

3. For Egypt, see Baines and Eyre 1983, 65–96. They estimate that the literacy rate was ca. 1 percent or lower. For Mesopotamia, see Larsen, 1989, 121–48, esp. 134. Larsen believes that 1 percent is also a reasonable figure for Mesopotamia.

very strained argument. To put it positively, I am absolutely certain that a nation (Israel) that has a scribal apparatus that is capable of developing a national script and employing standardized orthographic conventions is certainly capable of producing literature.

CHAPTER 8

INSCRIPTIONS FROM THE MARKET: A PRECARIOUS BASIS
FOR STATEMENTS ABOUT THE NATURE OF THE
EPIGRAPHIC RECORD, SCRIBAL PRACTICES,
AND LITERACY

A SEA OF MARKET INSCRIPTIONS:
EXAMPLARS FROM ANTIQUITY AND MODERNITY

The number of Northwest Semitic inscriptions appearing on the antiquities market continues unabated. Some of these inscriptions are genuine (i.e., ancient) inscriptions, but have appeared on the market as a result of illicit excavations. Within this category are the Wadi ed-Daliyeh materials, the Qumran scrolls, and, in my opinion, the Idumean Ostraca (Rollston 2003, 2005). Some of these epigraphic objects, however, are modern forgeries. Within this category, I place inscriptions such as the Brazilian Phoenician Inscription, the Hebron Philistine Documents, Moussaieff Ostraca (Widow's Plea and Three Shekels), the Jehoash Inscription, the Ivory Pomegranate, and the Baruch Bullae (Rollston 2003; 2005). Of course neither pillaging nor forging is a recent development; both of these problems have been part of the equation for decades, even centuries.

THE TREASURE CHEST: PRODUCING A FINE FORGERY

The field has sometimes had the *a priori* assumption that modern forgers cannot produce "good forgeries," that is, forgeries that "appear ancient." However, I would argue that forgers have all of the resources necessary to produce superb forgeries (that "pass all the tests," or at least pass them to the satisfaction of many). To elucidate this point, it is useful to list some of the primary and secondary sources that would be most useful for a forger with a knowledge of biblical

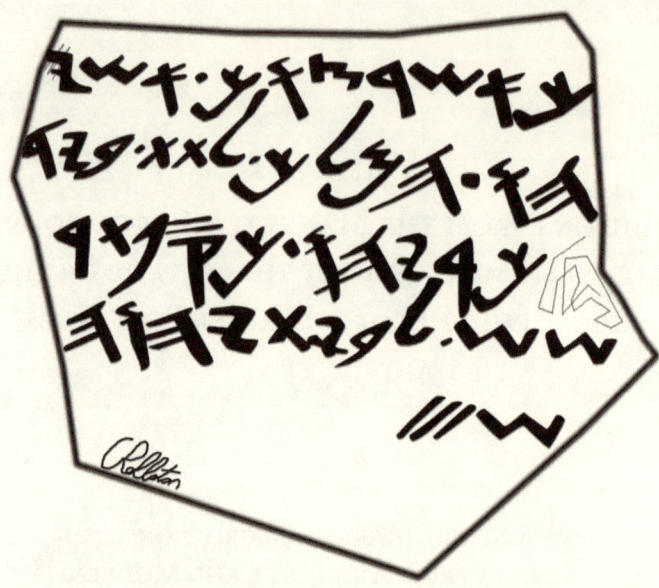

Fig. 8.1. Moussaieff ostracon 1. Drawing by the author.

Hebrew attempting to produce an inscription written in Iron Age Hebrew script and language (i.e., Old Hebrew):

- A standard dictionary of biblical Hebrew, Hoftijzer and Jongeling's *Dictionary of the North-West Semitic Inscriptions* (1995), and Davies *Ancient Hebrew Inscriptions* (1991);
- Cross and Freedman's *Early Hebrew Orthography* (1952);
- Waltke and O'Connor's *Introduction to Biblical Hebrew Syntax* (1990);
- Birnbaum's *The Hebrew Scripts* (1954–1971); Naveh's *Early History of the Alphabet* (1987a), and Cross's seminal articles on the Iron Age Hebrew script in *BASOR* (1961; 1962a; 1962b);
- Donner and Röllig's *Kanaanïsche und aramïsche Inschriften* (1973–1979);
- Freedman's *Anchor Bible Dictionary* (1992);
- Pardee's *Handbook of Ancient Ancient Hebrew Letters: A Study Edition* (1982);
- Avigad and Sass's *Corpus of West Semitic Stamp Seals* (1997).

Using such sources, a deft modern forger has the essentials regarding script, orthography, vocabulary, syntax, language, and culture to produce a fine Old Hebrew forgery. All of these sources are widely considered standard in the field and are readily available; therefore, knowledge of, and access to, the proper resources is not an issue (and, of course, such sources are available for all the Northwest Semitic languages, not just Hebrew). It should also be affirmed that forgers also now have available software programs (e.g., Adobe Photoshop) that can be used to facilitate accurate "script production."

Naturally, some of the remaining requirements would often be adequate time; some knowledge of, or expertise in, chemistry or ancient metallurgy (or an associate with such expertise); access to various materials such as potsherds, ancient metals, stone of Levantine quarry, small pieces of ancient papyrus or vellum, some carbonized remains (for the production of "ancient" ink); and sufficient finances. None of these necessities is problematic, however. Because non-provenanced epigraphs often sell for thousands (or tens of thousands) of dollars, funding is a non-issue; that is, the sale of one forgery could fund the production of several additional forgeries. Moreover, ancient materials of various sorts (e.g., potsherds, papyri, carbonized remains used for the production of ink, etc.) are readily available to those participating in, or associated with, excavations (or those dealing with the market). In addition, the chemical composition of ancient patinas can be "replicated." The point is that specialists and non-specialists in epigraphy and biblical studies must come to terms with the fact that the production of a good forgery in the contemporary period is not facile, but neither is it *now* as difficult as specialists and non-specialists within the guild would have affirmed in *the past*. Forgers have all the tools needed to produce a rather impeccable forgery. Fortunately, of course, forgers often make mistakes (and these can be detected), but it is imprudent to assume that this is always the case. The point is that forgers have ample "means."

Some have suggested (or assumed) that the primary motive for forgers is economic. However, I am confident that various motivations can be posited (with some certitude) for the production of forgeries. Of course, venality is certainly a component present in the production and sale of forgeries. Non-provenanced inscriptions routinely sell for four, five, and even six figures. Some recent non-provenanced inscriptions have been valued at seven figures. Some forgeries are arguably the result of "sour grapes" (e.g., a student purged from a Northwest Semitic epigraphy program) or professional rivalry, with the forger hoping to "dupe" the "offender." Naturally, sometimes a forgery can be a prank. For example, the forger of the Hebron Documents was probably a prankster (or a dolt, or both). Moreover, there is a certain amount of prestige associated with being the person who "collects," "vets," or "finds" a significant "ancient epigraph" from the market. Indeed, the public (and even scholars within the field) can sometimes lionize such people because of "sensational" non-provenanced epigraphs. For this reason, it is my position that forgers may sometimes produce inscriptions so as to be lauded as the one who "found" "vetted," or "owns" a sensational epigraph.

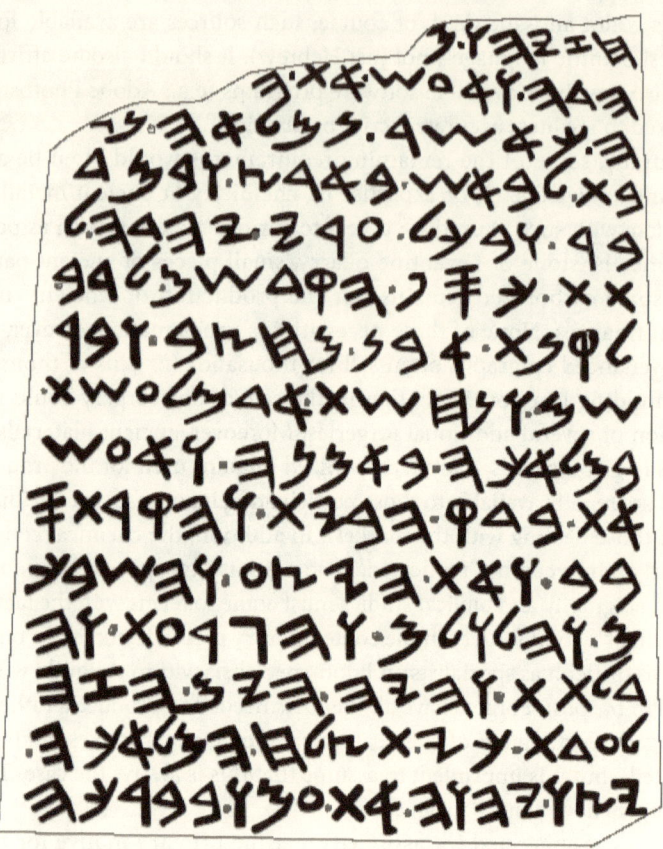

Fig. 8.2. Jehoash inscription. Drawing by the author.

Religion and politics are also strong motives for the production of a forgery. For example, there was arguably a strong religious motivation for the production of the Shapira Fragments (and the initial aura surrounding them). The fact that the Jehoash Inscription was "reported to have been found in the region of the Temple Mount" has political and religious overtones. Ultimately, forgers are arguably motivated by a combination of such factors, and, of course, with each success, hubris is fostered. The main point is that forgers have substantial "motive." The result is that scholars must be very careful about basing arguments about the epigraphic record on inscriptions from the market. With rare exceptions (e.g., Dead Sea Scrolls, Wadi ed-Daliyeh Papyri) it is methodologically imprudent to rely on Northwest Semitic inscriptions from the market for assumptions about the epigraphic record.

Retaking the Ship: Epigraphic Detection of
Modern Forgeries

Several methodological points regarding forgeries and forgery detection can be articulated at this juncture. Modern forgeries are often "reported to have come" from specific locations to increase the credibility of the objects' authenticity (e.g., Hebron Documents, Jehoash Inscription [fig. 8.2], Brazilian Phoenician Inscription). Therefore, epigraphers must not consider information about purported sites of discovery for non-provenanced inscriptions to be useful in and of itself for making determinations regarding authenticity.

Modern forgers have traditionally relied heavily upon provenanced epigraphic and biblical materials for a number of reasons. Sometimes this information is damning (Hebron Documents), but sometimes (Moussaieff Ostraca) this information is more suggestive, or even of no absolutely necessary consequence. Also of significance in this connection is the fact that although forgers have been predisposed intentionally to use attested words and phrases, they are sometimes ignorant of the semantic evolution of these words (Jehoash Inscription). Ultimately, knowledge of forgers' tactics assists epigraphers in assessing the possible antiquity of a non-provenanced epigraph.

Forgers often produce inscriptions with sensational contents (e.g., Moussaieff Ostraca, Jehoash Inscription, Ivory Pomegranate), perhaps because these create enormous interest (and irrational exuberance) and yield high prices.

Forgers are beginning to produce patinas that "appear ancient" (Jehoash Inscription, Moussaieff Ostraca). This fact, combined with the fact that some lab testing of epigraphic materials has reflected incompetence and collusion, has created problems. Lab tests must be scrutinized and protocols for lab testing must be put in place.

Modern forgers often commit serious palaeographic and orthographic errors (e.g., Phoenician Inscription from Brazil, Moussaieff Ostraca, Jehoash Inscription). Palaeographic and orthographic anomalies (and anachronisms) are of fundamental importance, and, in my opinion, egregious violations of attested ancient orthography and palaeography provide sufficient basis for complete rejection of a non-provenanced epigraph. Red flags should be noted, and not easily dismissed (even with the sample-size argument).

The end result is that the field of epigraphy should be capable of eradicating many, if not all, forgeries from the data set.

Laboratory tests are also of fundamental importance. I have discussed these at some length in print, suggesting that C^{14}, TL, radiography, SEM-EDS microscopy can all be useful. Nevertheless, there is an interpretive component to even these tests (as the GSI's flawed analysis of the Jehoash inscription demonstrated).

Moreover, those working within the humanities should be cognizant of the relevance and irrelevance of certain tests. For example, I recently saw someone argue in print that because a TL test performed on an ostracon demonstrated that the potsherd was fired in antiquity the ink on it must be ancient. This sort of naiveté is most problematic. The field must become savvy about the use and misuse of laboratory tests. Protocols must be developed.

Quarantine the Cargo

Some specialists might suggest that non-provenanced epigraphs should, therefore, be eliminated *in toto* from the Northwest Semitic dataset. I suggest that such materials can sometimes be used, but they must normally be subjected to the most rigorous epigraphic and laboratory analyses in order to determine with substantial reliability that they are ancient, and they should be separated from the provenanced corpus and also flagged as non-provenanced.

A. Non-Provenanced Epigraphs in Handbooks and Collections: The Principle of Separation

First and foremost, it is readily apparent that those discussing specific non-provenanced epigraphs should articulate the fact that the source of such an epigraph was not a controlled archaeological excavation. Nevertheless, scholars have sometimes been remiss in this regard. This practice is particularly problematic because some readers might reasonably conclude, therefore, that such inscriptions are definitively provenanced and ancient. Ultimately, I would suggest that those discussing an epigraph should clearly refer to the "circumstances of discovery and recent history" in a precise manner so as to avoid causing readers to make erroneous conclusions about the actual or putative origins.

For some time, there has been a tradition of including non-provenanced epigraphs side-by-side with provenanced materials. Not separating provenanced and non-provenanced materials was a convenient utilitarian practice in the past. However, I would posit that combining the data in this fashion is problematic: it implicitly (and erroneously) suggests to many readers that the data from non-provenanced materials and provenanced materials is on a par. Therefore, I would argue that at this juncture, for methodological reasons, provenanced and non-provenanced epigraphs should be separated, placed in distinct sections of handbooks and collections, and be given descriptive labels such as "Provenanced Epigraphs" and "Non-Provenanced Epigraphs." In short, the field must simply be(come) very intentional about "presentation" in handbooks and collections.

B. The Principle of "Flagging"

Within certain types of works (e.g., lexica), it may not be practical to "present" the provenanced and non-provenanced materials separately (i.e., with completely separate entries of some sort for the provenanced and non-provenanced evidence). Therefore, I would suggest that non-provenanced epigraphs cited in the entry be "marked" or "flagged" in some fashion so as to signify their status as non-provenanced. This system will allow the reader immediately to understand that this non-provenanced epigraphic data may need to be weighted differently (i.e., it is not necessarily of the most pristine sort). Several potential methods of "marking" are possible. For example, the reference could be preceded (or followed) by the mathematical symbol Ø, signifying in this case the absence of provenance. Hence, "ØMoussaieff Ostracon 1" would convey to the reader that this particular ostracon is non-provenanced, as would something such as "[non-prov]Moussaieff Ostracon 1." The section on sigla or abbreviations within the volume or article could be used to communicate the author's system of flagging. I have been campaigning for this for some time and am pleased to see that some works are beginning to separate and flag non-provenanced materials.

C. The Principle of Relegation

It is readily apparent that epigraphic materials without secure provenance and without certain antiquity are normally compromised, problematic, and precarious bases for "reconstructing" the past (e.g., scripts, orthography, languages, religion, and culture). Nevertheless, scholars sometimes do continue to base certain conclusions about various aspects of antiquity on non-provenanced materials. For example, Heltzer authored a recent article (2003) about property rights of women in ancient Israel, but his article is based predominantly on non-provenanced epigraphic materials, and one of the epigraphs he mines heavily for ancient data is actually a modern forgery.

D. The Principle of Categorization

Although several caveats and provisos must be present, I would suggest that specialists must begin to be more intentional about categorizing non-provenanced inscriptions. That is, although it is not pragmatic to ignore non-provenanced inscriptions, neither is it prudent to assume that all non-provenanced inscriptions are of equal status (e.g., in terms of possible authenticity). I would propose the following general categories of assessment regarding the antiquity or modernity of (an) inscription(s): (1) Modern Forgery, (2) Probable Modern Forgery, (3) Possible Modern Forgery, (4) Probable Ancient, (5) Ancient. Inscriptions that reflect no real aberrations (in terms of script, orthography, etc.), and for which it is certain that laboratory anomalies are absent, can be considered probable ancient, or ancient inscriptions. Inscriptions that reflect serious or egregious problems or deviations from the provenanced corpus are to be considered modern forgeries or probable modern forgeries.

Of course, sometimes palaeographers will differ about the authenticity of an inscription, however, substantial disagreement of palaeographers, in print, is not nearly as common as is agreement. Genuine disagreement in print, when it does occur, can often be attributed to the high quality of a forgery or a genuine inscription with modest aberrations and the relative competency of a palaeographer with the relevant script series. Sometimes palaeographers are misled by problematic or erroneous laboratory tests, causing a palaeographer to assume the inscription is genuine and then to account for the anomalies with tenuous or strained arguments. Sometimes a sensational epigraph will cause such exuberance that critical judgment becomes impaired and declarations of authenticity are made on the basis of tenuous evidence. In any case, the views of specialists should be cited, and an assessment of the possible or probable antiquity should be made.

Salvage Work: Flotsam and Jetsam

Some have suggested that epigraphers and archaeologists should not use inscriptions from the market. Some have suggested that these inscriptions can be used without compunction. Polar perspectives, though, are often difficult to sustain, within the complicated nexus of this epigraphic crisis. Nuanced policies and protocols must become the norm, for this is the best means of navigating this problem.

Glossary

Abecedary. An inscription that consists of the writing of the alphabet, in order (i.e., in a standard sequence).

Alphabet. A term denoting a writing system in which a single letter (or "grapheme") basically signifies a single phoneme (cf. syllabic and logographic writing systems).

Antiquities Market. A general term denoting the "place" where looted and pillaged antiquities (including inscriptions) are sold to collectors and the public. In many countries, this practice is entirely illegal, but some countries regrettably still allow it.

Archaic. A feature of a text or script that is genuinely old. See archaizing.

Archaizing. A feature of a text or script that is made to appear older than it actually is. See archaic.

Boustrophedon. A term that refers to the direction of writing, namely, multi-line inscriptions that have a dextrograde line, followed by a sinostrograde line, etc. This term literally means "as the ox plows." See dextrograde and sinistrograde.

Bulla (plural: bullae). A small lump of clay (usually about the size of a fingernail) impressed with a stamp seal. Important legal documents were often rolled (e.g., papyri), a string was tied around the rolled document, and a lump of clay would be placed on the string and then impressed with a stamp seal. The impressed clay is called a bulla.

Ceiling line. Northwest Semitic inscriptions of the Iron Age were hung (i.e., "suspended") from an upper line called a "ceiling line" (sometimes still visible in stone inscriptions), rather than being written on a "base line" (as is the case with most Latin-based writing systems of the modern period).

Chiseled. Inscriptions in hard media (e.g., stone, fired pottery) were sometimes made using a chisel, hence, the term "chiseled inscription." See incised.

Cursive. A term that signifies a form of a script that developed so as to be written rapidly (but also written well). This form of a script was the norm for inscriptions written with ink on pottery, and also very commonly used for most incised inscriptions (cf. lapidary).

Damming. Sometimes inscriptions were incised in wet clay (i.e., before the clay was fired or allowed to dry). Most letters required multiple "strokes" with the writing instrument. Damming is a term coined by the author to signify the manner in which the wet clay of a second or third stroke (etc.) will often be (of necessity) pushed into a portion of the incision of a previous stroke. Damming patterns are often useful for determining ductus.

Dextrograde. A term that refers to the direction of writing, namely, writing from left to right. See boustrophedon and sinistrograde.

Ductus. This term refers to the number, direction, and sequence of strokes that are used to form a letter.

Epigraphy. Within the field of Northwest Semitic, the term "epigraphy" is used as a general term for the reading and analysis of ancient inscriptions. See palaeography.

Forgery. Within this book, the term "modern forgery" is used to refer to an inscription that was made in the modern period, although the forger intended for it to be understood as a genuine ancient inscription.

Grapheme. This is a common means of referring to an alphabetic "letter."

Heterograph. Literally, "a different writing." I use the term "national script heterograph" to refer to a "letter form" that is diagnostic for a script series.

Incised. Sometimes inscriptions were incised (e.g., in stone, clay before firing, and clay after firing) with a sharp stylus.

Lapidary. This is a broad term, but is often used to refer to inscriptions chiseled into stone, especially very formal inscriptions (e.g., monumental inscriptions that were placed in or around a temple or palace). A lapidary script is normally a very carefully executed, with emphasis placed upon precise letter morphology, stance, and spacing. See cursive.

Mater Lectionis (plural: *matres lectionis*). The earliest Northwest Semitic alphabet signified consonants, but not vowels. However, during the course of time, the practice developed of using certain consonants to signify certain vowels (e.g., certain "long vowels"). Consonants used to signify vowels are referred to as *matres lectionis*.

Morpheme. A unit of meaning. For example, the word "epigraphist" consists of three morphemes: /epi/ (upon); /graph/ (write); /ist/ (one who specializes in).

Mutterschrift. This is a German term that refers to a script that is the ancestor of a descendant script. For example, the Old Hebrew script derives from the Phoenician script so the Phoenician script is referred to as the *Mutterschrift*.

Orthography. The rules and conventions of spelling.

Ostracon (plural: ostraca). This term is used to refer to ink inscriptions written on potsherds.

Palaeography. Within the field of Northwest Semitic, this term is used to refer to the careful analysis of a script, so as to discern the ductus of a script or script series, its diachronic development, and synchronic variation. See epigraphy.

Papyrus (pl: papyri). This is a type of reed plant that was cut and then arranged together in such a fashion that it could be used as a good writing surface.

Phoneme. A meaningful unit of sound.

Prosopography. The science of attempting to determine the kinship relationships of those attested in an ancient document, corpus, or corpora. Often this term is also used to refer to the attempts to identify a person attested in the epigraphic record with someone attested in the biblical text or classical literature.

Scriptio continua. Inscriptions often have "word dividers" in them. Those that have no word dividers or spaces are said to have been written in *scriptio continua*, a Latin term meaning "continuous script."

Script series. Epigraphers refer to the "Phoenician script series," the "Aramaic script series," the "Old Hebrew script series," etc. That is, this term is used to refer to distinctive national scripts.

Seal. This term is used of both "cylinder seals" and "stamp seals." Stamp seals were used frequently in the Iron Age Levant. Some were epigraphic (contained an inscription) and some were anepigraphic (contained no inscription). Some were iconic (contained an image of some sort) and some were aniconic. See Bulla.

Sherd (Potsherd). Often the medium used for writing, this term refers to a broken piece of pottery.

Sinistrograde. A term that refers to the direction of writing, to be precise, inscriptions written from right to left. See boustrophedon and dextrograde.

Stance. A term that refers to the direction the letter is facing, as well as the position of a letter vis à vis the ceiling line and the letters around it (e.g., upright stance, recumbent stance, etc.).

Stela or stele (plural: stelae). A prepared, formal stone surface upon which something is inscribed.

Stylus. A writing instrument that could be made of metal, wood, or bone (etc.).

Vellum. Animal skin prepared in a particular fashion so as to be used as a writing surface.

Word divider. Many ancient texts used word dividers, such as a short vertical stroke or a dot, to separate the words of a text (so as to aid the reader). Note: word dividers are often not used in a consistent manner in ancient texts, but their presence is always most useful. See *scriptio continua*.

Bibliography

Abou-Assaf, A.; Bordreuil, P.; Millard, A.
  1982   *La Statue de Tell Fekherye et Son Inscription Bilingue Assyro-Araméenne.* Études Assyriologiques 7. Paris: Éditions Recherche sur les Civilisations.
Abu Taleb, M.
  1985   The Seal of ploy bn m͗š the mazkīr. *ZDPV* 101: 21–29.
Aharoni, Y.
  1975   *Investigations at Lachish: The Sanctuary and the Residency (Lachish V).* Publications of the Tel Aviv University Institute of Archaeology 4. Tel Aviv: Gateway.
  1981   *Arad Inscriptions.* Jerusalem: Israel Exploration Society.
Albenda, P.
  1978   Of Gods, Men and Monsters on Assyrian Seals. *BA* 41: 17–22.
Albright, W. F.
  1941   New Light on the Early History of Phoenician Colonization. *BASOR* 83: 14–22.
  1943   The Gezer Calendar. *BASOR* 92: 16–26.
  1947   The Phoenician Inscriptions of the Tenth Century B.C. from Byblus. *JAOS* 67: 153–60.
  1960   Discussion. Pages 94–123 in *City Invincible: A Symposium on Urbanization and Cultural Development in the Ancient Near East.* Edited by C. H. Kraeling and R. M. Adams. Chicago: University of Chicago Press.
  1966   *The Proto-Sinaitic Inscriptions and Their Decipherment.* HTS 22. Cambridge, Mass.: Harvard University Press.
Alexandre, Y.
  2006   A Canaanite-Early Phoenician Inscribed Bronze Bowl in an Iron Age IIA–B Burial Cave at Kefer Veradim, Northern Israel. *Maarav* 13: 7–41.
Avigad, N.
  1953   The Epitaph of a Royal Steward. *IEJ* 3: 137–52.
Avigad, N., and Sass, B.
  1997   *Corpus of West Semitic Stamp Seals,* with revisions by B. Sass. Jerusalem: Israel Exploration Society.
Athas, G.
  2003   *The Tel Dan Inscription: A Reappraisal and a New Interpretation.* London: T&T Clark.
Aufrecht, Walter E.
  1989   *A Corpus of Ammonite Inscriptions.* Lewiston: Edwin Mellen.
Baines, J., and Eyre, C. J.
  1983   Four Notes on Literacy. *Göttinger Miszellen* 62: 65–96.

Baker, L.; Fernandez-Fein, S.; Scher, D.; and Wiliams, W.
    1998   Home Experiences Related to the Development of Word Recognition. Pages
            263–87 in *Word Recognition in Beginning Literacy*. Edited by J. L. Metsala and L.
            C. Ehri. Mahwah: Erlbaum.
Barkay, G.
    1992   The Iron Age II–III. Pages 302–73 in *The Archaeology of Ancient Israel*. Edited
            by A. Ben Tor. New Haven: Yale University Press.
Beit-Arieh, I.
    1999   *Tel 'Ira: A Stronghold in the Biblical Negev*. Nadler Institute of Archaeology:
            Monograph Series 15. Tel Aviv: Yass Publications in Archaeology.
Beckerath, J. von
    1999   *Handbuch der aegyptischen Königsnamen*. Mainz: von Zabern.
Ben-Dov, M.
    1994   A Fragmentary First Temple Period Hebrew Inscription from the Ophel. Pages
            73–75 in *Ancient Jerusalem Revealed*. Jerusalem: Israel Exploration Society.
Biran, A, and Naveh, J.
    1995   The Tel Dan Inscription: A New Fragment. *IEJ* 45: 1–18.
Birnbaum, S.
    1954–71 *The Hebrew Scripts*. 2 Vols. London: Paleographia.
Black, J.; Cunningham, G.; Robson, E.; Zólyomi, G.
    2004   *The Literature of Ancient Sumer*. Oxford: Oxford University Press.
Bongenaar, A. C. V. M.
    1997   *Neo-Babylonian Ebabbar Temple at Sippar: Its Administration and its Prosopog-
            raphy*. PIHANS 80. Istanbul: Nederlands Historisch-Archeologisch Instituut te
            Istanbul.
Brunner, H.
    1957   *Altägyptische Erziehung*. Wiesbaden: Harrassowitz.
Byrne, B.
    2005   Theories of Learning to Read. Pages 104–19 in *The Science of Reading: A Hand-
            book*. Oxford: Blackwell.
Caminos, R. A.
    1954   *Late Egyptian Miscellanies*. BES 1. London: Oxford University Press.
Carr, D. M.
    2005   *Writing on the Tablet of the Heart: Origins of Scripture and Literature*. Oxford:
            Oxford University Press.
Catling, H. W.
    1977   The Knossus Area, 1974–1976. *Archaeological Reports* 23: 3–23.
Civil, M.
    1985   Sur le 'livres d'écolier' à l'époque paléobabylonienne. Pages 67–78 in *Miscella-
            nea Babylonica: Mélanges offerts à Maurice Birot*. Edited by J.-M. Durand et J.-R.
            Kupper. Paris: Éditions Recherche sur les civilizations.
Clermont-Ganneau, C.
    1903   Inscription égypto-phénicienne de Byblos. Pages 378–83 in *Comptes rendu, Aca-
            démie des inscriptions et belles-lettres*. Paris.
Crenshaw, J. L.
    1985   Education in Ancient Israel. *JBL* 104: 601–15.
    1998   *Education in Ancient Israel: Across the Deadening Silence*. New York: Doubleday.

Cribiore, R.
  1996   *Writing, Teachers, and Students in Graeco-Roman Egypt*. Atlanta: Scholars Press.
Cross, F. M.
  1961   Epigraphic Notes on Hebrew Documents of the Eighth-Sixth Centuries B.C.: I.
          A New Reading of a Place name in the Samaria Ostraca. *BASOR* 163: 12–14.
          Repr. pages 114–15 in *Leaves from an Epigrapher's Notebook*. Winona Lake, Ind.:
          Eisenbrauns, 2003.
  1962a   Epigraphic Notes on Hebrew Documents of the Eighth-Sixth Centuries B.C.: II.
          The Murabba'at Papyrus and the Letter Found near Yabneh-Yam. *BASOR* 165:
          34–46. Repr. pages 116–24 in *Leaves from an Epigrapher's Notebook*. Winona
          Lake, Ind.: Eisenbrauns, 2003.
  1962b   Epigraphic Notes on Hebrew Documents of the Eighth-Sixth Centuries B.C.: III.
          The Inscribed Jar Handles from Gibeon. *BASOR* 168: 18–23. Repr. pages 125–28
          in *Leaves from an Epigrapher's Notebook*. Winona Lake, Ind.: Eisenbrauns, 2003.
  1973   Notes on the Ammonite Inscription from Tell Siran. *BASOR* 212: 12–15. Repr.
          pages 100–103 in *Leaves from an Epigrapher's Notebook*. Winona Lake, Ind.:
          Eisenbrauns, 2003.
  1980   Newly Found Inscriptions in Old Canaanite and Early Phoenician Scripts.
          BASOR 238: 1–20. Repr. pages 213–30 in *Leaves from an Epigrapher's Notebook*.
          Winona Lake, Ind.: Eisenbrauns, 2003.
  1982   Alphabets and Pots: Reflections on Typological Method in the Dating of Human
          Artifacts. *Maarav* 3: 121–36. Repr. pages 129–32 in *Leaves from an Epigrapher's
          Notebook*. Winona Lake, Ind.: Eisenbrauns, 2003.
  1995   Palaeography and the Date of the Tell Fahariyeh Inscription. Pages 393–409
          in *Solving Riddles and Untying Knots: Biblical, Epigraphic, and Semitic Studies
          in Honor of Jonas C. Greenfield*. Edited by Z. Zevit, S. Gitin, and M. Sokoloff.
          Winona Lake, Ind.: Eisenbrauns. Repr. pages 51–60 in *Leaves from an Epigra-
          pher's Notebook*. Winona Lake, Ind.: Eisenbrauns, 2003.
  2003   *Leaves from an Epigrapher's Notebook: Collected Papers in Hebrew and West
          Semitic Palaeography and Epigraphy*. HSS 51. Winona Lake, Ind.: Eisenbrauns.
Cross, F. M., and Freedman, D. N.
  1952   *Early Hebrew Orthography: A Study of the Epigraphic Evidence*. AOS 36. New
          Haven: American Oriental Society.
Crowfoot, J. W.; Kenyon, K. M.; and Crowfoot, G. M.
  1957   *The Objects from Samaria*. London: Palestine Exploration Fund.
Cunningham, A. E., and Stanovich, K. E.
  1998   The Impact of Print Exposure on Word Recognition. Pages 235–62 in *Word Rec-
          ognition in Beginning Literacy*. Edited by J. L. Metsala and L. C. Ehri. Mahwah:
          Erlbaum.
Darnell, J. C.; Dobbs-Allsopp, F. W.; Lundberg, M. J.; McCarter, P. K.; Zuckerman, B.
  2005   *Two Early Alphabetic Inscriptions from Wadi el-Hôl*. AASOR 59. Boston: Ameri-
          can Schools of Oriental Research.
Davies, G. I.
  1991   *Ancient Hebrew Inscriptions: Corpus and Concordance*. Cambridge: Cambridge
          University Press.
Dearman, A., ed.
  1989   *Studies in the Mesha Inscription and Moab*. SBLABS 2. Atlanta: Scholars Press.

Dever, W. G.
1969–70 Iron Age Epigraphic Material from the Area of Khirbet el-Kom.
2005   *Did God Have a Wife? Archaeology and Folk Religion in Ancient Israel.* Grand Rapids: Eerdmans.

Deutsch, R., and Heltzer, M.
1994   *Forty New Ancient West Semitic Inscriptions.* Tel Aviv: Archaeological Center.

Dion, P. E., and Daviau, P. M. M.
2000   An Inscribed Incense Altar of Iron Age II at Ḥirbet el-Mudeyine (Jordan). *ZDPV* 116: 1–13.

Donner, H., and Röllig, W.
1973–   *Kanaanäische und aramäische Inschriften.* 4th ed. 3 vols. Wiesbaden: Harrassow-
1979   itz.

Dunand, M.
1930   Nouvelle Inscription Phénicienne Archaïque. *RB* 39: 321–31.
1937   *Fouilles de Byblos* 1. Bibliothèque archéologique et historique. Paris: Geuthner.
1945   *Biblia Grammata: Documents et Recherches sur le Dévelopment de L'écriture en Phénicie.* Beyrouth: Direction des Antiquité.

Duncan, L. G., and Seymour, P. H. K.
2000   Socio-Economic Differences in Foundation-Level Literacy. *British Journal of Psychology* 91: 145–66.

Dussaud, R.
1924   Les inscriptions phéniciennes du tombeau d' Ahiram, roi de Byblos. *Syria* 5: 135–57.
1925   Dédicace d'une statue d'Osorkon 1er par Elibaal, roi de Byblos. *Syria* 6: 101–17.

Ehri, L.
1997   Learning to Read and Learning to Spell are One and the Same, Almost. Pages 237–69 in *Learning to Spell: Research, Theory, and Practice across Languages.* Edited by C. A. Perfetti, L. Rieben, and M. Fayol. Mahway: Erlbaum.
2002   Phases of Acquisition in Learning to Read Words and Implications for Teaching. Pages 7–28 in *Learning and Teaching Reading.* Edited by R. Stainthorp and R. Thomlinson. British Journal of Educational Psychology: Monograph Series 1. Leicester: British Psychological Society.

Eran, A.
1996   Weights and Weighing in the City of David: The Early Weights from the Bronze Age to the Persian Period. Pages 204–56 in *City of David Final Report IV.* Edited by D.T. Ariel and A. DeGroot. Qedem 35. Jerusalem: Hebrew University.

Eshel, E.; Puech, E.; and Kloner A.
2007   Aramaic Scribal Exercises of the Hellenistic Period from Maresha: Bowls A and B. *BASOR* 345: 39–62.

Evans, H. M., and Seymour, P. H. K.
1997   Genetic Constrains on the Development of Alphabetic Literacy: A Cognitive Study of Two 48, XXXY Cases. *Cognitive Neuropsychology* 14: 225–91.

Fitzmyer, J. A.
1995   *The Aramaic Inscriptions of Sefire.* Rev. ed. BibOr 19/A. Roma: Editrice Pontificio Istituto Biblico.

Freedman, D. N.
1992   *The Anchor Bible Dictionary*. New York, NY: Doubleday.
Frost, R.
2005   Orthographic Systems and Skilled Word Recognition Process in Reading. Pages 272–95 in *The Science of Reading: A Handbook*. Oxford: Blackwell.
Gardiner, Alan H.
1906   Serabit. Pages 129–32 in *Researches in Sinai*. Edited by W. M. Flinders Petrie. London.
1916   The Egyptian Origin of the Semitic Alphabet. *JEA* 3: 1–16.
Garr, R.
1985   *Dialect Geography of Syria-Palestine, 1000–586 B.C.E.* Philadelphia: University of Pennsylvania.
Gass, S. M., and Selinker, L.
2008   *Second Language Acquisition: An Introductory Course*. 3rd edition. New York: Routledge.
Gasse, A.
2005   Catalogue des ostraca litteraires de Deir el-Medina. Tome V. Cairo: Institut français d'archéologie orientale.
George, A.
2005   In Search of the é.dub.ba.a: The Ancient Mesopotamian School in Literature and Reality. Pages 127–37 in *An Experienced Scribe Who Neglects Nothing: Ancient Near Eastern Studies in Honor of Jacob Klein*. Edited by Y. Sefati, P. Artzi; C. Cohen; B. L. Eichler; and V. A. Hurowitz. Bethesda, Md.: CDL.
Gitin, S.; Dothan, T.; Naveh, J.
1997   A Royal Dedicatory Inscription from Ekron. *IEJ* 47: 1–16.
Gogel, S. L.
1998   *A Grammar of Epigraphic Hebrew*. SBLRBS 23. Atlanta: Scholars Press.
Golka, F. W.
1993   The Israelite Wisdom School or "The Emperor's New Clothes." Pages 4–15 in *The Leopard's Spots: Biblical and African Wisdom in Proverbs*. Edinburgh: Clark.
Gropp, D. M.
2001   *Wadi Daliyeh II: The Samaria Papyri from Wadi Daliyeh*. DJD 28. Oxford: Oxford University Press.
Hackett, J. A.
1980   *The Balaam Text from Dier 'Allā*. HSM 31. Chico: Scholars Press.
Hamilton, G. J.
2006   *Origins of the West Semitic Alphabet in Egyptian Scripts*. CBQMS 40. Washington, DC: Catholic Biblical Association.
Haran, M.
1988   On the Diffusion of Literacy and Schools in Ancient Israel. Pages 81–95 in *Congress Volume, Jerusalem 1986*. Edited by J. A. Emerton. VTSup 40. Leiden: Brill.
Harris, W. V.
1989   *Ancient Literacy*. Cambridge, Mass.: Harvard University Press.
Heltzer, M.
2003   About the Property Rights of Women in Ancient Israel. Pages 133–38 in *Shlomo: Studies in Epigraphy, Iconography, History and Archaeology in Honor of Shlomo Moussaieff*. Edited by R Deutsch. Tel Aviv: Archaeological Center Publications.

Henderson, E.
    1985   *Teaching Spelling.* Boston: Houghton Mifflin.
Hermisson, H.
    1968   *Studien zur israelitischen Spruchweisheit.* WMANT 28. Neukirchen-Vluyn: Neu-
            kirchener.
Herr, L. G.
    1998   The Palaeography of West Semitic Stamp Seals. *BASOR* 312: 45–77.
Herzog, Z.
    2002   The Fortress Mount at Tel Arad: An Interim Report. *Tel Aviv* 29:3–109.
Hess, R. S.
    2002   Literacy in Iron Age Israel. Pages 82–102 in *Windows Into Old Testament His-
            tory: Evidence, Argument, and the Crisis of "Biblical Israel".* Edited by V. P. Long,
            D. W. Baker, and G. J. Wenham. Grand Rapids: Eerdmans.
Hoftijzer, J., and Jongeling, K.
    1995   *Dictionary of the North-West Semitic Inscriptions.* Leiden: Brill.
Huehnergard, J.
    1989   Remarks on the Classification of the Northwest Semitic Languages. Pages
            282–93 in *The Balaam Text from Deir 'Alla Re-evaluated. Proceedings of the Inter-
            national 84 Symposium held at Leiden 21–24 August 1989.* Ed. J. Hoftijzer and G.
            van der Kooij; Leiden: Brill.
Jamieson-Drake, D. W.
    1991   *Scribes and Schools in Monarchic Judah: A Socio-Archaeological Approach.* JSOT-
            Sup 109. Sheffield: Sheffield Academic Press.
Janssen, R., and Janssen J. J.
    1990   *Growing Up in Ancient Egypt.* London: Rubicon.
Kaufman, S. A.
    1982   Reflections on the Assyrian-Aramaic Bilingual from Tell Fakhariyeh. *Maarav* 3:
            137–75.
    1986   The Pitfalls of Typology: On the Early History of the Alphabet. *HUCA* 57: 1–14.
Kramer, S. N.
    1981   *History Begins at Sumer.* 3rd ed. Philadelphia: University of Pennsylvania.
Larsen, M. T.
    1989   What They Wrote on Clay. Pages 121–48 in *Literacy and Society.* Edited by K.
            Schousboe and M. T. Larsen. Copenhagen: Akademisk.
Lehmann, R. G.
    2005   *Dynastensarkophage mit szenischen Reliefs aus Byblos und Zypern: Teil 1.2: Die
            Inschrift(en) des Ahiro-Sarkophags und die Schachtinschrift des Graves V im Jbeil
            (Byblos).* Mainz: von Zabern.
Lemaire, A.
    1981   *Les écoles et la formation de la bible dans l'ancien Israël.* OBO 39. Göttingen: Van-
            denhoeck & Ruprecht.
Lichtheim, M.
    1973   *The Old and Middle Kingdoms.* Vol. 1 of *Ancient Egyptian Literature.* Berkeley
            and Los Angeles: University of California Press.
    1976   *The New Kingdom.* Vol. 2 of *Ancient Egyptian Literature.* Berkeley and Los Ange-
            les: University of California Press.

Lindenberger, J. M.
  2003   *Ancient Aramaic and Hebrew Letters*. 2nd ed. SBLWAW 14. Atlanta: Society of
         Biblical Literature.
Lipiński, E., ed.
  1991   Introduction: Phénicie et la Bible. Pages 1–10 in *Phoenicia and the Bible*. OLA
         44. Studia Phoenicia XI. Leuven: Peeters.
Lundberg, M.
  2004   Editor's Notes: The Ahiram Inscription. *Maarav* 11: 81–93.
Macalister, R. A. S.
  1908   Communication. *PEFQS* 40: 271–89.
Marcus, M.
  1991   The Mosaic Glass Vessels from Hasanlu, Iran: A Study in Large-Scale Stylistic
         Trait Distribution. *The Art Bulletin* 73: 537–60.
McCarter, P. Kyle, Jr.
  1975   *The Antiquity of the Greek Alphabet*. HSM 9. Missoula, Mont.: Scholars Press.
  1980   The Balaam Texts from Deir "Alla. *BASOR* 239: 49–59.
  1987   Aspects of the Religion of the Israelite Monarchy: Biblical and Epigraphic Data.
         Pages 137–55 in *Ancient Israelite Religion: Essays in Honor of Frank Moore Cross*.
         Edited by P. D. Miller, Jr., P. D. Hanson, and S. D. McBride. Philadelphia: For-
         tress.
  1996   *Ancient Inscriptions: Voices from the Biblical World*. Washington, DC: Biblical
         Archaeology Society.
McDowell, A.G.
  1996   Student Exercises from Deir el-Medina: The Dates. Pages 601–8 in *Studies in
         Honor of William Kelly Simpson: Volume 2*. Edited by Peter Der Manuelian.
         Boston, Mass.: Museum of Fine Arts.
  1999   *Village Life in Ancient Egypt: Laundry Lists and Love Songs*. Oxford: Oxford Uni-
         versity Press.
  2000   Teachers and Students at Deir el-Medina. Pages 217–33 in *Deir el-Medina in
         the Third Millennium AD: A Tribute to Jac J. Janssen*, eds R. J. Demarée and A.
         Egberts. Leiden: Nederlands Instituut voor het Nabije Oosten.
Meshel, Z.
  1978   *Kuntillet 'Ajrud: A Religious Centre from the Time of the Judaean Monarchy on
         the Border of Sinai*. Jerusalem: Israel Museum.
Milik, J. T.
  1961   *Les grottes de Murabba'at*. Discoveries in the Judean Desert II. Oxford: Oxford
         University Press.
Milik, J. T., and Cross, F. M.
  2003   Inscribed Arrowheads from the Period of the Judges. Pages 303–8 in *Leaves from
         An Epigrapher's Notebook: Collected Papers in Hebrew and West Semitic Palaeog-
         raphy and Epigraphy*. HSS 51. Winona Lake, Ind.: Eisenbrauns.
Millard, A.
  1972   The Practice of Writing in Ancient Israel. *Biblical Archaeologist* 35: 98–111.
  1985   An Assessment of the Evidence for Writing in Ancient Israel. Pages 301–12 in
         *Biblical Archaeology Today: Proceedings of the International Congress on Biblical
         Archaeology, Jerusalem, April 1984*. Jerusalem: Israel Exploration Society.

1995   The Knowledge of Writing in Iron Age Palestine. *Tyndale Bulletin* 46: 211.

Naveh, J.

1960   A Hebrew Letter from the Seventh Century B.C. *IEJ* 10: 129–39.

1962   More Hebrew Inscriptions from Meṣad Ḥashavyahu. *IEJ* 12: 27–32.

1968   A Palaeographic Note on the Distribution of the Hebrew Script. *HTR* 61: 68–74.

1970   *The Development of the Aramaic Script.* Jerusalem: Israel Academy of Sciences and Humanities.

1987a   *Early History of the Alphabet: An Introduction to West Semitic Epigraphy and Palaeography.* 2nd ed. Jerusalem: Magnes.

1987b   Proto-Canaanite, Archaic Greek, and the Script of the Aramaic Text on the Tell Fakhariyah Statue. Pages 101–14 in *Ancient Israelite Religion: Essays in Honor of Frank Moore Cross.* Edited by Patrick D. Miller, Jr., Paul D. Hanson, and S. Dean McBride. Philadelphia: Fortress.

Niditch, S.

1996   *Oral Word and Written Word.* Library of Ancient Israel. Louisville, Ky.: Westminster John Knox.

Olson, R. K., and Gayan, J.

2002   Brains, Genes, and Environment in Reading Development. Pages 81–94 in *Handbook of Early Literacy Research.* Edited by S. B. Neuman and D. K. Dickinson. New York: Guilford Press.

Pardee, D.

1982   *Handbook of Ancient Hebrew Letters: A Study Edition.* SBLRBS 15. Chico: Scholars Press.

in press A Brief Case for the Language of the Gezer Calendar as Phoenician.

Parker, B.

1955   Excavations at Nimrud, 1949–1953: Seals and Seal Impressions. *Iraq* 17: 93–125.

1962   Seals and Seal Impressions from the Nimrud Excavations, 1955–58. *Iraq* 24: 26–40.

Peckham, B.

1968   *The Development of the Late Phoenician Scripts.* HSS 20. Cambridge, Mass.: Harvard University.

Pestman, P. W.

1990   *The New Papyrological Primer.* Leiden: Brill.

Phillips, B. M., and Lonigan, C. J.

2005   Social Correlates of Emergent Literacy. Pages 173–87 in *The Science of Reading: A Handbook.* Edited by M. J. Snowling and C. Hulme. Oxford: Blackwell.

Porten, B. and Yardeni, Y.

1989   *Textbook of Aramaic Documents from Ancient Egypt.* Vol. 2: *Contracts.* The Hebrew University Department of the History of Jewish People. Texts and Studies for Students. Winona Lake, Ind.: Eisenbrauns.

Pritchard, J. B.

1959   *Hebrew Inscriptions and Stamps from Gibeon.* Philadelphia: University Musuem, University of Pennsylvania.

1969   *Ancient Near Eastern Texts Relating to the Old Testament.* 3rd ed. Princeton, N.J.: Princeton University Press.

Puech, E.

1988   Les écoles dans l'Israël préexilique: Données épigraphiques. Pages 189–203 in

Congress Volume: Jerusalem 1986. Edited by J. A. Emerton. VTSup 40. Leiden: Brill.

Reisner, G. A., Fisher, C. S., Lyon, D. G.

1924   *Harvard Excavations at Samaria: 1908–1910.* Vol. 1: *Text.* Cambridge: Harvard University Press.

Röllig, W.

1999   Appendix I – The Phoenician Inscriptions. Pages 50–81 in *Karatepe-Aslantas.* Vol. 2 of *Corpus of Hieroglyphic Luwian Inscriptions.* Edited by H. Çambel. UISK 8.2. Berlin: de Gruyter.

Rollston, C. A.

1999   The Script of Hebrew Ostraca of the Iron Age: 8th–6th Centuries BCE. Ph.D. dissertation, The Johns Hopkins University.

2001   Ben Sira 38:24–39:11 and the *Egyptian Satire of the Trades*: A Reconsideration. *JBL* 120: 131–39.

2003a   Non-Provenanced Epigraphs I: Pillaged Antiquities, Northwest Semitic Forgeries and Protocols for Laboratory Tests. *Maarav* 10: 135–93.

2003b   The Rise of Monotheism in Ancient Israel: Biblical Epigraphic Evidence. *Stone Campbell Journal* 6: 95–115.

2004   Non-Provenanced Epigraphs II: The Status of Non-Provenanced Epigraphs Within the Broader Corpus of Northwest Semitic. *Maarav* 11: 57–79.

2005   Navigating the Epigraphic Storm: A Palaeographer Reflects on Inscriptions from the Market. *NEA* 68: 69–72

2006   Scribal Education in Ancient Israel: The Old Hebrew Epigraphic Evidence. *BASOR* 344: 47–74.

2008a   The Pheonician Script of the Tel Zayit Abecedary and Putative Evidence for Israelite Literacy. Pages 61–96 in *Literature Culture and Tenth-Century Canaan: The Tel Zayit Abecedary in Context.* Edited by Ron E. Tappy and P. Kyle McCarter. Winona Lake, Ind.: Eisenbrauns.

2008b   The Dating of the Early Royal Byblian (Phoenician): A Response to Benjamin Sass. *Maarav* 15: 57–93.

2009   Prosopography and the Yzbl Seal. *IEJ* 59 (2009): 86–91.

Routledge, B.

2003   *Moab in the Iron Age.* Philadelphia: University of Pennsylvania Press.

Sass, B.

1988   *The Genesis of the Alphabet and Its Development in the Second Millenium B.C.* AAT 13. Wiesbaden: Harrassowitz.

2005   *The Alphabet at the Turn of the Millennium: The West Semitic Alphabet ca. 1150–850 BCE.* Tel Aviv Occasional Publications 4. Tel Aviv: Yass Publications in Archaeology.

Schniedewind, W. M.

2000   Sociolinguistic Reflections on the Letter of a 'Literate Soldier' (Lachish 3). *Zeitschrift für Althebraistik* 13: 157–67.

2004   *How the Bible Became a Book.* Cambridge: Cambridge University Press.

Seymour, P. H. K.

2005   Early Reading Development in European Orthographies. Pages 296–315 in *The Science of Reading: A Handbook.* Edited by M. J. Snowling and C. Hulme. Oxford: Blackwell.

Share, D. L., and Levin, I.
    1999   Learning to Read and Write in Hebrew. Pages 89–111 in *Learning to Read and Write: A Cross-Linguistic Perspective*. Edited by M. Harris and G. Hatano. Cambridge: Cambridge University Press.
Shiloh, Y.
    1984   *Excavations at the City of David 1978–1983: Interim Report of the First Five Seasons*. Qedem 19. Jerusalem: Hebrew University.
Shoham, Y.
    1994   A Group of Hebrew Bullae from Yigal Shiloh's Excavations in the City of David. Pages 55–61 in *Ancient Jerusalem Revealed*. Edited by H. Geva. Jerusalem: Israel Exploration Society.
    2000   Hebrew Bullae. Pages 29–57 in *City of David Excavations: Final Report VI*. Edited by D. Ariel et al. Qedem 41. Jerusalem: Hebrew University.
Sjöberg, Å.W.
    1972   In Praise of the Scribal Art (Examination Text D). *JCS* 24: 126–31.
    1973   Der Vater und sein missratener Sohn. *JCS* 25: 105–69.
    1975   Der Examenstext A. *ZA* 64: 137–76.
Smith, Mark S.
    2002   *The Early History of God: Yahweh and the Other Deities in Ancient Israel*. Grand Rapids, MI: Eerdmans.
Sznycer, M.
    1979   L'Inscription Phenicienne de Tekke pres de Cnossos. *Kadmos* 18: 89–93.
Tappy, Ron E., and McCarter, P. K. Jr., eds.
    2008   *Literate Culture and Tenth-Century Canaan: The Tel Zayit Abecedary in Context*. Winona Lake, Ind.: Eisenbrauns.
Teale, William H.
    1986   Home Background and Young Children's Literacy Development. Pages 173–207 in *Emergent Literacy: Writing and Reading*. Edited by William H. Teale. Norwood, N.J.: Ablex.
Thompson, T. L.
    1992   *Early History of the Israelite People from the Written and Archaeological Sources*. SHANE 4. Leiden: Brill.
Tinney, S.
    1998   Texts, Tablets, and Teaching: Scribal Education at Nippur and Ur. *Expedition* 40: 40–50.
    1999   On the Curricular Setting of Sumerian Literature. *Iraq* 61: 159–72.
Tov, E.
    2004   *Scribal Practices and Approaches Reflected in the Texts Found in the Judean Desert*. STDJ 54. Leiden: Brill.
Treiman, R., and Kessler, B.
    2005   Writing Systems and Spelling Development. Pages 120–34 in *The Science of Reading: A Handbook*. Oxford: Blackwell.
Turner, E. G.
    1971   *Greek Manuscripts of the Ancient World*. Princeton: Princeton University Press.
Tur-Sinai (Torczyner), H.; Harding, L; Lewis, A.; and Starkey, J. L.
    1938   *Lachish I (Tell ed-Duweir): The Lachish Letters*. London: Oxford University Press.

Ussishkin, D.
  1978   Excavations at Tel Lachish – 1973–1977: Preliminary Report. *Tel Aviv* 5: 1–97.
  1993   *The Village of Silwan: The Necropolis from the Period of the Judean Kingdom.* Jerusalem: Israel Exploration Society.

Van der Toorn, K.
  2007   *Scribal Culture and the Making of the Hebrew Bible.* Cambridge, Mass.: Harvard University Press.

Vanstiphout, H. L. J.
  1995   On the Old Edubba Education. Pp 3–16 in *Centres of Learning: Learning and Location in Pre-Modern Europe and the Near East.* Edited by J. W. Drijvers and A. A. MacDonald. Leiden: Brill.
  1997   Social Dialogues. Pages 588–93 in *The Context of Scripture: Canonical Compositions from the Biblical World.* Edited by W. W. Hallo. Leiden: Brill.

Vaughn, A. G.
  1999   *Theology, History, and Archaeology in the Chronicler's Account of Hezekiah.* SBLABS 4. Atlanta: Scholars Press.

Veldhuis, N.
  1996   The Cuneiform Tablet as an Educational Tool. *Dutch Studies* 2: 11–26.
  1997   Elementary Education at Nippur: The Lists of Trees and Wooden Objects. Ph.D. dissertation, University of Gronigen.
  2003   Mesopotamian Canons. Pages 9–28 in *Homer, the Bible and Beyond: Literary and Religious Canons in the Ancient World.* Edited by M. Finkelberg and G. G. Stroumsa. Leiden: Brill.
  2004   *Religion, Literature and Scholarship: The Sumerian Composition "Nanše and the Birds."* CM 22. Leiden: Brill.

Waltke, B. K., and O'Connor, M.
  1990   *An Introduction to Biblical Hebrew Syntax.* Winona Lake, Ind.: Eisenbrauns.

Wasik, B. H.; Dobbins, D. R.; Herrmann, S.
  2002   Intergenerational Family Literacy: Concepts, Research, and Practice. Pages 444–58 in *Handbook of Early Literacy Research.* Edited by S. B. Neuman and D. K. Dickinson. New York: Guilford Press.

Weeks, S.
  1994   *Early Israelite Wisdom.* Oxford: Oxford University Press.

Whybray, R. N.
  1974   *The Intellectual Tradition in the Old Testament.* BZAW 135. Berlin: de Gruyter.

Young, I. M.
  1998a   Israelite Literacy: Interpreting the Evidence Part I. *VT* 48: 239–53.
  1998b   Israelite Literacy: Interpreting the Evidence, Part II. *VT* 48: 408–22.

Zayadine, F., and Bordreuil, P.
  1986   Coupe. P. 146 in *La Voie Royale: 9000 ans d'art au royaume de Jordanie.* Luxembourg: Musée du Luxembourg.

Zevit, Z.
  1980   *Matres Lectionis in Ancient Hebrew Epigraphs.* ASOR Monograph Series 2. Cambridge: American Schools of Oriental Research.

Zuckerman, B.
  2003   Pots and Alphabets: Refractions of Reflections on Typological Method. *Maarav* 11: 89–133.

Subject Index

Scripture Index

Author Index